START YOUR OWN BUSINESS 2010
The Ultimate Step-By-Step Guide

START YOUR OWN BUSINESS 2010
The Ultimate Step-By-Step Guide

crimson

This edition first published in Great Britain 2010 by
Crimson Publishing, a division of Crimson Business Ltd
Westminster House
Kew Road
Richmond
Surrey
TW9 2ND

First edition published by Crimson Publishing 2009
Second edition published by Crimson Publishing 2010

A catalogue record for this book is available from the British Library.

ISBN 978 1 85458 489 2

Printed and bound by MPG Books Ltd, Bodmin

CONTENTS

CONTENTS

INTRODUCTION

WHAT'S IN THIS CHAPTER

■ What are the elements of a successful business?
In this chapter we profile four successful, inspiring
businesses, learning what drove them to start up,
the challenges they faced along the way and the key
lessons they learnt.

Still a good time to start up...

If you have picked up this guide and are reading this page, the chances are that you are thinking about starting your own business. And, despite whichever direction the prevailing economic wind is blowing in, you are not alone. Until the recession in 2008, more and more people were feeling the entrepreneurial urge. More than 200,000 new businesses registered for VAT (value-added tax) in 2007, according to the latest government statistics in November 2008 – a rise of 23,700 over 2006. Although the 2008 figures won't be available until late 2009, indications are that there will be only a small decline in VAT registrations, despite de-registrations – those companies going out of business – expected to increase significantly, according to the Department of Business, Enterprise and Regulatory Reform. This is because many people who have lost their job are starting up on their own.

Despite the downturn, small- and medium-sized businesses remain a key driver of the UK economy. The days of hundreds of large companies employing thousands of staff are no more. The number of aspiring entrepreneurs starting small businesses has surged in recent years, and their companies now make up 99.9% of the total businesses in the UK, and are responsible for almost half of the UK's workforce.

> **Despite the downturn, small- and medium-sized businesses remain a key driver of the economy**

Starting a business in a recession – pros and cons

Reasons not to start in a recession

1. People are spending less money
2. It will be harder to raise money
3. It feels risky at a time when everyone is scared of risk

Reasons not to start in a recession

1. It is cheaper to start now than at any other time
2. So it needs less cash to start than at any other time
3. Your opportunity cost is small
4. People and businesses still consider some new options
5. Creative non-cash deals easier to do e.g. partnerships
6. Easier to hire great staff/consultants
7. Your positive energy amid a sea of depression will stand out
8. Cheap acquisitions

Technology has advanced to such a stage, it's now possible to start a global business from a laptop, forcing the entrepreneurial doors wide open to everyone from teenagers to the retired and those who quite sensibly want to dip their toes in the water (or at least on eBay) before taking the plunge. There's also a greater range of finance available to help make your entrepreneurial dreams a reality than ever before. Even though some of the key sources of finance, such as banks and equity investors (which take a stake in your company in exchange for finance) have been badly hit by the credit crunch, and are investing less in new businesses, money is still available. So if your idea is good enough – and presented in the right way – people will want to invest in you. (For a detailed discussion of finance options, see Chapter 4). What's more, if you can gain investment in tougher economic times, it's tantamount to a rubber stamp of success.

There has also never been so much help and information for people who are thinking about striking out on their own, and the government has never been so geared to encourage enterprise. The National Enterprise Academy, which will open its doors in September 2009, will deliver the UK's first full-time accredited courses in Enterprise and Entrepreneurship. It is the brainchild of *Dragon's Den* entrepreneur Peter Jones and its aim is to give students – aged from 16 to 18 – the skills, experience and support to learn how to set up and run successful and innovative businesses, or to become enterprising employees, helping to grow existing businesses – skills that can be used across any business sector, and skills for life.

CONTACT

The National
Enterprise
Academy
www.thenea.org

Prime-time television shows such as *Dragon's Den*, *The Apprentice*, *Tycoon* and *Risking It All* have pushed the idea of running your own business to the forefront of the national psyche – no longer is it exclusive to the daring or the pinstriped, it's for everyone. Of course, startups.co.uk has been championing business pioneers and helping those inspired to follow in their footsteps for some time now, through its website, awards and other events. As such, startups.co.uk has been more aware than many of the rise in interest in entrepreneurialism. But even we were surprised when our first book *How They Started*, telling the startup stories behind some of the UK's best-loved brands, from Innocent Drinks to Pizza Express, hit Amazon's Top 20 on its release in 2007, and garnered considerable media coverage. Such is the current buzz around business.

The startups.co.uk website has become a font of knowledge and debate on starting your own business, and *Start Your Own Business 2010* draws all this vital information together in a definitive guide to starting your own company. The book is presented in the readable, sharp, jargon-free style that characterises startups.co.uk, with key tips, action points and engaging case studies to help you on your way. Whether you have designs on becoming the next Richard Branson or simply want to go it alone and be your own boss, you have come to the right place. The following pages will guide you through choosing the right business to run and deciding whether you are up to the job of launching your own company, to drawing up your business plan and everything else involved in preparing you for take off.

So fasten your seatbelt and get ready for the ride of your life...

Entrepreneurs are people like you

For some people, the word 'entrepreneur' automatically brings to mind Peter Jones and his ilk – those high flyers who set up and run more successful businesses than most of us could manage in several lifetimes. But in reality, an entrepreneur is anyone who chooses to go it alone and make the most of a business opportunity for themselves, no matter how big or small.

Nowadays, being an entrepreneur is becoming a legitimate career choice for more and more people. Gone are the days when you had to have years of business experience under your belt before you might even consider taking the plunge with a startup of your own. Before getting down to the nuts and bolts of how to start a business, here's a brief insight into why a selection of successful entrepreneurs decided to start their own business.

People choose to become entrepreneurs for a variety of reasons. For some it's an opportunity to escape their mundane nine-to-five existence and to commit their working life to something that is a lot closer to their heart. For the 'lifestyle' entrepreneurs, the important part of the deal is not how much their business grows, but the effect it has on their life.

David Creswell, the 27-year-old founder of the comics website ComicDomain.co.uk falls into this category. 'I don't care if I'm a comic geek, it's my hobby and I've turned that into a small business,' he says. 'I'm proud of the service we provide and our customers are also happy.' For others, the motivation for starting up will come from spotting a gap in a market they know well. Self-confessed 'ski bums' **Tim Slade** and **Jules Leaver** spotted an opportunity for 'been there done that' T-shirts to sell to skiing holidaymakers, and started the highly successful high-street chain Fat Face.

And for **Dee Edwards**, 29, the same kind of insight helped her to launch internet company Habbo. 'I really believed internet business could be made successful by using technology to run a company effectively, and leveraging the different way people were changing their communication,' she says. Whether it's T-shirts or technology, the world is littered with those who've been able to see a business opportunity others simply can't. In fact, a lack of business experience could well give you the kind of perspective those with a blue-chip curriculum vitae would struggle to attain. Nowhere is this better

> " Gone are the days when you had to have years of business experience under your belt before you might even consider taking the plunge with a startup of your own "

illustrated than by **Lena Bjorck**. Arriving in the UK from Sweden with no qualifications she landed a job as a kitchen porter, but quickly realised the country's service industry was just not up to scratch. So without a pound in her pocket or even the most basic equipment, she quit. She now runs one of the country's most successful catering companies, Inn or Out.

To help inspire you, here are profiles of four companies, started by entrepreneurs with quite different backgrounds and ideas, who took the decision to launch a business for the first time and succeeded.

Betfair

When **Andrew Black**, co-founder of Betfair.com says: 'I've had a very varied career and done a lot of job hopping', he's making somewhat of an understatement. If ever there's an entrepreneur who's trodden an unlikely path to fortune and success, it's Black. He's had to overcome being expelled from university, being sacked and a personal tragedy to rise to the head of a business that's giving the likes of established bookies William Hill and Ladbrokes a real run for their money. But every experience, Black insists, whether it be stocking shelves at B&Q, caddying on the European golf tour, dealing on the stock exchange, gambling for a living, or caring for his dying brother, contributed to the day he thought up Betfair while working on a secret project for GCHQ.

Building up experience

Black's working life was delayed when his brother developed a serious brain infection. Having only had a handful of dead-end jobs, Black stopped working to care for his brother for the final two years of his life. Following his brother's death, Black had a brief, and unsuccessful, sojourn onto the European golf tour, before landing his first serious job at 26, working in software. In the following four years, Black's natural flair for figures saw him flourish, as he wrote heavy computer code and saw how big business, particularly the stock market, worked. The high-risk stakes of stocks and shares captured Black's imagination, and prompted him to start gambling.

'When you're at the sharp end of trading you're trading very much in the short term and it is very, very similar to gambling,' he says. 'When I left, I didn't have enough money to go trading.' Instead, Black turned to more conventional forms of gambling for his kicks – and his income. 'I won £25,000 on a £20 bet on a horse and then had a £30,000 win from a £1,000 bet on a race,' he recalls. 'I'd won about £50,000 in three months. Compared to what I was earning at the time it was a lot of money.'

Black programmed his own models for betting on football and golf, and also played bridge for substantial figures. But despite doing 'pretty well', it wasn't enough to keep him occupied. So he moved back to buying and selling shares. 'I was seeing the whole mechanics of the New York stock exchange first hand and getting fantastic experience in this incredibly exciting environment,' he says. But Black's excitement was cut short – he was fired after a disagreement over business ethics – and he returned to programming, 'earning ridiculous amounts of money for very little work' in a period where IT skills were in demand. However, his obsession with the stock market and intellectual thirst for a challenge or bet never went away. While working on a secret GCHQ project, he had the time to contemplate how this passion could be twinned with his IT skills.

'We started work at nine and finished at five, and if you weren't out of the office on the dot they got rid of you,' he explains. 'So I had a lot of spare time. I was living in a small remote farmhouse and was lonely.' But the solitude gave Black precious time to turn things over in his head and come up with 'the idea'. It was conceived from the way the stock exchange works. 'It's simple,' he explains, 'Betfair is a cross-section of taking stock exchange technology to the gambling market using the internet. In my career I've worked directly with the stock exchange, I've been a professional gambler and I've built websites. I've been there on all three of them.'

> " Betfair is a cross section of taking stock exchange technology to the gambling market using the internet "

The big gamble

As Black's IT contractor job was going well, he was undecided whether it was worth giving up for the risk of starting his own business. Did he really want to leave his excellent lifestyle behind by going out on a betting venture? 'In my heart I knew I had to do it because I couldn't face the thought of going to my grave having had one great idea and not actually putting it into action,' he says. However, before doing anything Black wanted a partner. 'I wanted someone who understood business,' he says. But finding one proved difficult, until he met **Ed Wray**, the brother of a friend. 'Ed was talking about a horse he'd bet on but was complaining he hadn't won much,' says Black. 'I said: "Well it shouldn't have been like that, soon bookmaking will all change." Ed said: "Tell me more," so I explained the idea.'

A short time later, Wray got in touch to find out if Black had done anything about the idea and Black asked if he'd like to be his partner. Wray agreed in principle, but not without certain changes. He said Black had the right product and the idea was great, but he thought the business plan was totally wrong. He thought if it was going to be done, it needed to be done properly and that they needed to raise some serious finance. The pair spent the next five months working on the idea and carefully planning the business. In the end, Betfair was born. Black and Wray wanted conventional venture capital investment, but it turned out they had missed the boat. 'A company called Flutter had got there before us,' says Black. 'They were selling the eBay of betting and had got a lot of funding. They didn't have the knowledge or substance we had, but it was still terrible news.'

Breaking ahead of the game

The rival in the marketplace ruled out interest from venture capitalists, and the pair were about to quit. Then they came up with an idea to present their concept to wealthy individuals they knew in the city who had money to invest. 'We'd pick a bank, do a presentation and two or three would leave the room having invested £25,000,' says Black. 'It soon added up and we cobbled together the £1 million fairly

> **I couldn't face the thought of going to my grave having had one great idea and not actually putting it into action**

quickly.' They added £30,000 each and didn't pay themselves for the first eight months. The site was created and launched in June 2000, the day before Derby Day – one of the biggest days in the horseracing calendar. As funds were tight, Betfair deployed guerrilla tactics to promote the launch.

'We led a procession with coffins saying "Death of the bookmaker" through the city and held fake demonstrations with "Betfair – unfair" protestors to try and get some publicity,' explains Black. The antics made the front page of *The Times* business section. In its first week Betfair traded £30,000, but really hit the big time after merging with rival Flutter. 'There was a big fuss when they launched and they had all this money, but it wasn't until six months down the line that it became obvious people were using us,' says Black. 'They had a huge advertising budget, but they also had a message board where people were discussing Betfair. Punters were coming into them and leaving to us. About eight months later, they realised we had 97% of the market, despite the fact they'd spent 10 or 20 times what we had. At that point they realised the only way forward was our way.'

A merger was negotiated with Betfair reportedly securing favourable terms, along with access to a 'top-class' chief technology office, the hardware and most importantly, 'the big punters' that were essential to driving the business forward. Since then Black and Wray haven't looked back, establishing Betfair as the leading online betting website.

So rather than the establishment of their rival Flutter being the end of their dream, it proved to be the catalyst to their huge business success.

Jigsaw Research

Sue Van Meeteren and **Ann Morgan** struck out on their own to do the same as they were doing in the company they left with the aim of replacing the bureaucracy and board meetings of the corporate world with a fresh balance of home and egalitarianism – almost their own utopian view of how a business should be run. Their goal was a unique company, individual in its approach, setting itself out as a small fish in a big pond.

Dissatisfaction to motivation

The duo's business was market research and together they launched Jigsaw Research in 1998. What's particularly interesting is that Van Meeteren and Morgan weren't exactly minions within a great corporate machine. Van Meeteren was managing director at their former employer, the sector giant Research International (and had been with the company for seven years), while Morgan had been her deputy. They had both been members of the UK board of directors and were highly influential in the context of a company that was part of a larger group. But both wanted to break free of their corporate trappings, and had to make a decision that would shape their future. Should they simply jump ship to another leading agency or give up their safe, secure and lucrative jobs – and risk it all – by launching a brand new name in the already crowded market research sector. Confident that they would be able to attract business quickly and sure of the support of some of their existing clients they decided to go it alone. Their aim was to devise a new model; a new way of working. The seed for their new concept was sown when some Research International (RI) clients complained to them that they were not satisfied with the larger agencies' approach and wanted greater access to more senior researchers. So Meeteren and Morgan felt there was room for a small company that focused more single-mindedly on its clients' needs.

Coping with the culture shock

However, before Jigsaw Research was launched, there was one remaining piece to be slotted into the puzzle. A former RI colleague of Van Meeteren and Morgan, **Jo McDonald**, had remained in touch with them and it was her encouragement that steered them towards setting up a new business rather than going freelance. She completed the launch team. Of course, there were other small market research companies, so it was vital for Jigsaw to establish itself as unique. It did this by tackling the two main types of market research (qualitative and quantitative), offering an integrated approach, while most small agencies specialised in one or the other. This was clearly going to be a challenge, but with strong marketing and business qualifications behind them, along with several years' experience on the job, Van Meeteren and Morgan were convinced they could pull it off. Their personal lives had also reached a crossroads, with both Van Meeteren and Morgan starting families. This made them more determined than ever to rid themselves of the 12-hour corporate days they were putting in at RI. They wanted a business where they could control the growth rate; that was flexible enough to be able to accommodate their family commitments. 'At the start, our ambitions were very low-key,' stresses Morgan. 'We certainly weren't trying to take on the world.' Their goal was to generate a decent amount of business, have some good clients on the books and do a good job for them. If they wanted to take more time to focus on family life and less on expanding, or if they wanted to take on a small or charitable client that would not be very profitable, they could.

> "We certainly weren't trying to take on the world"

The concept seemed sound and timing appeared to be right, but what the Jigsaw founders hadn't planned for was the culture shock. Sure, they were keen to lose the corporate lifestyle, but they found the drop in status tough to handle at first. From their positions at the top of the corporate tree, Morgan describes the stark contrast of finding herself sitting around wondering if a client might phone them. The prestige and professional self-esteem they were used to had vanished. They also found that they had to make big financial sacrifices for a number of years. Just like any new business, they had to be frugal at first, so gone were the fat cat salaries – and despite the cultural shift, the team was determined to run a tight ship at the start. They launched Jigsaw with £40,000 of savings between them, which is relatively modest for a startup. This allowed them to avoid an overdraft or bank loan, and the associated repayments that can hit cashflow in the early days. They kept overheads low, only spending on what they perceived to be essentials, such as serviced office space, computers and a letterhead. This meant they were able to pay themselves back the £40,000 within the first couple of years, but salaries remained suppressed for longer.

The key to Jigsaw's initial success was its founders' contacts and experience. They knew certain RI clients who were looking for new suppliers, and American Express, Shell and PricewaterhouseCoopers were soon on board – but with small projects initially, so Van Meeteren, Morgan and McDonald could cope and deliver the right standard of service. Meanwhile, word was spreading and drawing more clients to the business. This meant they were in the privileged position of not having to do any marketing.

The balance of the team also proved crucial, with McDonald setting up the administration and financial side of the business, leaving Van Meeteren and Morgan to focus on developing their new business model and, consequently, the client work that they actually wanted to do. 'She has become a sort of unofficial financial director, but with operations and facilities manager also being part of the job description,' explains Morgan, who is keen to stress that having good support can make or break a company. 'Getting Jo on board was the single most sensible thing we did,' she adds.

Although Jigsaw had a dream start from a business perspective, the early client wins coupled with Morgan's pregnancy meant they had to take on staff earlier than they would have done to provide the necessary maternity cover. Recruiting two former colleagues made the process far easier than it might have been, and by the end of the first year the company had five employees. Of course, experienced performers require salaries to match, but with business flourishing, Jigsaw could afford to pay market rates. However, that certainly wasn't the case for the founders, who took less money than they could have commanded as employees elsewhere. But this sacrifice was well worth it according to Morgan. 'The advantages massively outweighed the drawbacks,' she says. Jigsaw has grown into an established and successful medium-sized agency. But despite its size and continued growth, the principles on which the founders built the business have never been compromised, with the focus still firmly on

> " The advantages of launching Jigsaw massively outweighed the drawbacks "

client care, excellent service – with the minimum of bureaucracy and not a board meeting in sigh.

Bigger feet

Many business opportunities arise from everyday frustrations, but it still takes a shrewd entrepreneur to exploit such gaps in the market. When you achieve this when you are just 16 years old, however, you are an inspiration to anyone who is considering starting their own business – and it's little surprise that the media beat a path to your door.

Oliver Bridge, a schoolboy from Cambridgeshire, has found himself in front of the cameras of the BBC and CNN, as well as seen his face staring back at him from various newspapers, since starting up Bigger Feet. Despite his tender years, Bridge has not been daunted by the exposure he has gained, displaying a business brain that belies his years. He has a plan and has put it into place – and he understands the importance of gaining good publicity.

'We're not interested in getting a venture capitalist on board, because they would want a big part of the business, but there are other ways of expanding the business,' he says. 'We could get a private investor on board by saying: "We've been on the BBC and CNN and got massive coverage – do you want a piece of the pie?"'

Seeing opportunity in frustration

Bigger Feet is an online shoe retailer for people who are larger than average below the ankle. The business was born from Bridge's own frustrating experiences. 'I was sitting in a shop saying it's annoying that I couldn't get any shoes and that someone should sell them,' he explains. 'My mum just said: "Why don't you just start up your own business then?" When I thought about it, I decided it was a distinct possibility.'

Besides knowing that he was only one of several people at his school who required large shoes, Bridge did some research and found that about a million people in the UK have large feet – men over size 12 and ladies upwards of size nine. So having pretty much established there was a market for his idea (or rather his mum's), he decided to go for it. Also he knew someone who had started his own business, so he thought it was a realistic idea. (The person in question, **Paul Wilkinson**, is now Bridge's business partner and adult guarantor for banks who get jumpy dealing with under-18s they can't retrieve money from.)

From the off, Bridge faced some of the same problems that adults looking to start a business encountered. Just as many people find it tough to work on a launch while holding down a day job, Bridge was concerned about how he was going to find time. 'At first I was a bit worried, I thought I wouldn't be able to run the business and do my schoolwork at the same time and that I should put it off until I was older,' he confesses. 'But I thought I should go for the opportunity, it can't do any harm, it's not going to cost that much money and if it gets too busy, we can always hire staff.' Wise thoughts for someone not yet out of their teens.

Another fear that older entrepreneurs don't come up against was that people wouldn't take him seriously due to his age. Luckily, this was largely unfounded. 'There's been a great response,' says a relieved Bridge. 'There's only been a few comments about my age. People seem to treat me as an adult, and, if anything, they respect me more because I'm young and going for it.'

Jumpstarting the modern way

Setting up in the family home with a small office space to store the shoes, Bigger Feet could be held up by internet providers as a demonstration of the low-cost flexibility of the web. 'So far, we've only put £4,000 into the business from our savings, which is a really tight budget,' Bridge reveals. 'A website allows you to put something across very professionally at a very low cost. Our website probably rivals a medium-sized business, when in fact we're working from a tiny office. It's so flexible. Because it's all internet-based, we are going

> "At first I was a bit worried, I thought I wouldn't be able to run the business and do my schoolwork at the same time"

> "People respect me more because I'm young and going for it"

on holiday to Barcelona in a couple of weeks and are going to be running the company from Spain.'

Finding stock

Key to the success of any retail business is finding the right supplier and striking a good deal with them so that you can maximise the profit margin. When you hear about the deal Bridge cut with a wholesaler to supply him with shoes, it's again hard to believe he can't yet legally vote or drink. After going to various trade shows in the UK and Europe, he agreed with UK distributors to sell him shoes as and when he needs them. He, therefore, rarely has more than 30 or 40 pairs of shoes in his possession, cutting down on overspend. An almost perfect situation to be in as a retailer.

'Because we weren't ordering massive quantities in advance, they said that would be OK – we are not a credit risk to them,' Bridge explains. 'We are only placing relatively few orders, so if it all goes belly up, they are only going to lose a bit of money. We get them in as we need them, so we cut down on liability. If we get no orders for a month, all it costs us is our phone bill – we won't go out of business, we'll simply be stagnant for a month.'

A significant headache for Bridge has been the reluctance of Nike and Reebok to supply him with trainers. Despite approaching them directly, he got short shrift. 'They didn't want to hear it at all,' he says. 'We went up to a representative of Reebok at a trade show and he gave us a business card and basically told us to get lost. We wrote a few letters to Nike, and they just shoved us from department to department. The big brands aren't interested in small business because they think it tarnishes their image. It's silly really, they should be selling to everyone they find, because ultimately people are going to get hold of Nikes directly or indirectly. They would surely make a better profit if they sold directly to us.'

The media interest (and Google advertising) has understandably boosted sales, which means that generally his age has been a benefit rather than a hindrance. Meanwhile, Bridge insists that Bigger Feet is a 'friendly, personal company', and has certainly benefited from the niche market and cheap prices he is able to generate, although he insists on quality. 'We don't import stuff from China that's rubbish,' he insists.

Staying ahead with personal development

With his family happy to step into the breach when his workload increases with A levels, and an array of impressed school friends, Bridge would be forgiven for thinking he has a career made. But he plans to go to university before making any definite decisions – so clearly his feet are firmly on the ground. 'The business may be able to pay off my tuition fees, which would be great,' he says. 'I don't think that it will grow into a multi-million pound business empire, although you never know.' And he could be right, because there certainly aren't many big shoe retailers out there.

Bebo

For proof that persistence is a key entrepreneurial trait, look no further than **Michael Birch**, founder of social networking website Bebo. About 28 million 'young' people signed up as members within 18 months of its launch in 2006. But this was no overnight success for Birch. Since quitting his IT job, he had been grafting away for years, and Bebo was his sixth venture.

Climbing up the learning curve

'It took three years of trying before three years of success,' he recalls. 'It's a learning experience. Just because something fails, it isn't a complete waste. You learn from it, perhaps realise one element that works well, and leverage that into a new business.'

Birch had always dreamt of being an entrepreneur and the rise of the internet gave him the boost he'd been waiting for. 'I quickly realised it was the prefect medium,' he says, 'and I already had half of the equation, because I understood the IT side of it.'

Birch had experienced some success with one of his earlier websites BirthdayAlarm.com, a diary alert website that reminds

> **Just because something fails, it isn't a complete waste. You learn from it**

you of key dates by email to stop you forgetting people's birthdays and anniversaries. Once this was up and running successfully, he started experimenting with online social networks, which have now become hugely popular. 'I was fascinated with the early ones like Sixdegrees.com,' he says. 'I had ideas on how that content could be improved.' This resulted in Ringo.com, which proved an instant success, surprising Birch and his team. It had quickly become the second biggest social network and needed time and resources that Birch couldn't afford.

Unable to keep up with the growth, Birch quickly sold Ringo. com just three months after starting it. 'We decided to sell and focus on other things we were running at the time,' he explains. But Birch was far from finished with social networking, which was building momentum as household internet connections approach critical mass for the first time. 'I saw how people inter-acting with each other could integrate with other types of media, such as music and video, and how whatever suddenly becomes hot fits easily into it,' he recalls.

Finding the right niche

Birch knew that he couldn't just launch any old social networking website. He had to find a niche – a unique proposition – to give himself the best possible chance of success. The sector was growing rapidly, and that meant so was the competition. So he decide to target young people with a product that matched their demands and understood exactly what they wanted – and didn't want – from a network host. Initially, this meant being as inclusive as possible. 'We always intended Bebo to be a broad social network,' says Birch, who intentionally made the website less complex and with fewer features than some of its competitors.

'It's designed to be simple,' he says. 'You can register, get a homepage and be up and running in minutes. Other sites put people off by being too tricky.' The key was to create an environment that encouraged young people to network with each other. 'It's about trying to foster a healthy community, without trying to dictate how that community behaves,' Birch explains. 'We control things like pornography, or it would escalate, but we won't delete anything just because we think it's silly. If you want to create profiles for your pets, that's fine by us. We've also been careful about using the right language, treating people with respect, while making it light-hearted and fun.'

Focusing on the customer

Birch knew getting it right would take a lot of thought, as the youth market can be a harsh critic, so he put more emphasis on tailoring the environment to the people who were going to use it rather than making it hi-tech, all singing and all dancing – the customer was the absolute focus. He insists that Bebo's modest aesthetics and simple functionality, along with its very limited advertising spaces and casual controls, was fundamental to building its credibility among its target market. 'It was crucial that we weren't too corporate,' he says. 'If you're too corporate, the social network society will backlash against it.'

This made promoting the website tricky – mass marketing was clearly a no go. In the end Birch took a major risk and did almost no advertising or promotion for Bebo when it went live in July 2005. He posted a link to Bebo on BirthdayAlarm.com, the social website he had created years earlier, for just two days, and let the internet take its course. 'We literally seeded it with the first few people and let it just grow on its own.' And how it grew!

> **The customer was the absolute focus**

Forward financial planning

With no marketing spend or major premises and equipment expenditure to worry about, launching Bebo proved very inexpensive. Initially, his and his co-founder wife **Xochi's** wages, along with the fees of two technical programmers that he used, were covered by BirthdayAlarm.com profits. The main costs were new computer servers to support the anticipated new traffic, as Birch was determined that he wasn't going to repeat the experience he'd had with Ringo.com.

'Within a month Bebo was generating revenue from advertising,' reveals Birch. 'It took another month for that money to come through, so in eight or nine weeks it was cashflow positive.' The advertisements were sold by specialist online ad agencies that specialise in selling advertisements on other people's websites, which helped keep costs down and let Birch do what he does best, and concentrate on developing the website.

Another good move proved to be using off-the-shelf software to post the advertisements on the website, rather than Birch developing it from scratch. The common platform also meant advertisements could be sold in different countries, even though Birch and his team were only based in one. This capitalised on the fact that Bebo soon had substantial numbers of users across the globe.

From startup to growth business

So rapid was the growth of Bebo's membership that within a year the site had 28 full-time staff, and Birch found that recruiting was one of the biggest challenges he had ever faced. 'It has been difficult,' he says. 'Recruitment and interviews is something we really focus on.'

Although keen to maintain a small-business culture, in May 2006 Birch took the big step of taking $15m of venture capital investment from Benchmark for a stake in the company that remains undisclosed. 'We raised it because it's good to have a cash buffer even though you're profitable,' he explains. 'It gives us the confidence and ability to grow aggressively if we need to.'

Bebo's revenue comes solely from advertising, but Birch isn't prepared to threaten de-stabilising his growing community by selling too much advertisement space or making it overly intrusive. He realises that Bebo's members are its lifeblood and would rather build profits slowly. 'Clearly we could make a lot more money in the short term by throwing advertising at it, but it terms of growing a community that wouldn't be right and people wouldn't react well,' says Birch. 'We're aiming to make money, but not as much as we possibly can. The aim is to grow the business, and we think we can do that more quickly by not being greedy and, ultimately, we'll then have a much bigger business that we can make more money from.' And with millions of members already online, and more signing up daily, it looks like Birch's careful customer-focused approach is paying dividends.

EXPERT OPINION

STAY AHEAD OF THE GAME

The National Register has some tips on how to make the most of the tools available to give your startup a headstart

In today's competitive environment, a catchy, quirky name and image isn't enough to launch a business and capture the attention of potential customers. With an overcrowded and sometimes saturated market, many other factors have to be addressed.

Online presence and business name issues

Although it wasn't so long ago when many were suspicious of the e-commerce revolution, today in a business sense, if you are not online, you are not alive. Nor is it a straight choice of 'Do I get a .com or a .co.uk?' There are so many domain suffixes to choose from, including .eu,. tv and .mobi, and the list will only get bigger and bigger! Then there are the numerous website design options to be considered 'Do I want Flash? Do I need a shopping basket? How much web-space do I need?' The list goes on and on…

Once you are finally up and running online, you are competing with literally millions of websites to be seen, and this is where search engine optimisation comes in. It is no longer enough to just 'have a website', you have to make sure it can be found through the many online search engines. So you have to consider metatags, pay per click and sponsored listings among other options.

Of course all of these preferences can be expensive, coupled with sorting out branding and trademarks, business names and company names. You will need to find out whether your chosen business name, company name, domain name and trademark is already in use in relation to your chosen nature of business and intended market area. You then need to consider registration to protect your corporate identity.

Time management

Time is one commodity that is very precious in today's commercial arena and usually in very short supply. Most owner-managers would just want to run and manage their business within their area of expertise and not get bogged down with additional responsibilities. But unfortunately, in the real world, you can't run a business without paying attention to them and you will have ensure adequate time is set aside for them – either by you or someone else.

Staying ahead of your competitors

Just as important is to ensure that you are one step ahead of your competitors and constantly monitoring and evolving where required. This can involve repeatedly checking to see if your current trading style is being copied and updating your corporate image periodically, making sure it does not become tired or outdated. The modern business environment is continually changing and if you are not moving forward you might soon be overtaken by your rivals who are.

Keeping up with business news

In keeping with the last point, it's essential that owner-mangers of businesses, whether sole traders, partnerships or limited companies, keep up to date with the latest business news, changes in legislation and financial updates. Whether business is good or bad, the economic climate is optimistic or pessimistic it is important to keep informed of current trends.

Use the free tools available on the internet and don't be slow in seeking the advice and guidance of experts in the areas that you may not have the time or knowledge to fully embrace.

Contact: The National Business Register can help you and your business.
For more information on business names, trademarks or company formation, call freephone 0800 069 9090.

10 REASONS TO START A BUSINESS

1. Being your own boss

If you have your own business, the only person you have to answer to is yourself. Being your own boss gives you the freedom to do things your way and implement your own plans. Of course, you live or die by your decisions, but that's what's good about it, isn't it?

2. Doing what you love – or at least have a keen interest in

The good thing about being an entrepreneur is that you can choose what kind of firm you start up, and where. So, provided that you've done your research properly and there is a gap in the market, you can turn a hobby or interest into a profitable enterprise.

3. Playing by your own rules

Start your own firm and you get to set and meet your own deadlines. Of course, you won't be able to just lie in bed until 2pm – you will need self-discipline. But meeting your own targets can be a huge motivation to work hard and drive the business forward.

4. The freedom to express yourself

If you have considered going it alone, you will have thought out how you would do things your way. You will have the freedom to express yourself and develop your concept in any way you choose. Of course, there may be financial constraints, but you will have the opportunity to be as creative as you like.

5. Plenty of support available

The news is full of stories about the amount of red tape and taxes that small firms have to face on a daily basis. However, over the past few years, several measures have been introduced that should make it easier to go it alone. From the Small Firms Loan Guarantee (see page 160) to various inner-city projects, the government certainly can't be accused of doing absolutely nothing for budding entrepreneurs. With the Prince's Trust, Shell LiveWIRE and other support organisations also up and running, you should be able to secure the help and funding needed to get you started.

6. Make a fortune – or at least enough to live

There are countless stories of entrepreneurs hitting on a great idea, exploiting it successfully and being well on their way to their first million by the end of the year. Although the startup process can be tough, with long hours and little money not uncommon, if you run your business well, the rewards can be huge. And, from a purely selfish point of view, you will get most of the profits yourself.

7. Doing a variety of things

Dealing with spreadsheets one minute, suppliers the next and then having a look around your new office – an entrepreneur's work is not just busy, it is also extremely varied. If you want a career where every day is different, going it alone could be for you.

8. **Have a second career**

Of course, if you don't want to give up a regular income, you can always get the best of both worlds and remain as an employee while running your own firm. Although juggling the two can be tricky, having a successful sideline should be a profitable option. Do something that you are interested in and go for it.

9. **Cutting commuting by setting up close to home**

Although most small firms operate from offices, many entrepreneurs find that operating from home helps keep costs down in the early stages. As well as having familiar, comfortable surroundings to work in, you don't have to endure the daily tangle with public transport or clogged up roads.

10. **Realising your big dream**

You may feel that starting up a small firm won't lead to anything more than having your own desk and taking on a few extra staff. However, it's possible to make it really big – just think of the late Anita Roddick, who became a Dame thanks to her entrepreneurial achievements. She started a small shop in Brighton on a shoestring in the 1970s. Before long, she had a chain of Body Shop stores across the UK and was launching her concept in the USA. So, don't dismiss your dreams as a mere fantasy – it really could happen. What are you waiting for?

Can you do it too?

The case studies in the previous section highlight the qualities required of an entrepreneur – of which one of the most important is passion. No matter how much potential your business might have for making money, unless you believe in it, how can you expect anyone else to? A bit of self-belief can go a long way. Hand in hand with passion comes commitment to the cause. From day one you will need to work hard, often forgoing friends and family to get your venture off the ground. Ask yourself whether you are prepared to make that kind of sacrifice and whether you can keep yourself motivated to put in those long, long hours. If you are the sort of person whose new year resolution lasts until 2 January you might want to think again whether you've got what it takes, particularly when things might not be going your way.

Also, as you've probably realised, the chances are you will be going through all of this on your own. While escaping the office might seem like paradise now, you could soon be missing that office gossip and backchat. You'll need to dig deep to find the kind of emotional resilience to keep you from losing the plot when there's no one around to lend a helping hand. So while you don't need qualifications on paper, not just anyone can become an entrepreneur. But if you think you've got what it takes then it could be one of the best decisions you ever make.

IDEAS FOR STARTUPS

WHAT'S IN THIS CHAPTER

■ Not everyone starts a business following a 'eureka!' moment – in fact few people actually do. Some simply want to work for themselves. But, of course, to do this you need to find the right business for you, and hopefully one that has a good chance of success. Starting up is likely to take quite a bit of your time, energy and money, so it pays to think carefully about the kind of business to launch. This chapter should provide some inspiration…

The right startup for you

Although thousands of people dream of escaping the nine-to-five grind and becoming their own boss, many are unsure of what sort of business they want to start up and how they can ensure their new venture is a success. Ultimately, this is your choice, but it can help if you initially think about what you want from your business. Before **Kirsty McGregor** launched her web-based company Entertainthekids.com, which provides inspiration for parents looking for ways to keep their children entertained, she laid down her vision of 'business utopia', as she puts it.

'I had quite a strict list of what I wanted any business to be for me, in my circumstances,' Kirsty says. 'These were my requirements:

- The business shouldn't be reliant upon my input as the limiting factor in the growth of the business. This is a personal thing, as I wanted to start and grow the business and then be able to get "time freedom" as quickly as possible. It's the whole point of being able to run my own business – flexibility for the family while being financially comfortable and secure.
- It either had to provide a product or service that was niche and high value, or have mass-market appeal with a low price.
- The business needed to be scalable, without any major scarce resource, such as fixed employee or machinery hours, etc.
- Overheads/fixed costs had to be as low as possible, so that I could break even on a fairly low turnover.
- The product should preferably not be a fashionable item or have laws or regulations that will change quickly.
- The business should not have to deal with any stock issues, such as storage, delivery and suppliers – it had to be a service!
- It had to have low startup costs (unfortunately that also means low barriers to entry for competitors).'

To find out how McGregor went on, look out for the 'Kirsty's Story' boxes in this guide. Of course, your vision could be completely different from hers, but getting it down on paper can give you key pointers about the kind of business you would like to launch. To give you some food for thought, this chapter gives you 20 business ideas. Some have popped up recently due to certain trends, while others have been around for some time, but all are either very popular now or growing rapidly in popularity. If none of them appeals to you, then at least you know what you don't want to do – and they might inspire you to find the business that is right for you.

A big problem for many people who want to start a business is being able to afford to do it, especially in these current difficult financial times. But don't let a lack of financial resources put you off. Starting a business on a shoestring seems like an impossible task, conjuring up visions of compromises and cutting corners that will ultimately undermine your best efforts. But it doesn't have to be that way as many industries are well suited to budget beginnings. This is not a case of restricting yourself to mean margins. There are several steps you can take to keep overheads down:

> " **Many industries are well suited to budget beginnings** "

- The most obvious costs in the early days are premises and staffing. If you start by working from home, your office space or workshop budget can go elsewhere. Obviously, this is easier if you are in a desk-bound profession. If it doesn't matter where you are based, rents on out-of-town premises or those in unfashionable areas will also keep costs down. And if you don't have the money for staff immediately, don't forget friends and family. Provided that you don't abuse their goodwill, most will be prepared to help you out on the odd occasion.
- It's inevitable that you will have to put 120% into the business at first, so try to become competent in as many tasks as possible. It will save you money if you can do things such as basic desktop publishing and accounting yourself. You will also gain a better understanding of the day-to-day running of the business.
- Where possible, lease rather than buy and purchase second-hand. Tools, machinery and ovens, for example, are widely available to lease if you can provide assurance that payments will be made. You can also make great savings if you opt for used desks, chairs

---

! TOP TIPS
CHOOSING THE RIGHT BUSINESS

! Base it on a key skill or interest

! Draw up a list of what you are looking for from your ideal business

! Search out the most successful businesses nationally and locally

! Find a gap in your local market

! Canvas opinion from friends and family about your idea

! Consult business contacts about your idea, such as your accountant

! Check out local competition and decide if you can do it better

! Look into the level of finance you will need and whether you will be able to secure it

! Find out if anyone likes your idea enough to go into business with you

---

and filing cabinets. Search on the internet or in the *Yellow Pages* for outlets and warehouses. Most large offices refurbish reasonably regularly, so the second-hand market is generally well stocked.

Half of the business ideas that follow are relatively inexpensive to launch, while the other 10 require more capital input. But no matter how much money you have, the points above are worth bearing in mind, because during the startup phase of a business, every penny counts.

Shoestring startups
An eBay business

Setting up a company on eBay is an increasingly popular choice among would-be entrepreneurs. With millions of potential customers

> **The most important thing is to find a niche that few other people are competing in**

just a couple of clicks away from your products, setting up an eBay store is a cheap and easy way to do business online.

Once you've created a business account you can set up an online shop for just £6. It then costs between 15p and £2 to list an item on eBay, depending on the opening value or reserve price of the item. eBay takes a slice of the selling fee once an item is sold, depending on how much the item is worth. For items under £30, eBay takes a 5.25% share. For items between £30 and £599.99, eBay's share is 3.25% for the part of the bid above £30, and for items over £600, eBay takes 1.75%. Making and receiving payments through Paypal, eBay's online payment system of choice, also incurs a small transaction charge.

Julie King, from Newcastle, gave up her job as an IT consultant after she found she could buy and sell designer shoes and handbags on eBay for a profit. Her eBay business, **Killer Heels**, now makes more than £6,000 a month buying shoes and bags from wholesalers and selling them on eBay. Meanwhile, **Wilmamae Ward** set up a vintage clothing business, **The Gathering Goddess**. 'The most important thing is to find a niche that few other people are competing in,' she says. 'Start with selling something that you know about and/or love doing. Then research the eBay market in your particular sector, as well as on the internet in general, to see what the competition is doing and what is being offered. This will mean you can find a point of difference that will set you apart from your competitors.'

'It's also important to build up your positive feedback, as this is the bedrock of eBay and is what sets you apart as a good seller,' she continues. 'Excellent customer service equals great positive feedback, so never slack on processing orders.'

Personal trainer

Despite the government's on-going drive to cut obesity and encourage people to get fit, recent figures show that gym membership is falling. According to the *Leisure Report*, people are seeking out a 'wellness' lifestyle – and who better can help than a personal trainer, who will

ACTION POINT
LAUNCH AN eBAY BUSINESS

Start with selling something that you know about and/or love doing: This will help to drive your motivation and will be vital in maintaining your work levels, which will be heavy to start with.

Research the eBay market: In particular, do this in your sector, as well as on the internet, to see what the competition is doing and what is being offered. Find a point of difference that will set you apart from your competitors.

Be committed to it: It isn't easy, but it can be extremely rewarding.

Build up your positive feedback: This is vital for successful selling on eBay because it lets potential customers know exactly where you stand among the competition. And remember that excellent customer service will automatically get you this all-so-important positive feedback. Always aim to provide the best possible customer service.

Always keep track of your competition: Don't just research them once or occasionally. Remember they are looking at you and as your business steams ahead, they are plotting and planning to take over. Half of Wilmamae's eBay time is spent researching competitors and new marketing techniques.

Be as transparent as you can with your potential customers: Don't hide costs, and describe your items clearly and honestly. Building trust builds business on eBay.

Don't spend huge amounts of money on stock and setting up: Start small and grow it slowly. The world of eBay is quite complex and the best way of discovering this world is by experiencing it. If you plough in with a huge store full of stock without knowing the ins and outs of how eBay works, you risk falling quickly on your face.

take you outside the stuffy, artificial atmosphere of the gym and into the fresh air? There's no doubt that as the government gears itself up for the battle against obesity, and the UK set to showcase its sporting prowess in 2012, the next few years will see a peak of sporting activity – and those helping the population to achieve that goal could be set to reap the rewards.

If you think this could be for you, first you need to decide which area you want to specialise in, for example helping people to lose weight

> **The low overheads associated with the profession does mean that it can prove quite profitable**

by combining fitness and nutrition, working with pregnant women or training elite athletes. Next, find a suitable and respected course that will give you the training and qualifications you need. Although there is no singular qualification that you need to gain for becoming a fitness instructor, some courses are better respected than others, so it is worthwhile weighing up the alternatives.

Other than the cost of training, which can range from £300 to £5,000 depending on your specialty and prior knowledge, other overheads are limited. Public liability insurance is a must, and will often be in the region of £100 a year. Transport is also vital, but other costs depend on you. Most personal fitness trainers work from their clients' homes, so investment in the necessary equipment, such as free weights or a blood pressure machine, for example, is usually an early outgoing.

Linda Grave, a personal fitness trainer based in Suffolk, says, 'Most of my clients know each other because friends have recommended me to them.' How much you will earn will depend on several factors, not least how hard you want to work, but the low overheads associated with the profession does mean that it can prove quite profitable. **Steven Jones**, sales manager at Premier Fitness, says the average hourly rate charged by fitness trainers is between £20 and £50. 'It depends on several factors, such as how well known you are, your location, your specialist skills, etc.,' he explains. 'I know one guy in London who charges £100 an hour.'

> **Introductions can be made at organised social events such as dinners or drinks, or in lunch appointments as opposed to evening dates**

Dating agency

Rising divorce rates and the scarce social time enjoyed by hard-working employees have resulted in a large increase in the number of single people in the UK looking for partners. However, to run a dating agency, you need to be able to deal well with other people's emotions, and be both diplomatic and supportive.

Introductions can be made at organised social events such as dinners or drinks, or in lunch appointments as opposed to evening dates. In addition, many people prefer to meet those in the same situation as themselves, for example, single, widowed or divorced parents. An agency can offer any combination of these services, but you may do better to specialise in order to offer a good service, particularly if you are starting very small. Organised dinners, for instance, can be a good way of starting to build up a database of people. Each guest will have a friend to recommend you to, who will recommend you in turn and so on. To help decide which area to specialise in, check out the local competition for a gap in the market.

Bringing people together in the more traditional 'one-to-one' basis can be achieved in one or a combination of three ways:

- Personal introductions, where all clients are personally interviewed
- Computer comparison, where software compares submitted client details for suitability
- Lists method, where the clients receive a list of selected members.

This obviously makes for an agency with a local focus. To start small, but have a national clientele would mean running a largely computer and internet-based agency. So, you need to decide this from the start as the routes are very different. Costs will revolve around setting up a website with a payment-processing facility, and initial marketing. An agency might charge £50 for computer matching up to £2,000 plus for executive or hand-picked selection.

Driving school

With approximately 1.6 million learner tests conducted annually the demand for new instructors is very much there, so if you have the time, patience, skill and concentration, and can gain the required competence to teach other people to learn to drive, you could consider this as a career. You will also need a healthy sense of humour. You will need to pass a three-stage exam to become an approved driving instructor (ADI). Then you can choose to start out on your own or train with and sign up to a pre-established franchise that already has a list of pupils, contacts and trainers. In both cases you will be self-employed but with varying degrees of individuality and support.

If you have your own car, costs are fairly minimal. If not, you will have to either invest in one with dual controls, which will be a major expense, or be supplied with one by the franchise you work under. You will spend a large amount on fuel each week so it may be worth opening an account with a petrol station. However, the major cost is the training (up to £2,500 plus training licence, £100; ADI licence, £200; literature, £50), the three-part exam (under £200) as well as the on-going franchise fee (£40–£300), which, with a larger brand name, may be a high percentage of the work they supply you with. Against these costs, **Nick Zapettis** of A2Z Motoring gives a rough indication of what you can expect to earn. 'If you charge around £15–£16 an hour, which is the going rate, take between 30 and 50 lessons a week, including weekends and evenings, and take into account the franchise fee, then you could be earning a net salary of roughly between £15,000 and £22,000 per year,' he explains. This can be more if you go it alone, and of course the idea is that ultimately you will have your own school and franchisees.

Tutoring

If you are a good communicator and enjoy passing on your skills, then you may find tutoring attractive. Essentially, you will be offering extra tuition that provides children and young people (from primary to A level) with one-to-one or few-to-few attention they can't get in school or college. This is a profession that is ideal for people who need to be at home for certain times of the day, for example those with children. It can be operated from home, although by travelling to your clients' homes, you can increase your appeal and income. You must have a comprehensive knowledge across the complete range of your subject, and be at least one level in advance of the level you are tutoring. It isn't essential to be a qualified teacher, but having some teaching experience can reassure parents.

Cost-wise you will need access to the correct year's syllabus (around £2), sample exam papers (50p to £1) and a range of up-to-date relevant textbooks (£10 upwards). Lessons are generally charged by the hour and fees vary across the country and for different levels, but you might charge between £15 and £20 at home, plus a few extra pounds for travel. This isn't a big money business, but it can easily be built up into much more than a part-time one if you can work at weekends and do longer evenings. To make tutoring a success, it's vital to keep up to date with the curriculum, and as word-of-mouth is so important for generating more business in this field, make sure you get on well with your pupils and that they get better grades than predicted.

Public relations

A public relations (PR) and communications agency promotes and represents businesses in the general marketplace, in their specialist fields and within the media. That is, it is concerned with creating a name for its client and helping it succeed. As a PR agent you will work closely with a variety of companies, identifying their needs, while focusing on an area of personal interest and increasing relevance to each client's core business. You will need to understand the objectives of your client's business and identify a strategy for achieving them through increasingly diverse communication channels. Then you have to sell that story effectively to a chosen audience.

The bare essentials are: office premises (£650 a week), computers (£2,000), printer (£300), desks and other furniture (£700), telephones (£200), print costs (£1,000) and legal expenses (£120). But initially you could run this business from home. A sample hourly rate for executive time is £70 and you should focus on securing retained clients on a regular monthly income. In theory, therefore, two executives should be able to generate an annual income of around £150,000.

It is essential that you identify a market area to focus on that is not only new, but also experiencing growth, as this indicates that there is a

> **You will need to understand the objectives of the client's business and identify a strategy for achieving them**

> Identify a market area to focus on that is not only new, but also experiencing growth

proven market and also competition, so that companies will need help to stand out. For example, **Tim Lewis** and **Greg Moore** of Synapse Communications specialise in corporate social responsibility (CSR), working with companies that promote responsible practices to benefit business and society. Remember that this is a 'people' business, so you and your staff will need good communication skills, and the ability to be both friendly and persuasive.

Dog walking

It's often said that Britain is a nation of animal lovers, but with the credit crunch, animal care has taken a backseat as many people are putting longer and longer hours in at work in an attempt to pay off their debts.

There's no doubt, then, that Britain's dogs are crying out for attention, and if you are an animal lover with an entrepreneurial streak who empathises with these oft-overlooked victims of the economic downturn, then starting a dog-walking business could be the right business for you.

> Startup costs are relatively low for a dog-walking business

Despite reports that dog walkers have suffered from the effects of the credit crunch, a report by insurance company Insurantz.com has found that with 6.5 million dogs in the UK, dog walkers can earn up to £8 an hour per dog from time-strapped workers.

William Taylor, from industry body the National Association of Registered Petsitters ('NARP'), agrees. 'Although people might not have so much disposable income to spend on a pet sitter, they will have to work longer hours so they will need one in that instance,' he says. There's good money to be made in the business, according to Taylor. A recent survey by NARP revealed that demand rose by almost 60% in 2008. In Philadelphia, USA, one dog-walking business grossed US$650,000 (£377,800) in 2008.

Startup costs are relatively low for a dog-walking business. Your major expenditures at the beginning will be public liability insurance (£80–£150 a year); a police CRB (Criminal Record Bureau) check –

which is recommended as it will reassure your clients you are reliable – costing just over £30; flyers and business cards to spread the word in your local area (you can get 5,000 flyers printed for around £100).

It's also a good idea to join NARP, from which you will get insurance and all the forms and paperwork you will need to get the business going for around £450 a year. NARP members are advised to charge around £10 an hour per dog. 'That does vary somewhat, though,' advises Taylor, so do some research into how much competitors in your area are charging before you decide on your fees.

Debt collection

Debt collectors chase so-called 'delinquent debts', through snail mail, telephone and email, for businesses. The older the debt, the higher the commission you can collect. And with rates running as high as 60%, the earning potential of this business is clear. Although this may not be the first business opportunity that springs to mind nowadays it as an essential service to businesses and you should ignore any stigma that people may attach to it. Then you need market it in the same way as you would any other business.

Debt collection today requires good interpersonal skills and careful organisation. The 'old school' heavy-handed approach is no longer relevant, as businesses want subtlety, so that they can maintain their business relationships with the companies that owe them money.

It could be argued that debt collection is certainly a business for these times. First, it is a prime example of a sustainable business, requiring nothing more than a telephone in the first instance. Second, these are tough times, and as customer debt grows, the demand for non-court action debt collection is increasing. Also, companies are realising the value of this service more and more, as sufficient cashflow becomes increasingly vital. Many debt agencies operate from a home base, and if you network well, and establish good word-of-mouth, you can quickly build up a client base.

> **Debt collection today requires good interpersonal skills and careful organisation**

So if you are self-motivated, enjoy dealing with people and can think quickly on your feet, debt collection could be the right business for you.

Cake making

Although cake making has been hit by everything from high flour costs to aggressive supermarket pricing, the British cake market was worth close to £1.8 billion in 2007, and according to Euromonitor, this figure is forecast to grow by almost 5% by 2012. So if you are interested in cake making as a business, and can ride out the current economic conditions, the demand seems to be there for you to reap the rewards when the good times return.

Keeping your head above water in this industry will require organisation, a good head for figures and a certain amount of artistic flair. 'We work long hours and it's tiring, because you've got to hit delivery times spot on,' explains **Lynn Oxley**, who has been running Oxley's of Morpeth and its accompanying website, Cake Perfect, since 2003.

" Your cakes will need to look as professional as possible "

Your cakes will need to look as professional as possible, so training in all aspects of the industry, from sugarcraft to marzipan techniques, is essential if you want to compete in a busy market. However, there are several courses available for all levels of cake making, so you should find one which will suit your commitments. Courses start at around £190 for 10 weekly sessions, rising to around £500 for a 30-week NVQ course. Alternatively, The Bakery School has an online course that you can complete at your own pace. A one-year licence for the downloadable software costs £250 plus VAT.

Shaz Yousaf's preparation for starting up his own organic cake making business, The Healthy Dessert Kitchen, included testing his creations out on friends and work colleagues, and noting down comments and reactions. He also looked for key opportunities to publicise his enterprise, such as appearing on Asian TV channel Sunrise.

Your startup costs will depend on how big an operation you wish to run. The fewer overheads you have, the lower your expenditure, so working from home initially is a good idea. But you will soon need to trade up to professional catering equipment, and follow the required hygiene and health and safety guidelines.

Pricing is tricky, but you can charge from around £30 for a simple 10-inch diameter sponge to up £900 for an intricate, five-tiered wedding cake.

Landscape gardener

The Horticultural Trade Association's figures show that the landscape gardening industry employs over 60,000 people and has an annual turnover of approximately £3bn – and it is growing. This presents a great opportunity for greenfingered entrepreneurs, but there is real hard graft involved – most landscape gardeners start off as one-person operations. According to **Kath Walker**, field officer for the Association of Professional Landscapers, there is far more to the job than people generally think.

'You have to have training. It's a diverse industry and you have to have expertise in lots of different areas,' she says. Areas in landscape gardening include water features, building, paving, stonework, wind structures, decking, joinery, groundsmanship, draining and irrigation. You also need fairly comprehensive knowledge of plants and what can grow where.

As landscape gardener **Mark Gregory** of Landmark puts it: 'At its simplest it's doing garden makeovers. At its best it's an art form.' This, of course, means there's plenty of scope to develop a landscape gardening business to match your skills and ambitions. The key to success is building a strong reputation which leads to most business coming through recommendations.

So, if you like getting your hands dirty and being creative, then perhaps it's time to start thinking.

The business is sensitive to the weather, with excessive rain making work difficult, and it is also seasonal. So you need to be resourceful

> " At its simplest it's doing garden makeovers. At its best it's an art form "

and plan carefully. **Warren Hall**, who runs his own landscape gardening business in Kingston-upon-Thames, Surrey, explains: 'The first year was exceptionally difficult; I had to do lots of maintenance work, but as the days got sunnier, the work picked up. It's ideal to squirrel the money away: the summer may be busy, but you need to cover yourself over winter.'

Landscape gardening can be one of the cheaper businesses to go into. In fact, Gregory estimates the average startup cost to be somewhere between £5,000 and £10,000. This will cover everything

---

VALUEFLORA AND THE CHEAP SHOT

Company: Valueflora
Owner-manager: Russell Hirst

Russell Hirst was just 21 years old when he set up his online flower delivery service from a bedroom at his parents' home in Manchester. Hirst's 'one room, one computer' company is now selling flowers to 120 countries.

Hirst says he is self-taught when it comes to the internet and attributes his success with Valueflora to noticing a gap in the market. By putting customers in touch with the farms that grew the flowers, he could cut out the middle man (high street florists). Customers choose their flowers from the website, their order is sent directly to the flower farms, where the flowers are packaged and sent off directly to the customer. There are no call centres – everything is done online, and Valueflora has just six members of staff.

The flowers come from all over the world, from the UK to Thailand and Cost Rica, while Valueflora's customers are also global. Amazingly, Hirst claims his global enterprise cost under £10 to start. 'It was done on a shoestring,' says Hirst. 'I paid £8 for the domain name and it was pretty much just me for the first 18 months, cold calling people and getting in touch with the farmers.'

Living at home kept overheads low. 'I was fortunate in that respect,' says Hirst, 'because it's not easy living without a wage for two years.' Hirst says the biggest obstacle to overcome was cashflow. Because virtually no money was spent on starting up the company, every penny of profit was invested back into the business to ensure its growth. Hirst also dedicated a great deal of time to search engine optimisation (SEO), spending up to 60 hours a week looking to establish Valueflora's search ranking.

With a current annual growth rate of 700% and a turnover of more than £1m, Hirst is planning to branch out into providing flowers for events, and remains keen to extend the Value brand further.

from an array of light and heavy tools to a second-hand van. At the outset, charging around £100 a day and allowing for four days ruled out a month through the weather, while taking into account petrol and insurance costs, you can generate an income of around £15,000 a year.

Other popular options
Online businesses

Starting an online business can be as simple as setting up a basic shop on eBay (see 'Shoestring startups', above) to sell a few wholesale items, to coming up with a completely new online concept with a novel way of monetising it.

The beauty of the online business is that it's suited to just about anyone. You don't need to be an MBA graduate based in London to succeed. You can start your operation from anywhere, as long as you've got access to an internet connection and a bit of business acumen. You can start off small, work on it part-time or even view it as a hobby before you decide whether to commit to it.

Claire Lewis and **Pat Wood** started their online retro T-shirt shop Truffleshuffle.com as a part-time venture. 'It all started after Pat bought a retro T-shirt in the States and friends kept asking where he'd got it,' explains Claire. 'Truffleshuffle was only ever intended to be a hobby – something to bring in a bit of spare cash. It was only when the site went live and started growing that we thought: "There's mileage in this."'

At the other end of the scale, **Sophie Cornish** and **Holly Tucker** did a five-year profit-and-loss feasibility plan before they started work on their website, Notonthehighstreet.com, an online marketplace where customers can buy from a whole range of independent, quirky and specialised small businesses in a single transaction.

Key factors to consider for an online business are: making sure your domain name reflects your business; choosing the right hosting

> " Truffleshuffle was only ever intended to be a hobby – something to bring in a bit of spare cash "

ONLINE BUSINESS MODELS

After you have decided how much time, money and resources you want to put into your online venture, there are three basic online business models you can follow:

- E-commerce – which means that customers buy directly from your website
- Advertising – which means you get as many visitors as possible, increasing the amount of customers your advertisers reach
- Subscription – which means users pay to access all or part of that content.

You can of course base your website around a combination of two or all of these models.

service; adhering to online trading rules; working carefully on the design and functionality of the site and optimising it for search engines to maximise exposure.

Startup costs for online businesses vary widely from very little for an eBay set-up to thousands of pounds for a hosted, e-commerce site.

Crafts

If you are creative and enjoy making things, then you could put these talents to good use and enjoy real job satisfaction by starting up a crafts business. For example, you could launch a blown glass design company, which would involve individually designing and making glass awards, vases, bowls, paperweights and commissioned sculpture. Alternatively you could work with other materials such as metal (designing and making popular items such as wrought iron gates, curtain poles, bases for tables), wood (using your carpentry skills to make furniture), or clay (creating crockery and ornaments).

A crafts business can be relatively cheap to start up, as you can set up a workshop at home so that you only have to buy tools and materials. To go into the glass blowing business, for example, it is possible to rent a studio one day a week (around £130) to blow the glass and give yourself enough work for the rest of the week. **Susan Nixon** of Susan Nixon Design established a workshop for under

£4,000, including £500 for a compressor and £500 for a sandblaster. If you do this, however, remember you need to follow the necessary health and safety guidelines.

To be taken seriously in your field you will need formal design training either from a university or college. Nixon spent over two years on a glass blowing scholarship, demonstrating in a museum. Learning in someone else's business can also be invaluable practical experience. But you may be able to study part-time while working, and this is also a business that you can start while in another job to build up contacts and examples of your work.

The demand for individually designed artefacts is booming, but this also means there is plenty of competition. Getting along to and exhibiting at national and international craft fairs and events can help you build key contacts. However, bear in mind that it will take time to establish yourself as a known artist.

You will earn money through individual commissions, selling directly through trade shows or, if you hit the big time, creating pieces for retail chains. Studio glassware starts at around £20 rising to £1,000 upwards. For exclusive pieces, £150 upwards is not uncommon, and around £100 for retail vases.

> " You will need formal design training either from a university or college "

Photography

For many amateur photographers, running a professional photography business would be a dream come true, and now it can be. The photography industry offers many opportunities for keen amateurs who want to make a living from it.

Wedding photography is the most high-profile money-maker. It is generally recognised by most photographers as being a highly skilled job – not only in terms of taking photographs, but handling all kinds of people at a potentially emotional time. It tends to be seasonal, too. May to September is the busiest time – accounting for 80% – 90% of the work – with the rest of the year being relatively quiet, when many wedding photographers will turn to other sources of income, such as

> " The photography industry offers many opportunities for keen amateurs who want to make a living from it "

passport and portrait work, or commercial and industrial photography. This means it pays to be flexible.

Photography is a business you can run from home, but you will need to set aside some space for administration and storing equipment. Many home-based photographers convert a garage into an all-in-one studio, admin, storage and reception facilities. A double garage attached to your home is ideal for doing this. Budget around £5,000 for your conversion costs. Alternatively, you can rent a small shop with a display area and a small studio; prices will vary depending on your location. But, of course, a shop will give you a higher public profile and you may not need to spend as much on marketing your business. You will also need photographic equipment – a reasonable camera and lens, studio lights and back-drops will cost around £5,000. Then there's general administration and marketing, which could rise to between £4,000 and £8,000 over the year.

You can learn your trade through a college course or if you are a gifted amateur you can pick up professional tips by offering your services to a local business.

Your potential earnings will depend on many factors, not least your range of services and your ability to market yourself as a top-notch photographer. However, a reasonably established photographer should expect to earn an least £20,000 a year, with weddings, for example, potentially generating a profit from around £50 to £750 each, depending on the size of the event.

> "
> It won't be until you have a large operation that you start bringing in good money, so it could be worthwhile to start up part time "

Catering

Whether it's a major sporting event or a low-key wedding, food and drink at gatherings will always be in fashion. In fact, with a growing population of foodies and people becoming more nutritionally aware, it is increasingly a key part of an event. The key to success in catering lies in a passion for excellent quality food and service, along with exploiting any gap in the catering marketing that may exist in your area.

As an independent there are two main sectors you can target – private and corporate events. The former category consists of, for example, family occasions such as weddings, birthday parties, dinner parties and funerals. In serving the corporate world, you are more likely to provide food for business breakfasts, business lunches, board meetings and evening receptions. Some caterers specialise in one or the other, while others try to cover both.

Taking into account the professional equipment you will need, you are looking at between £20,000 and £50,000 to start up, depending on the size of business and whether you are starting up at home or moving into premises. It won't be until you have a large operation that you start bringing in good money, so it could be worthwhile to start up part-time. **Sue Roberts** did this and has grown Bristol-based Topline Catering gradually over 20 years, moving from sandwich delivery to business lunches, and finally to corporate and private events for up to 1,000 guests. From first-day takings of £13, the business now turns over £300,000 a year. It obviously takes several years to build up to this size, but a small yet successful business could nevertheless turn over £100,000 and earn a net profit of £40,000.

> **You will start bringing in good money once you go big time, so it could be worthwhile to start up part-time**

Florists

Opening a florist business may be the result of a gardening hobby, but even if you are new to the sector you can start up and make a success of this business. Of all retail businesses, this is one that could probably be almost recession-proof, as people always want to send, and appreciate getting, flowers, whether the occasion is happy or sad. But an online presence is practically a must these days.

The flower market has been on the increase since the early 1990s with UK fresh flowers and indoor plants representing £1.5bn at retail level. Before setting up, carry out thorough market research of the area you want to cover, the people who live and work there and the existing competition. 'Any kind of specialisation is beneficial. Florists should also emphasise the additional design input and technical skill

> **Floristry has the classic retail cost base of premises and stock, so the initial outlay can be significant**

that goes into their work,' says **Andrea Caldecourt** of the Flowers and Plants Association. 'This often has a personal touch – just as artists and clothes designers are recognisable by their work.'

Of the 6,700 florist businesses in the UK, around 80% are members of relay organisations such as InterFlora, Teleflower or Flowergram, which allow people in one part of the country to 'send' flowers to a someone in another part of the country or abroad through a network of florists. The benefit of this membership is that you will receive support in marketing and sales, and product and design, and as a result of the organisations' international links, you may compete with multi-national firms, and respond to a changing market. Floristry has the classic retail cost base of premises and stock, so the initial outlay can be significant. As with clothing retail, risks are high, but if you get it right, the rewards can be substantial.

CONTACT

Flowers and Plants Association
www.flowers.org.uk
☎020 7738 8044

Running a hotel

The types of client you attract depend, to a large extent, on the hotel's location

Whether it's just a simple bed and shared bathroom or full en suite luxury, somewhere for the weary traveller to stay for the night is always in demand. Obviously, location is the key to success, but the rise of boutique establishments means that many people are increasingly going for style and ambience over five-star blandness.

The first thing to consider is what type of hotel you want to run. Is it going to be a small, cosy affair catering for couples seeking a romantic weekend break, or a larger, metropolitan establishment servicing the corporate market? Some hotels pitch for both business and private clients. The types of client you attract depend, to a large extent, on the hotel's location. The size of the hotel, its location and the clientele you are aiming to attract will all determine costs. It is possible to rent, but buying means you keep more of the profits.

As an example, **Stephen Hipwell** bought a 20-year lease on the Granville Hotel in Brighton for £350,000, with the total expenditure, excluding VAT, expected to be £280,000 a year. There are basically two schools of thought when it comes to turnover. The first is to keep earnings below the VAT threshold, which is £54,000, which at a usual 40% profit margin you are looking at clearing £20,000. The alternative is to go all out to earn as much as possible. To make it worthwhile you need to earn considerably more than the VAT threshold, which means taking £100,000+. Hipwell is forecasting a turnover of £400,000 this year.

Hairdressing

If there was a service that was always in demand, this could be it. Having said that, competition is fierce, and you do need to train hard to gain the necessary qualifications; it also involves long hours. But if you find the right location you are almost certain to make money. With the variety of customers, from children to adults, it pays to be a people person in this business. However, unless you open your own chain of shops, it's unlikely to make you a millionaire. But as **Linda Heald** from Keeping Up Appearances in Chichester, West Sussex, says: 'Getting paid for something you love doing and working with friends in a nice atmosphere can't be beaten.'

A look at hairdressing companies currently for sale over the internet indicates that purchasing such a business can cost anywhere between £5,000 and £59,000, including fixtures and fittings. If you are starting from scratch, there'll be the usual outlay for either renting or buying premises, plus fixtures, fittings and equipment. Keeping it basic, Heald spent £1,000 on basic salon fittings and a further £3,000 on chairs and dryers. Having sat down and costed all the equipment she had to buy to fully kit out her salon, she found out that it set her back £1,800. But this could be a lot more expensive depending on the level of ostentation. 'You could stagger these costs though and just get essentials and then buy extras as you begin to make a profit. Also, you must remember to set aside money for the taxman right from day one,' she says. On a good week, Heald can earn around £1,300. But when you take away costs, she will be left with a figure more likely to be between £300 and £400.

> **If you find the right location you are almost certain to make money**

Running a day nursery

Day nurseries are a vital service for the many families that can't afford to give up a regular income to stay at home. Clearly, you need the ability to spend long hours with children as well as patience and other child minding skills, but this is a growing area and one that appears to be increasingly in demand. It is a business that tends to attract working parents – usually either because they have found a gap in what nurseries in their area offer or because there is nothing available in the area at all.

Running a nursery will not make you quick money. But, if you want a job – and a business – that offers hourly challenges and a lot of rewards then this could be right for you. Finding suitable premises is a must. The regulations set out how much space you will need per child, so once you have worked out how many children you want to have you will know the minimum space required. You can either rent or buy, or build from scratch, but this can be expensive. Some local authorities allow modular nurseries, which are much cheaper to build and can be up and running quickly – for 25–30 children they cost around £80,000.

Freya Derrick set up Hopscotch Day Nursery for £600,000 and is now turning over £50,000 per month with 82 children currently attending the nursery. 'You've got to decide right from the beginning if you want to run the business as a lifestyle choice, or as a profit-making thing, and that will determine the size of the operation,' she says. 'I wanted to have the freedom to spend time with my children, but I also wanted to run a successful business.'

> " **Finding suitable premises is a must** "

Running a restaurant

Despite the downturn, eating out remains big business with a huge variety of restaurants now inhabiting British high streets. However, whatever the climate, many new restaurants won't survive for long due to the sheer amount of competition. But if you can think strategically and find the right niche for your location, the rewards can be great in terms of both job satisfaction and money. For his restaurant, which seats 40 people, **Stephane Luiggi**, owner of the French Living restaurant in Nottingham, spent £5,000 on kitchen equipment, some of which was second-hand, and £5,000 on tables and chairs. Then there's the premises. 'You need to have quite a lot of money, particularly in central London, where an 80-seater restaurant would cost you about £1m,' explains restaurant consultant **Torquil Macleod**. However, if you are going for something slightly more modest, a restaurant on a suburban high street for example, then you should have between £70,000 and £150,000 in your pockets, explains **Mike Rogers**, director of startups and small businesses at Barclays.

Aside from the equipment, staff will be one of your biggest fixed costs. If you are open seven days a week, you will need more than one chef. Head chefs can these days command salaries of between £30,000 and £40,000 per year – and getting a good chef will be critical to your business. To avoid being just another restaurant casualty, be prepared to run a business rather than merely indulge a hobby. Market research is essential. 'You need to check out the location and the competition,' says Rogers. 'What's your catchment area? What's more, you can't charge a premium when you first open. You need to know what will make people want to come and spend their money with you. With local research you can see what is popular whether it be Mexican, Thai, Japanese, whatever.' There are also all the hygiene and health and safety regulations to negotiate, and initially long hours to cope with, but if you think strategically and implement your business plan carefully, you will find that there is money to be made.

Internet café

Although the number of households with a broadband connection is soaring, internet cafés are still highly popular among people who need to get online while on the move. And even though wifi is increasingly available, those with laptops still need somewhere comfortable to

> " If you are open seven days a week, you will need more than one chef "

> " Many of our users have a PC at home and work and yet still use us… simply because they are so used to using it "

base themselves between appointments or simply to while away a few hours. So this business could make a tidy profit.

'Many of our users have a PC at home and work and yet still use us or other cafés, simply because they are so used to it,' says **Jason Deane** of Quarks (www.quarks.co.uk), a chain of internet cafés in and around London. 'Once you have chosen a suitable space for your café, you will need to set a budget for all the equipment and add-ons you plan to provide customers.'

BEATTHATQUOTE.COM AND THE COPY CAT PRINCIPLE

Company: BeatthatQuote.com
Owner: John Paleomylites

Launched in 2005, and winner of the 2006 Startups Awards, price comparison site Beatthatquote.com continues to plough, behemoth-like, past its competitors. It was recently crowned the fastest-growing site on the web, with monthly figures for unique visitors growing by 1,165%, beating Facebook, which came second with a measly 781%. Serial entrepreneur **John Paleomylites** is ever the ambitious business owner: 'There's still plenty more growth that we are on target to achieve,' he says.

Paleomylites started up to compete with MoneySupermarket.com and is quite convinced that you don't have to have an original idea to succeed in business. In fact, he thinks it can be a hindrance. 'The business model was entirely copied,' he says. 'What we aimed to do was better it, so we looked to see what they did, saw where we could improve on that process, and then employed it – with much more effective technology.

'I think it's easier to make money from an unoriginal idea than it is an original idea. If you look at it in the way a venture capital company would, an original model is a market risk. If the market has accepted the product that you are trying to sell or the service you are trying to sell, there's no market risk.

'With a new idea, you don't know whether you can develop the technology to meet the business requirements because it's the first time that business requirement has been influenced, so there's a technology risk there. You don't necessarily know whether you can get skilled staff to move from something they haven't done before to something entirely new, so there's a management risk there.

'With my last company, everything was new. Every time you sold something to a client you had to explain to that client what it is that you do – there was a six-month sales cycle before they even understood what it was that you were selling. This time, all that work has been done and everyone understands what it is that we do.'

'Our own branches have cost between £17,000 and £150,000 to start, so the amount is hugely varied,' Deane continues. On top of this, you are also likely to have to pay out for internet access (£4,000 a year), PCs (£400 a year), networks (up to £1,000 a year), timing systems to ensure customers do not go over their time limit (£500 a year), a website and hosting (£1,000 a year), plus equipment such as printers, fax, scanners and CD burner (around £1,000 depending on requirements). These costs are just a guide as internet cafés vary in size and what they provide. To make money with an internet café, you must plan carefully and meet public demand for additional services. Research the businesses that will surround your café – do they offer the services that you could offer, such as gaming, printing, scanning and, most importantly, web surfing? If no companies in your area offer these things, you should consider incorporating them into your internet café. This market is very competitive and internet access is a commodity, nothing more. Therefore your service has to be different and priced accordingly.'

Protecting your business ideas

Once you have come up with an idea for a new business, it's important to think about protecting any original aspects of your concept that could prove invaluable to its success. This is known as your intellectual property. The main reason for guarding this is to prevent others from using your key business ideas without your permission. Failing to protect the intellectual property of your business can mean that ideas vital to your product or service could be used by competitors, and this could severely affect the performance of your company in the future.

Your intellectual property could be rooted in your product, which may contain a feature that makes it different from other similar products and vital to its appeal to your customers. This may also be the case for a particular service. You may also want to make sure no other company uses the original name or brand of your specific product or service.

The UK Intellectual Property Office can help you to identify the key elements of your business that you may need to protect, from trademarks to designs and processes. It will also provide advice on how best to go about doing this, such as applying for a patent or copyright.

CONTACT

UK Intellectual
Property Office
www.ipo.gov.uk

Protecting your intellectual property is also vital from an investment perspective. When starting up and as your business develops, you are likely to need financial backing to help your company grow. This could be for anything from boosting cashflow to taking on new staff and moving to new premises. Any investor, whether a bank or private equity company, will carefully examine your business before lending any money, to make sure that the business is sound and that their investment will be safe. During this 'due diligence' process, if an investor discovers that you have not adequately protected your intellectual property, they are unlikely to provide the required financial support. This is because, not only does this open your business to outside competition and therefore risk, but it also reflects badly on you as the proprietor for not having considered protecting your intellectual property in the first place. Further down the line when you come to selling your business, your intellectual property can have a significant influence on its value, as well as its appeal to prospective buyers.

So, as you develop the idea for your business towards a possible launch, it's important to bear in mind any potentially valuable intellectual property that you may need to protect.

KIRSTY'S STORY

My lightbulb moments

The website Entertainthekids.com was set up by **Kirsty McGregor** and her brother Gregg. It provides a one-stop shop for parents and carers looking for some inspiration when it comes to the difficult job of keeping kids entertained, and is proving highly successful. Throughout this guide Kirsty will be giving you an insight into setting up her business and some of the problems she has faced. Here she describes the moment she came up with the idea, and how beforehand she had listed the criteria her business had to meet:

'My lightbulb moments came in early January 2005, both of them borne out of sheer frustration at trying to entertain my own baby, then only 12 months old. After the initial idea popped into my head, I started researching the market (namely, the internet) and found that what I wanted to do appeared to be fairly unique. Most of the "competition" was more general sites, offering a whole range of things for parents, but no site appeared to specialise in just providing activity ideas… We have amended the product slightly since those early days. For example, we thought about recommending books and toys, but then decided that we were straying away from our core focus area, and to provide personal opinions could alienate some members who didn't agree with our tastes.

We also considered a chat room or message board, but again decided that it wasn't for us. There are plenty of great "community" sites that do this really well, and we didn't want to compete with them. We knew what we wanted, and we just had to see if it was viable. As well as provide parents and carers with inspirational activities for children, we also wanted the site to be:

- Quick to load and easy to use
- Clean, uncluttered (the company's strapline is "… and now you can relax!")
- No banner advertising or pop-ups, instead the business model is based on members paying a subscription
- Original content, not just a myriad of links to other sites
- Focused on traditional entertainment activities for children aged 0–11, not straying into other areas, such as advice, health or education.'

the accountancy network you can count on

The abacus accountancy network is an affiliate member of the British Franchise Association (BFA) and is the only accountancy network that is specifically for qualified accountants.

abacus was established in September 2004 and to-date has over 50 practices in the UK representing the network.

What does this mean to you the client?

abacus can offer a local service but with the specialist support associated with a national organisation. Furthermore, being part of a network enables abacus accountants to offer a cost effective "Value for Money" service to all its clients.

All our accountants gained invaluable experience working in various industries before joining the abacus network and they therefore have a greater understanding of your financial and accounting requirements.

This experience has helped us to build an enviable reputation for providing excellent advice and a first class service to our business and personal clients alike. We have amassed a portfolio of over 2,000 clients across many industry sectors covering individuals', start up business and medium and large organisations within the SME market arena.

Industry sectors in which we currently have clients, covers:-

- Pubs, restaurants and hotels;
- the Professions;
- the Service Sector;
- the Construction Industry;
- Manufacturing;
- Retailing and Distribution.

In addition to traditional auditing, accounting and tax services we also provide advice on how to improve and develop your business. Whether you need an integrated business strategy, access to corporate finance or specialist tax advice we are here to help you achieve your goals.

We understand that the needs of a business change from company to company and throughout the life cycle of an organisation, we therefore take the time to talk with our clients to establish their requirements and tailor the services we provide to optimise the accounting and financial solution.

Please visit our website: **www.abacusnetwork.co.uk** to view the wide range of services abacus has to offer.

abacus Franchising Company Limited, 3a Colima Avenue, Sunderland Enterprise , Park West, Sunderland, Tyne and Wear, SR5 3XB
Tel: 0844 050 2254 Fax: 0844 050 2255
Email: enquiries@abacusnetwork.co.uk Web: www.abacusnetwork.co.uk

Zepter International is a global enterprise which produces, sells and distributes exclusive, high-quality consumer goods around the world. Principally this is achieved by way of direct sales. Zepter uses 'direct sales' as a way of passing the products from the manufacturer to the end user / customer by personal recommendation through an Independent Consultant. We insist that our Consultants use, appreciate and can honestly verify the benefits of using our products before they recommend them to anyone else.

The UK branch of Zepter International was renamed 'Tuttoluxo Ltd' in January this year as a way to shine the light of Zepter in this country as a larger and more dynamic presence here.

Zepter International manufactures its products to the highest possible qualities in Italy, Switzerland and Germany. The range of the Zepter products is wide to suit every person and every home.

Zepter stainless steel Cookware:
A revolutionary cooking system made from stainless steel 18/10 and produced in Italy. As well as the traditional way of cooking, you can cook without having to use water or fat and oil.

Zepter Food Preservation System VacSy®:
A patented Vacuum System that saves fresh and cooked food, thus keeping its natural organic properties and vitamins.

Bioptron Light Therapy Medical Devices:
Unique and patented Swiss made light therapy devices for the treatment of wound healing, pain management, varying skin conditions and general well being.

Skin care products:
Swisso Logical: This range offers a large choice of skincare products for the whole family. Perfect for women, ideal for men and essential for babies.
LaDanza: Perfect for the mature skin and helps combat premature skin ageing.
Active Spa: Natural products with active formulas coming from selected gardens and unpolluted waters.
Swiss Nature: This range is based on fresh Edelweiss extract.
Swiss Nature Sun: This range, not only includes Edelweiss extract but also vitamins A,C and E plus coconut and monoi oils.

Being in direct sales with Zepter enables you to start your own business and create an extra income working part or full time, at your own pace, to suit you.

Whether you decide to work and retail our products on your own or to combine that with building a team, Zepter has a unique marketing plan that is designed to generate the best income from your work and efforts. Every consultant who starts working with Zepter has an immediate starting income of 25% on all their net personal sales. Our additional commission percentages start from 4% on your net personal sales and up to 26% on your net group sales.

To become an Independent Consultant and start retailing and earning money, you need to register and purchase a starter pack containing a smart carrying case and catalogues. The cost of this will be £30.00 + postage and you will have 14 days money back guarantee (£30.00) if you change your mind.

"I'll Guarantee You'll Be On Over £70,000 Within 12-Months If You Follow My Proven Step-By-Step Guide To Starting Your Own Carpet Cleaning Business!"

If you're looking for a business opportunity with all the benefits of owning a franchise, with ready-made marketing and support – BUT without paying any franchise fee, then becoming a **Professional Cleaner with ALLTEC Network i** s the logical choice for your future.

How can I be so sure? – Well, a several years ago I found myself in pretty much the same position as you are probably in now. I was working long hours, yet was poorly paid - I derived little or no job satisfaction and had few job prospects to look forward to.

I decided to start my own business, as I wanted...

- ✓ **To work from home**
- ✓ **Low start-up costs**
- ✓ **Low overheads**
- ✓ **Easy to learn and run**
- ✓ **Work hours to suit me**
- ✓ **High profit margins**

Like you, I came across something that suggested professional carpet and upholstery cleaning might be the opportunity I was looking for, and although at the time it seemed an unlikely solution, it subsequently proved to fulfil all the ideals that were important to me.

To cut a very long story short, after a lot on money spent on the wrong marketing, I found a formula which worked and my company started to grow, and now I've gone from carpet cleaner to owning one of the largest manufacturing and supply businesses for carpet cleaning in the UK.

Now I Can Help You Make £1,500 - £2,000 Per Week From Cleaning Carpets!

I can offer you everything you need to start-up your own carpet cleaning business from the machines, detergents, training and marketing … in fact all you need to do is follow my tried, tested and proven step-by-step guide.

Soon you can be making an average of £250 per job and you can easily do two jobs a day – making you £500 per day for 3 or 4 days cleaning and just one day 'quoting' in customers home.

Robert Saunders
Managing Director
ALLTEC Network,
Butts Business Units, Fowlmere, Royston, Herts, SG8 7SL.
Tel 01763 208222
www.alltec.co.uk

Unique Solutions in Promoting Your Image

Nigel Toplis, managing director of Recognition Express and past chairman of the British Franchise Association, explains the increasing appeal of franchising.

It can be argued that franchising is neither an industry in its own right nor in fact a business.

Rather it is one of the fastest growing and most consistently successful methods (a marketing concept) for distributing products and services, with some 467,000* people employed and a market turnover in excess of £11 billion per annum*.

Franchising is the answer to many people's dreams of becoming their own boss – a proven business system with a supportive framework.

It is a crazy mixture of conformity and individuality and combines the very best elements of big business and small operation. To be successful a Franchise Owner must comply with the franchise system and yet such compliance will enable the franchisee to achieve a level of self-fulfilment.

'In business for yourself, not by yourself' really does capture the essence of franchising.

A franchisor will always be on hand to provide knowledge and expertise on all the key areas of business which Franchise Owners can take as much or as little advantage of this as they require. Some have referred to the relationship of franchisor and Franchise Owner as a 'marriage'. It is the ideal option for both enterprisers and those less keen to take a big leap into the unknown.

Support

Due to the scale of this support, Franchise Owners come from a wide range of backgrounds and experience. Running a franchise is conducive to a variety of transferable skills, including project management, marketing, operations and sales, and the franchisor is there to help if you need to boost any skill sets.

Opportunity

Franchise Owners can often choose where their franchise is based and many can be run from home, meaning more time to spend with the family and no daily commute. This is a huge benefit for many franchisees, especially parents. Franchising is also ideal for people who have lots to offer, but who would find the structure of regular employment unsuitable, such as single parents or people with disabilities.

For young people too, franchising is an excellent way to launch their careers. A Coventry franchise was opened three years ago by Alex Newman former employee at our Recognition Express headquarters, and in his mid-twenties.

"Buying a Recognition Express franchise has given me a unique opportunity to become a business owner at such a young age. The market potential is massive, our product range extensive and the range of companies we access is huge. We expect to end our 3rd year at around £250,000 with a net margin of 25% plus and I am aiming for £350,0000 in my fourth year."

Alex Newman Recognition Express, Coventry

Rationale

There is a good quote from the book 'Growing Pains' that accurately differentiates between running your own 'independent' business and a franchise, stating that running your own business is

"about as easy as navigating unchartered waters in a leaking rowing boat with an inexperienced crew while surrounded by a school of sharks. The crew might be glad to know that others before them have made the voyage successfully and to hear (and learn) of the lessons that other voyagers learned in the process."

Franchising is very much a two way street where the franchisor can achieve faster expansion of his/her operation, make more money and gain a higher return on capital employed.

The Franchise Owner on the other hand gets a proven business system to include marketing, goodwill, training, support, trademarks etc to help them become a successful business person in their own right.

Selecting a franchise opportunity

Key questions to ask when considering a franchise

- Why do I want to run a business?

Personal ambition, getting just reward for effort, attaining greater job security, to learn new skills, building a capital asset and to work with the family are all well documented reasons.

- What am I good at?

Sit down and evaluate your strengths and weaknesses, your likes and dislikes. You should look upon a franchise as a long term tenure, more a vocation than a job.

- What sort of person am I?

It will help if you are positive, outgoing and energetic, if you like solving problems and see yourself both as a self starter and a team player.

- What can I afford?

Be sure you can afford both the initial fee and the time spent training (so not earning), as well as any shortfalls over the first months of trading.

If you think the venture is going to cost you £100,000 and you only raise £80,000 be very, very sure before you beg and borrow (usually from family) to go ahead.

Once you've identified a business that:
- interests you
- uses your skills/experience
- you can afford
- matches your aspirations
the next step is to find the right franchisor and to help here are

10 questions you should ask
- Do they have a solid trading history?
- Are they financially sound?
- Do they have a history of success?
- Is there a genuine Head Office support structure?
- What do they actually provide by way of support?
- If the franchisor supplies product, what are the T's and C's?
- What is their position in the market?
- Are projected cash flows realistic? Can they prove so?
- Does the company have a finance facility with the banks?
- How tough is their interview process?

You should now be in a position where you have decided to become a business owner, you know the type of business and industry you want to be in and you've chosen the franchisor to get into bed with.

Next do a Business Plan (possibly with the help of a good accountant) which explains what you hope to do, how much money you need to do it and how you propose to pay the money back. Finally approach the bank!

The magic of franchising is that it combines an individual skill set, ambition, drive and energy with the tools, training, branding, support and proven business system of the Franchise.

Remember, you're in franchising for yourself but never by yourself.

Ideas for Start-Ups

To aspiring business owners.

Whether you fancy starting a retailing business, a manufacturing company or something in the rapidly growing service industry, it's going to be hard work.
It's tough in the good times but in these uncertain times it's going to be much more demanding.

Getting financial support is more difficult. Banks are cautious and getting them to part with the required funding you need will take twice as long as usual

An exceptionally good business plan and a fully researched marketing plan will help your cause.

Hopefully you do a good job presenting your case to the bank and they eventually lend you the money.

Now, you're on your own to go market, advertise and hopefully, sell your product or service. Fingers crossed you get an order- or two!

Supply is another thing.

Let's hope the product or the service you provide is up to scratch. It needs to be.

Little tip- whatever business you end up running, ask the customers how they feel about you and your service or product. It means you can put the wrongs right, giving you another opportunity to show them just how good you can be.

If you don't ask it's probable they won't volunteer the information, and the first you know of their disenchantment is when they are giving business to a competitor.

Another tip - Treat your customers how you wish to be treated.

As I say, it's very tough starting and then running your own business, but you can make life a little easier- get a partner the best one you can find. Another company would be a good place to start looking. You should seek one with the right, proven product, the system to market and sell it, and one that knows about growing a business from scratch!

That company we've described is a franchise. A business concept designed to help people just like you.

Make life easier with someone alongside you, an organization that has the systems in place and a brand that's recognized. A company such as Chemex International for instance, a 'blue chip' opportunity, 24 years as a franchise and responsible for some real success stories.

Franchising in the UK is growing faster than most other businesses or industry. It speaks for itself. Do yourself a favor acquire yourself a good franchise, a vehicle to take you where you want to be. Chemex would be a great place to start if you really want a proper business.

To talk about your future aspirations phone me on 0121 565 6315 or email: ron.hutton@chemexuk.com

Ron Hutton

DECISION TIME

WHAT'S IN THIS CHAPTER

■ Having formulated your idea, or even if you are still trying to choose the right kind of business for you, you may feel ready to start taking the first steps to starting up on your own. But before you do so make sure you know what it takes to be an entrepreneur. This chapter will help you understand the commitment it involves and the kind of person you need to be to succeed, and when to take the plunge and quit your present job. By the time you reach the end of this chapter, you should know for certain whether you are cut out for entrepreneurialism, so read on…

What it takes to become an entrepreneur

Although it's critical to carefully consider what kind of business you would like to launch, having a good idea doesn't automatically lead to success. An original concept or devising a company that you are confident has a strong market is great start, but the key to making it a going concern is, quite simply, you. No matter how good your idea, it will only be a success if you have the necessary drive to turn it into a profitable business. Whether you have what it takes to be a successful entrepreneur ultimately comes down to three factors:

- Being certain you want to start your own business
- Being certain you can take the risk to give up a secure income
- Being certain you are cut out for it.

> " No matter how good your idea, it will only be a success if you have the necessary drive to turn it into a profitable business "

Are you sure you really want to start your own business?

You shouldn't view becoming your own boss as simply an escape route from your current job, and certainly not as an easy option. In all probability, you will be working harder than you are at the moment. You need to be prepared to do this and be totally committed to your business idea.

Is it too great a risk to give up a secure income?

Initially, starting up is likely to put pressure on your financial stability, as it will be a big risk, no matter how good an idea you've come up with. Be sure that you have the resources to survive, otherwise the fear, stress and an inability to support yourself can mean that your business never gets off the ground.

Are you really cut out for it?

Launching your own business will probably the most exciting and rewarding thing you have ever done – it's also likely to be the biggest challenge you have ever faced. So be honest about whether you think you will be able to cope. This is such an important factor that this chapter is dedicated to defining what qualities an entrepreneur needs and helping you recognise whether you have them.

The reality of starting up

Launching your own business will change your life, the way you think, the way you work, the way you spend money and the way you socialise. You will most likely need to work every hour possible to get your business off the ground, and even longer to keep it afloat during the early days. You probably won't have another holiday for a couple of years and virtually your entire life will become focused on making your business venture succeed. If you are in a relationship, it will likely feel the strain, and if you've got a family, prepare to be repeatedly torn between them and 'the business'.

This is the truth of starting your own business. However, if what you have just read hasn't curbed your desire, keep reading – you are now showing the attributes an entrepreneur needs when starting up in business. Sure, you will still have plenty of anxieties and unanswered questions, but like every successful entrepreneur starting a small business, the thought of a challenge excites and enthuses you.

If you are going to succeed, you will most likely need to concentrate all your energy into the new business, because it will be 'your baby' and you and your family will be the ones reaping the rewards. You will also need the enthusiasm and ideas to find solutions to the obstacles in your path. But remember, you won't be the first person to have to cope with anxieties or to face the obstacles involved in starting your own business. Every successful entrepreneur has overcome many barriers and continues to do so every week with whatever new business he or she is bringing to market.

Many successful entrepreneurs have no business qualifications or experience prior to starting up. And many spent months, even years, formulating their idea into a viable business proposition, and every single one will have made mistakes, accepted help and learnt lessons as they've gone along.

The average UK entrepreneur

The latest statistics on business startups in the UK reveal that the majority of entrepreneurs are white males in their forties, who live in the south-east. They are likely to have been educated to degree or A level standard and to have previous work experience in the same sector as their business – although they are not necessarily experienced in owning or managing a business. If you don't fit this profile, take heart: the greater part of entrepreneurs may be white, middle-aged and male, but figures suggest that there is considerable scope for increasing the extent of entrepreneurship among women, those from ethnic minorities and younger people. Existing women-led and minority ethnic group-led businesses are very likely to be startups, with around 90% at the micro-business level.

> **Many successful entrepreneurs have no business qualifications or experience prior to starting up**

The age factor

Most small business owners and co-owners fall into three age ranges: 35–44 (25%), 45–54 (31%) and 55–64 (26%). Starting a business is being promoted as a viable career option for young people more than ever before. But statistically, although this sector is likely to grow in the future, young people are more likely to consider starting up as a sideline venture or as a something to do later in life. This is borne out by survey findings which show that just 9% of small business owners and co-owners are aged under 35.

Gender – shouldn't count but does

Only 14% of small and medium enterprises are led by a woman or by a management team mostly comprising women. But the gender gap is slowly closing, with the figures up since 2005, when just 12% of startups were led by women. With the government keen to encourage women in business, there's every indication the upward trend will continue. On a wider level, the UK has some work to do, as figures released in 2008 revealed the UK to be thirteenth in the gender gap index out of 130 countries surveyed. Although this may seem a respectable position, this is down from eleventh in 2007. For more about female entrepreneurs, see later in this chapter.

> **Only 14% of small and medium enterprises are led by a woman**

Education – does it matter?

Educational background clearly has a large impact on entrepreneurship and rising levels of education can be associated with higher relative rates of enterprise activity. Figures show the highest proportion of owner-managers tend to be educated to A level or equivalent (29.4%) followed by a degree or equivalent (21.8%). However, a significant minority of owner-managers – 11% – have no educational qualifications whatsoever. Almost two-thirds of entrepreneurs say that before working in their business, they had no prior experience of owning or managing a company, although half of active entrepreneurs have previously worked in the sector they start a business in.

> **Most ethnic minority groups are far more entrepreneurial than their white counterparts**

Ethnic background – is the gap closing?

Although the majority of entrepreneurs may indeed be white, most ethnic minority groups are far more entrepreneurial than their white counterparts, according to the Global Entrepreneurship Monitor (GEM) UK 2004. But despite high levels of entrepreneurial activity, the reality is that many ethnic minority businesses are concentrated at the bottom of the value-added chain and located in some of the most deprived areas of the UK. Many minority ethnic groups report problems relating to access to finance and to public sector business support.

The most recent Department of Business, Enterprise and Regulatory Reform figures reveal that just 8% of UK small business employers are led by a member of a minority ethnic group (MEG) or have a management team with at least half of its members from MEGs. This figure has grown since 2004, however, when the figure was closer to 5%, and has almost returned to the 9% level recorded in 2003. London is the focus of MEG entrepreneurial activity, with 22% of small businesses run by MEG groups, compared with 8% across the UK as a whole.

CONTACT

Global Entrepreneurial Monitor www.gem consortium.org

Business prospects north of Watford Junction

London and the south-east is also the focus of nearly a third of all the entrepreneurial activity in the UK, boasting more than 1,400,000 businesses. In the GEM UK 2007, respondents in the 'South' – the area comprising London, south-east England, south-west England and the east of England – were much more likely to think they had the skills to start a new business than those living in Scotland and Northern Ireland. Similarly, a relatively high proportion of Londoners expect to start a business over the coming three years. So it seems as if the north–south divide still exists. However, government initiatives to decentralise enterprise funding mean there should be greater support for entrepreneurs outside the South East in coming years.

> **London and the south-east is the focus of nearly a third of all the entrepreneurial activity in the UK**

What really counts

Finally, unsurprisingly, the differing attitudes of entrepreneurs aren't recorded – but perhaps they should be. Regardless of your age, background, gender or ethnicity, your success as an entrepreneur is most likely to be down to your attitude to business. If you're determined, prepared to make personal sacrifices, have the ability to plan ahead and take on board advice while remaining focused on your goal and also, of course, have a decent business idea, you will have every chance of success wherever you're from and whatever age you are. The next section will take you through the personal traits that mark successful entrepreneurs.

The entrepreneurial personality

You need to be able to not only draw up a viable business plan, but also possess the essential skills and personal traits required to make that plan work. To help you decide, we have described the core skills you need to have or develop to make your business a success in the sections below, from commitment to self-motivation. But remember that although starting up does demand an array of talents, the trade-off is the freedom and flexibility of running your own show.

A sense of commitment

Can you work incredibly hard, all day, every day? Before you answer, think about the implications, bearing in mind the words of **Bob Pierce**, joint managing director of online style emporium Pupsnuts. com: 'There will be more work and it will be more difficult than you can possibly imagine. And it will be around you all the time.'

So, it isn't about putting in a couple of late nights, or making an extra effort for a one-off project. By launching your first business, you could find yourself on the wrong end of a potentially gruelling timetable that could go on for weeks and weeks, even months and months. Or, in the case of **Dylan Wilk**, a whole year. When Wilk was setting up Gameplay.com during the 1990s, he claims he was permanently 'doing 24/7… I was working every single second of every single minute,' he says. 'Sure I had to give up a few things, like sleeping and eating, but I was willing to do that.' Are you prepared to make the same commitment?

Motivation – without it there is no business

Linked to your level of commitment is your ability to be motivated, and most crucially, self-motivated. Being self-motivated is not the same as being pushed by someone else to do something. This motivation has to come from within you. It has to come from your energy, your discipline, your focus. This is difficult enough when things are going well, but what about when things are going badly?

'It's really tough,' admits Wilk, who recalls just a few things that went wrong in the early days. 'We were burgled around eight times; we had tens of thousands of pounds in stock stolen; we had someone register our name and then try to slap a writ on us – that was pretty hairy; we had moments where it looked like the business was going to go under. And, at times, I didn't really know what to do.' So even the most determined of entrepreneurs have moments when they are not sure what direction to take. Even if they do know, some have simply had enough and can no longer be bothered taking it.

'This can affect all of us,' admits **Alan Denbigh**, executive director of the Teleworkers Association. 'To succeed in self-employment you have really got to be a self-starter.' Wilk adds: 'You have to really believe in yourself and decide that, no matter what, you will not be beaten.'

Emotional resilience – beating the isolation

Belief in yourself is not enough though. You must also have a capacity to work for yourself, often by yourself. At first this might sound like

> " Sure I had to give up a few things, like sleeping and eating, but I was willing to do that "

> " You can feel, professionally at least, very isolated at times "

CONTACT

The Breakthrough
Centre
www.breakthrough
centre.net

bliss, with no more workplace politics and gossip. But what about the banter, the social life, and more seriously, the brainstorming of solutions and the bouncing around of ideas? If you are like most solo entrepreneurs, you will miss this. 'The simple fact is that it can be very lonely,' says **Andrew Ferguson**, founder of the Breakthrough Centre, which counsels people on new ways to work. 'You can feel, professionally at least, very isolated at times.'

AMBITION 24HOURS AND THE FLYING PIGS

Company: Ambition 24Hours
Owner-manager: Penny Streeter

If you looked around for someone who embodies determination and self-motivation, the virtues just discussed above, you would be hard-pressed to find anyone to top **Penny Streeter**, founder of Ambition 24Hours, an employment agency for medical staff that she launched in 1996.

Defying the odds, South African-born Streeter, a single mother, has overcome a lack of finance and negative attitudes to build up a company that, in less than 10 years, has an annual turnover of £60 million. Having your bank manager write the words 'Pigs will fly' on your business plan or experiencing clients looking over your shoulder as you enter a meeting, looking for a more senior man to talk to, would crush lesser people. But for Streeter, the adversity she faced did not dent her belief that she could start up on her own and develop her idea into a world-class, multimillion-pound business.

With successive bank managers looking down their noses at her business plan, Streeter had to build up her firm without any funding at all. To make ends meet, she worked weekends as a children's entertainer. 'It was essential for our funding,' she says. 'We've never had any outside investment or loans for the business – initially because no one was interested in financing us!'

Looking back at her early struggles, it seems slightly astonishing that Streeter has built up Ambition 24Hours into a business with such a big annual turnover, around 13,500 healthcare staff on its books and 19 branch offices. 'We relied very much on our own resources, with no outside help, so we made mistakes, but we never made the same ones twice,' she says. 'Ultimately, you have to rely on yourself and be prepared to make the big decisions, although now we have an excellent management team.'

EXPERT OPINION

WHAT MAKES AN ENTREPRENEUR?

Shell LiveWIRE www.shell-livewire.org, runs through the big attributes. See how you compare...

The problem

Entrepreneurship is something that seems to be on television screens constantly, and more people are becoming interested in the benefits of starting their own business, be it to try to make their fortune – or more often these days, to fit into their lifestyle. The word 'entrepreneur' seems to be bounded around everywhere! But, starting a new business is unlike any other job – it's an enterprise, it's an adventure, it's a once in a life-time decision. You will be in many new and often difficult situations which you need to be able to overcome. Your future will be in your own hands – you are well and truly in control!

Can you trust yourself with this responsibility? Will you give yourself the job?

The answer: thorough self-evaluation

You will have your own view of who you are. But what about how others see you? Your parents, your friends, your colleagues, your work mates, your boss may all have a different image of you, and there may be elements of truth in what they think. One great trait of entrepreneurs is to be reflective on themselves. There's no single stereotype, but experience has shown that there are some things that successful self-employed people often have in common. Think for a moment what qualities might be important; then compare your list with this one:

- Persistent, enduring, have loads of stamina
- Aware
- Positive, optimistic, enthusiastic
- Tenacious
- Logical, perceptive, organised, realistic, responsible – good at getting things done
- Patient
- Have a sense of humour
- Willing
- Creative, imaginative – always coming up with new ideas
- Assertive
- Out-going, confident, cocky
- Flexible, adaptable
- Open-minded – able to take advice
- Forgiving
- Sociable, approachable, good leader – can win people over instead of getting their backs up
- Single-minded, decisive, independent

- Communicator – able to get a point across
- Opportunist, risk taker, ambitious
- Hard working, committed, determined, 'get up and go' type
- Self-motivated
- Self-belief, individual – not afraid to stand out from a crowd, or of what others think
- Recognise importance of quality.

You don't need all of these qualities, but you may discover that you do possess many of them but have never had to demonstrate them before. It's not easy to get a true picture of yourself. You have to work at it. You need to do the following:

Be honest – You are not selling yourself to an employer. There's no point in conning yourself. Face up to what you really are, not what you wish you were. If you don't feel ready for self-employment now, perhaps you will in a few years time, with more experience and qualifications. Remember you need to do what the customer wants not what you think they want!

Get an opinion – Different people will have different views of you. Talk to someone whom you know well, and trust. Get a good range of views. Try to sort out when they have a point (even if it makes you feel uncomfortable) and when they are just trying to make you fit in with an image that happens to suit them. Often, it's a mixture of both.

Prove it – Wherever possible, look for an example of the qualities that you have identified. If you think you are an organiser, what have you organised? Remember to look at all aspects of your life, not just work experience and qualifications.

Keep notes – Everyone, young or old should have a file on themselves. It's useful for planning, as well as applying for jobs. The great thing about enterprise is that it helps you to grow and develop as a person. You need to keep tabs on yourself – what are your strengths and weaknesses? What do you need to learn?

The future for entrepreneurs in the UK is somewhere that will be immensely exciting, where more and more people make a specific choice on leaving education to start their own enterprise and create their own futures. New technology will allow relatively small businesses to flourish further, and because of their size they will be able to react to changes in the market and compete with larger established corporations, challenging them at every level. The small firm will dominate as time goes on, flourishing in a knowledge-based economy – not only in the UK but all over the world. Most importantly we will see entrepreneurs who care about their surroundings and environment, entrepreneurs who have a social conscience and a drive to make the world a better place. Have you got what it takes?

Gwen Rhys, founder and director of networking organisation EW agrees. 'But there is a solution,' she says. 'You need to build up a virtual team. You need to develop a circle of colleagues that you communicate with in much the same way you did in the office, except now it may be over the phone, via email, or face to face, but once a month rather than every day. You also need to make sure that you do get out there and mix with people. It is worth joining a professional group you connect with, even if it is only to learn that there are others who have been through what you are going through and identify with how you are feeling. In itself this can be a great source of support.' So be aware that there will be some lonely times.

Optimism and opportunism

All this talk about what can go wrong may sound daunting, and the last thing you will probably expect to be feeling is optimistic. However, Wilk says that this is exactly what you have to be. 'There is no point doing something if you think it will not work,' he says. 'But sometimes you just have to think of ways of making it work better.'

Ferguson is equally encouraging. 'It's an opportunity to do something you've always wanted to do but never quite found anyone to pay you to do it. It's your big chance to do something that makes you happy.'

How and when to quit your job

Like many entrepreneurs, you have probably come up with the idea to launch your own business while still in employment. As mentioned above, many people launch startups into a market similar to that in which they were previously working as an employee. Of course, starting up by yourself will have serious ramifications on your existing job, and you have probably decided to quit it. But what is the best time to hand in your notice, and what exactly do you say to your boss?

The right time to quit

> **Continuing to earn while you are planning the business will allow you to save up some cash to act as a buffer**

A lot of research and planning will need to be put into your business before you can give up that monthly salary. Continuing to earn while you are planning the business will allow you to save up some cash to act as a buffer. That way you will be able to focus your attention on the business rather than worrying about next month's gas bill.

Tina Jesson put away half her salary for two years before quitting her job to set up property development company Home Stages, so she had personal income to cushion her through the first year of the business. She spent two years researching and planning, so her move from employee to business owner was a gradual one. 'I was spending about 30 hours a week on the business. I told my company that I either wanted to go part-time or leave, and I guess they thought that by allowing me to work part-time they could keep my skills for a while,' she explains.

Before you make the leap to self-employment, get as much done as you possibly can. You may have been using your spare room to sell a couple of items a week through your website while you were working, but if you are going to make a living out of it, perhaps you need to think about commercial premises. You might also want to use this period to prove the business model, through an eBay shop, or some other form of e-commerce selling and marketing. Potential investors will have far more confidence in an idea that has been tested.

Ask yourself if your revenue predictions are accurate, too. If you've budgeted for selling more than is realistic, you could find yourself in a tight spot when your last pay cheque gets used up. 'You should have some idea of at least two or three potential customers who can provide the beginnings of an income stream,' says **John Lees**, author of *How to Get a Job You'll Love* (McGraw-Hill, 2006). 'Only when you get customers saying "yes" to your offer should you really consider making the leap.'

Jeremy Martin, co-founder of men's health drinks brand For Goodness Shakes, says he and his business partner **Stuart Jeffreys** did as much work as possible while still in full-time employment. But eventually you need to make the move. 'It was definitely the right thing to do,' argues Martin, adding that cutting the cord 'commits you 100%. When you make the leap, it's surprising how fear gets you working harder and makes you more committed than ever before.'

How should you do it?

If your business is going to compete with the company you work for, it's probably not a good idea to mention it until you've handed in your notice, if at all. 'It's best to say as little as possible if you are becoming a competitor,' recommends Lees. In addition, if you are likely to compete with the company you work for, you need to check your employment contract carefully for competition clauses, notice periods or anything else that could cause legal problems if you decide to start your own business. If there's nothing threatening in your contract, though, and your employer's biggest worry is losing your skills, it may help to talk about your idea. 'Thank your boss for his or her support,' says Lees. 'Make it clear that you are leaving for entirely positive reasons. Your previous employer could be in a position to refer you new business, so if you can, be as clear as possible about what you plan to do.'

When **Liz Jackson** left to set up Great Guns Marketing, her employers provided her with a few days worth of work a week, which gave her crucial income while she was trying to win new clients. The lesson here is don't burn your bridges. There are just as many risks as rewards when setting up your own business, but if you plan your exit carefully, you may just manage to tip the balance in your favour.

! TOP TIPS
LEAVING YOUR JOB WITHOUT BURNING THE BRIDGES

! Don't do it immediately after your 'eureka!' moment

! Get as much preparation done as possible first

! Consider going part-time for a period

! Make sure you have at least some customers before ditching your income stream

! Keep your venture quiet before you leave if it's in a similar market

! Check your contract for possible legal issues relating to your startup

! Talk to your boss about your idea if he could be a possible customer

! Leave on a positive note – thank your boss for their support, etc.

> " The important thing is to not focus on obstacles but on goals "

Women entrepreneurs

As a woman interested in starting your own business, you will be faced with several stiffer challenges than men, mainly due to your gender. The 2006 GEM report on women and entrepreneurship revealed some interesting facts about women's route to self-employment.

What the figures say

Female entrepreneurs worldwide, for example, are much more likely than men to start their businesses when still employed. This may not only have benefits in terms of resources and social capital, but also act as a safety net, as women often express less self-confidence in their entrepreneurial ventures than men (although perhaps men are simply far less willing to admit their fears).

Early-stage entrepreneurship in women continues to grow globally, although startup rates among men are still higher. More than a third of people involved in entrepreneurial activity are women. However, in high-income countries, men are almost twice as likely to be early-stage or established business owners than women.

Female entrepreneurship is an increasingly important part of the economic profile of any country. But the male/female gap is still significant, especially in high-income countries and technology-intense sectors.

In addition, the 2004 GEM Monitor showed that independent startup activity among women is 3.1% of the adult female population, but 6% among men. Russia is the only country where the rate of female early-stage entrepreneurship is significantly higher than the male rate.

Regionally, the highest number of female startups is based in London, where 8.4% of the female workforce is self-employed, and female entrepreneurs are least active in the north-east, according to the Labour Force Survey 2003. And finally, a recent White Paper, entitled *The Observed Characteristics of Outstanding Women in Business*, found that while businesses run by women contribute £70bn to the UK economy and employ more than one million people, there would be 750,000 more female-led startups if rates matched those in the USA.

> **More than a third of people involved in entrepreneurial activity are women**

Ability to find funding

Access to investment is unfortunately one of the biggest barriers facing female entrepreneurs. Recent eye-opening research from the Women's Enterprise Task Force showed the scale of the problem. The taskforce found that when starting up, businesses owned by women access an average of only £10,000 worth of funding, compared with £15,000 for men. The task force believes that this disparity is likely to 'constrain business performance'. Furthermore, it has been found that women tend to be charged higher rates of interest when taking out loans – an average of 2.9%, substantially more than the 1.9%

> **Women tend to be charged higher rates of interest than men, when taking out loans**

average charged to men. **Pam Alexander**, co-chair of the task force, says: 'The under-capitalisation of women-owned businesses results in under-performance and slower growth.' For this reason, the task force has said that its key priority will be creating better access to funding and appropriate investment for women.

'We need to work with business support providers and banks to encourage women to be ambitious in their business plans and investment ready,' says Alexander. But this isn't to say that women aren't finding funding opportunities. Female entrepreneurs generally make better use of alternative sources of funding, with the British Chambers of Commerce (BCC) finding that although women put in less of their own money than men in the startup stage (£10,106 compared with £13,500), 27% of women will obtain further funding from family, compared with just 17% of men. What's more, 33% of women-owned businesses, compared with 20% of men-owned firms, had used government programmes to fund their business startup.

For both men and women, however, the bank is still the main provider of startup finance, funding 46% and 43% of new businesses, respectively. The BCC found there is no statistically significant difference between men and women with regard to usage of bank finance. It makes sense then that there is evidence that banks are waking up to the growth of female entrepreneurship and making more effort to attract female clients.

CONTACT

Women's Enterprise Task Force
www.womensenter
prisetaskforce.co.uk

CONTACT

British Chambers of Commerce
www.british
chambers.org.uk
☎020 7654 5800

Prejudice – and pride

"

As an entre-
preneur, a
thick skin is
something
of a neces-
sity "

The world of business is changing. But there's still a lingering attitude that assumes that a successful business is owned by a man. Women, especially young women, often report coming away from meetings or pitches feeling patronised or not taken seriously. As an entrepreneur though, a thick skin is something of a necessity.

Claire Nicholson, co-founder of marketing agency More2, finds her job surprises people even in a social environment. 'When I meet new people socially they often assume you are at home bringing up the children and not running a business,' she says. It's not just Nicholson's gender, but also her age that surprises people, with the combination of the two causing looks of disbelief. 'We set up More2 when I was just 28 and so many people don't expect you to have your own business at that age,' she adds.

Despite these challenges, many female entrepreneurs never experience any form of prejudice or negative reaction on account of their gender. 'I do feel that male/female prejudice is a bit of a red herring – the main problem with startups is access to good advice and supportive subsidised incubators, as well as government bureaucracy, anti-competitive practices from large incumbents,' says **Katie Allcott** of FRANK Water. 'I am aware of a few situations where it has taken longer for me to gain respect, but I think this is not just because I am a woman, but also because I am considered to be young and that I run a very ethical, values-driven company.' It's important to remember that every entrepreneur faces specific problems, and whatever you battle through will leave you even more determined to succeed. As Allcott articulates: 'Varying problems exist for tall people, short people, thin people, fat people, men, women, young people, old people – if you look for them. But the important thing is to not focus on obstacles but on goals.'

> "
> Whether a man or woman, you do need a reasonable amount of self-confidence "

Being self-confident

Findings do show that women are more put off by the fear of failure when it comes to starting a business. Women are less positive about their skills, according to Prowess (an advocacy network for women's business) and perceive fewer opportunities than men. However, this may just demonstrate that women are more honest or realistic than their male counterparts! Entrepreneurs are by their nature confident people who like taking risks, and anyone with these qualities won't be held back long by a fear of failure. 'I think that as long as women have plenty of support around them they can be very successful,' says Allcott. 'That's support from friends and family as well as colleagues, support agencies, bank managers, suppliers and customers. Whether a man or woman, you do need a reasonable amount of self-confidence, even more so, total confidence and passion for the business or idea itself… then with good support networks you have a great start.'

BABYLICIOUS AND THE LAW OF HARD KNOCKS

Company: Babylicious
Owner-manager: Sally Preston

Many prominent entrepreneurs have suffered setbacks on the path to success. Some have had to overcome a severe lack of funds, others have had to battle against negative attitudes. But few business owners have had to deal with as much adversity as **Sally Preston**, founder of Babylicious.

Having endured an acrimonious divorce, she was diagnosed with skin cancer. She chose this turbulent period in her life to launch Babylicious, a frozen baby food business. But the knocks kept coming for Preston – someone deliberately tried to steal her business's name and a hoax caller untruthfully told her retailer customers that the company was under investigation by the Advertising Standards Authority.

Preston remains tight-lipped about the identity of the malicious character who plagued her business, but admits it was a dispiriting time. 'It was the ongoing knock-backs – you can take one and you can take two, but they keep coming at you and it's very wearing after a while and it begins to wear you down,' she says. 'I think you have to be like one of those Weeble things, you get pushed over and you constantly keep picking yourself back up again.'

To her credit, Preston has made a stunning success of Babylicious since the launch of the company in September 2001. The business has picked up a host of awards and expanded overseas. The various setbacks have certainly not defeated the ambitious and refreshingly honest Preston.

WOMEN ENTREPRENEURS HAVE THEIR SAY

CLAIRE YARWOOD-WHITE
Yarwood-White

'When I was younger, "entrepreneur" was a scary word! In my twenties, I thought business was a secret that no one had let me in on, and running a business was best left to the big boys. As I worked my way through various companies and bosses as an employee, I realised that much of the secret was common sense, making good decisions at the right time and that confidence played a huge part in success. As my own confidence grew, I began to think: "I could do that."'

GEMMA STONE
Rock and Ruby

'I am probably part of the smallest statistic of entrepreneurs – under 30, female, mother of two, without a degree. But I work hard, enjoy what I do and am motivated to be a loving and giving mother and a successful businesswoman. If there are barriers in my path then I say: "Bring it on!"'

CLAIRE NICHOLSON
More2 (integrated marketing agency)

'Within a few months of starting up the agency, I discovered I was expecting my first child. My husband was studying full-time, so money was extremely tight and life was very stressful. At the beginning, to succeed you have to work every spare hour and with a small team you have to be prepared to do everything. Even now that the agency is five years old I wrestle with how little I see my two daughters. My top tip is work on the train. I save work to do on my journey home so that when I step in the door I can be a mum. Once they are in bed I can open up my laptop and get back to work.'

SARAH TREMELLEN
Bravissimo

'I never saw a ceiling for it, I just thought it would be fun, setting up from scratch and making something from nothing.'

ANITA RODDICK
The Body Shop

'No one talks of entrepreneurship as survival, but that's exactly what it is.'

RACHEL ELNAUGH
Red Letter Days

'Key is understanding what type of entrepreneur you are, and then doing business in a way that is true to yourself, and above all, one that brings you personal happiness and fulfilment.'

So you've made your decision...

There's no better time to start planning your next move than the present

You started reading this chapter with an idea that you think you can turn into your own business, or because you simply want to be your own boss. If you now think that the trials and tribulations of entrepreneurialism are not for you, then simply close the book and walk away, safe in the knowledge that you've at least carefully considered setting up on your own. However, if the last few pages have made you even more determined to launch your own company, then it's fair to say that you have decided to join the ranks of entrepreneurialism, and there's no better time to start planning your next move than the present.

So where should you start? The next step is easy – simply keep on reading and you will be guided through the key steps of starting your own business, from researching your idea to writing a business plan and raising finance and how to deal with the upheaval. Work–life balance is an over-used term you will hear from every business coach and all the business startup services you will encounter. But if you've worked 20 hours a day for two months in a row you will be physically and mentally drained and appreciate the need for striking that balance.

The next chapter will take you through the research stage, to help you test drive your idea to see if it's commercially viable and if there's the market demand for it. Then you will learn how to make cost and revenue forecasts and to present your idea in the form of a business plan that you can then take to prospective business investors and partners. Further chapters deal with naming your venture and how to register that name, as well as the format your business should take, from a limited company or partnership to a sole trader. There is also advice on developing the key skills you will need when starting up. For instance, there's a guide on safely negotiating the minefield that is tax and the practices, products and systems that will help you organise your accounts efficiently. If you are raising finance, there are plenty of sources from which to choose. There's a rundown of the advantages and disadvantages of using different financiers, from high-street banks to venture capitalists and business angels – and how best to impress them while still getting a good deal. There's also guidance on whether to work from home or seek premises, along with the right space for your business and how to get the best from your chosen location.

You will also find advice on how to get the most from your working day and ways that you can ensure your time is put to good use, such as the best way to take calls when you are in a meeting with clients. Do you need to use a virtual secretary, and would it be cost effective? There are tips on tracking down reliable and affordable suppliers, which can be one of the hardest tasks for new business owners, as well as talking to other entrepreneurs. Networking is a word that often strikes fear into the hearts of new business owners. Walking into a room of people who've been in business for decades can be quite daunting. But select the right networking groups and a format that you are comfortable with, and it will help you build a valuable source of contacts that can help to drive your business forward.

Word of mouth may not be enough to get your business working to its full capacity and it's likely that you will need at least some marketing and public relations (PR). There are clear explanations of all the options available to you, what is most likely to prompt the best response rates and advice on how to handle PR companies. You will also gain an insight into the type of marketing and PR that you can do for yourself for very little money.

If you are launching an internet business, website design, marketing and internet connectivity will be important issues from day one. Even if you are not starting an internet business, you might want a website or even to sell online too. You will find guidance on the process of getting a website designed from one of the thousands of companies now specialising in the service. There's help on deciding the level of complexity your website needs, along with advice on how to drive traffic to it.

If you will need to take on one or two people straightaway, do you think you are experienced enough at recruiting? You might know a friend of a friend who can help out, but you need to make sure that you can entrust this person with your business's future. So read on and you will be taken through all the issues involved in recruiting and employing staff, along with health and safety issues, employer liability insurance, virus protection and general employment legislation. Red tape is the bugbear of every business owner, but the weight of the problem is significantly lessened if you are organised and know what's expected of you.

3.0

PRE-STARTUP RESEARCH

WHAT'S IN THIS CHAPTER

- Once you have decided that you are going to go ahead, the next step is to start planning your venture to help you gain any investment you may need, and to make sure everything is in place for a successful launch. Find out as much as you can about the market you propose to launch into, your potential customers and any rivals who are already trading in your chosen area. This information will tell you whether your idea is viable, provide key data for your business plan and prove invaluable when you start up. So read on to find out how to approach market research...

Market research

Properly targeted market research is the key to a thriving business and can make the difference between success and failure, say experts. Market research can be a cost-effective way of discovering what your customers want and matching products and services to this demand. Even better, it can help a business grow by keeping you up to date with current trends and with what your competitors are doing. Knowing the state of the market and how to improve your position within it can revolutionise your businesses but this can only be achieved by carrying out proper market research. 'Unfortunately, most companies shy away from market research, and then they wonder why they don't succeed,' says **Simon Wieremiej**, spokesperson for the British Market Research Association (BMRA).

If you are looking to start a company, it pays to carry out the necessary research into the potential viability of your venture. First, it will provide key material for your business plan, which is an essential part of attracting the investment you may need to launch your business. Second, it would help you assess the chances of success.

A lot of companies already succeeding in the area you'd like to enter, doesn't automatically mean you are on to a winner. It could mean the competition may be too fierce and there may not be a demand for what you are offering in the specific location you plan to launch your version of the business. Equally, you may have had a highly original idea and there may be little or no competition around, but this could be for a very good reason. In either case, marketing research can help provide the answers. One key area you need to look at is demand:

- Do people want what you plan to offer, and if not, is it simply down to their profile in the particular location where you planned to launch?
- If there is demand, can you put a figure on it?

> **Most companies shy away from market research, and then they wonder why they don't succeed**

You also need to examine the competition:

- What other companies are offering something similar to what you are proposing?
- How successful are they?
- Can you improve on their offer, or strategically differentiate your offer from theirs, while maintaining demand?

Other research can provide key information on pricing, location, size of premises , etc. Securing these data early on not only shows potential sources of investment that you are serious about your proposal, but also reassures them that you are organised and motivated, making them more likely to want to lend to you. And, of course, it also increases the chances of your launch being a success, if after carrying out the research you decide to go ahead.

For many would-be owner-managers of small businesses, the cost of commissioning a market research agency can be prohibitive, so you will most likely want to conduct the basic market research yourself for the purposes of informing your business plan and providing an early indication of the viability of your venture. But remember that it needs to cover all the points discussed above so, depending on the market you are considering entering, you may find the process too complex and time consuming, and that calling in the experts can save you money through producing more accurate results

How important are trends?

CONTACT

Department
for Business,
Enterprise and
Regulatory Reform
www.berr.gov.uk

Before discussing the key market research techniques, here are some useful official startup statistics, published by the Department for Business, Enterprise and Regulatory Reform (BERR), which offer a key insight into the types of business that are on the increase or decline. The BERR publishes a lot of business statistics, such as those in Table 3.1, which are a useful starting point for you to make a quick assessment of the viability of your idea before embarking on more thorough research, while also informing you of the most popular sectors for business startups.

...prises registering and de-registering for VAT by industry, UK,

| | Thousands | | | | | | |
| | Registrations | | De-registrations | | Stock | | |
	2007	change on 2006	2007	change on 2006	start of 2008	change during 2007[1]	% change during 2007[1]
All industries	205.7	23.7	147.8	3.5	2,031.1	57.9	2.9
Agriculture, fishing	4.0	0.0	6.1	1.1	153.7	−2.2	−1.4
Mining, energy, water	0.2	0.1	0.2	0.0	2.0	0.1	3.8
Manufacturing	10.1	1.0	10.5	−0.3	152.5	−0.4	−0.3
Construction	25.9	2.5	16.6	1.12	44.0	9.3	4.0
Wholesale, retail, repairs	34.1	0.2	29.6	−1.2	401.3	4.5	1.1
Hotels, restaurants	18.0	−0.7	14.2	−1.1	145.5	3.8	2.7
Transport, communication	8.5	0.2	6.9	−0.1	85.9	1.6	1.9
Finance	1.7	0.0	1.5	0.1	21.8	0.2	0.9
Business services	89.5	20.3	50.7	3.4	644.6	38.8	6.4
Education, health	3.2	0.4	1.7	0.1	32.8	1.6	5.1
Other services	10.6	−0.3	10.0	0.4	146.9	0.6	0.4

Source: BERR Enterprise Directorate (Statistics Team)

When looking at the sector you intend to enter, consider:

- How many businesses were started in the current year, and how it compares with the previous year. Is it a growing market?
- If so, has that now been fully exploited and will it drop in the coming year?
- If it's less than in the previous year, why is that?

Also consider the changes to the total number of businesses that occurred during the current year. For instance, while around 10,100 new manufacturing businesses were started in 2007, around 10,500 folded. If you are looking to enter a market that's losing businesses, you will need to consider why this is so and find out which particular firms are suffering and why.

> **Evaluating the statistics doesn't mean that you shouldn't enter into a sector that is shrinking, but it should alert you to whether important changes are afoot**

Evaluating the statistics doesn't mean that you shouldn't enter into a sector that is shrinking, but it should alert you to whether important changes are afoot. In addition, you should think about the outside influences that are likely to have affected startup business figures. For instance, how much have the fish, agriculture, hotel and restaurant trades been affected since the start of the economic downturn?

Starting up in the downturn

As the UK didn't officially go into recession until 2008, Table 3.1 will not provide an accurate indication of this, and new registration and de-registration statistics will not be published until November 2009. This is when a little more digging is needed. You might expect both startups and closures to be up during 2008, as a result of the downturn, but, according to the BERR, this will not necessarily be the case. In fact, it believes there has only been a minor drop in new company registrations, indicated by figures for the number of self-employed people in the UK, which early 2009 figures reveal has only fallen by 2% compared to 2008. This view is also supported by Barclays' new business bank account statistics, which rose by 1% during 2008. This can be explained by the rise in unemployed people, which has led to many who are out of work starting up on their own.

> **New business bank account statistics rose by 1% during 2008**

It's likely those companies closing, however, will reveal a completely different picture. BERR statistics for the fourth quarter of 2008 show that insolvencies were up 50% on the same period in 2007. Therefore, although there's every chance that startups for 2008 have only fallen slightly, closures look like they will have grown significantly on the previous year. The key here is which sectors have been worst hit, and Barclays' data unsurprisingly suggest that the financial, property and construction industries have borne the brunt of the closures, while health, education and social work have actually grown.

With so many companies going out of business, this is clearly a challenging time to launch your own company, particularly in the sectors highlighted above. However, projections by BERR for 2008 suggest that many people are still starting up. In fact, it's unwise to launch without preparation in any kind of economic climate, so as long as you have done the groundwork, there's no reason why you can't launch in a recession. And if you can turn over a profit in tough times, you should be ready to go full steam when the recovery arrives, and hopefully grow significantly. Also, there are some businesses that have been doing well in the downturn, and not just in the public sector areas mentioned previously. Pharmacists traditionally do well when times are hard, perhaps because people are feeling more down and under stress. There have also been reports that takeaway restaurants and home movie rental companies are performing well, as more people are staying in to save money.

> **The financial, property and construction industries have borne the brunt of the closures**

Relevance of trends to your circumstances

Although national startup statistics are important to consider, they are by no means relevant to every situation. For instance, trends may vary in different parts of the country and at different times. The local economy will also affect your chances of success. Unless you are about to launch on a national scale, probably the most valuable research you can do is to investigate what need exists for your business locally. Look how many other similar businesses are in the area; can you find an area where there are few companies offering the service or products you are looking to launch, or where there's room for competition, either in terms of better quality service or on price.

> **Trends should be made and not followed**

There's also the argument that trends should be made and not followed, and there's some truth to this. The telecommunications industry is full of very young, bold, and now wealthy, individuals who proved a lot of sceptics wrong, and it can pay to be at the forefront of the latest movement. However, over-confidence can also be perceived as arrogance or naivety, and it's always worth checking the state of the markets even if you then choose to ignore them.

The do-it-yourself approach to sizing up the competition

There's no better way of testing than by using the services and products directly. A good place to start assessing the potential of your

> **There's no better way of finding the quality of the competition and how successful they are than by sampling it**

startup idea is the internet. Make a list of keywords that people would use when looking for companies that provide your potential product or service. Remember to keep a note of these words and phrases as they will prove useful in the future to help with optimising your website. Internet searches should throw up the range of companies across the UK that you will be competing with if you launch. If there are none, you have an original idea – but is there a market for it? If there are lots of competitors, is there room for you? To find this out, assess the local competition, what they are offering and whether you can improve on this. You can get much of this information from company websites, initially.

Depending on the business you are proposing to launch, in the next level of assessment, get out of the office and check out the competition first hand, either personally or by enlisting the help of others. There's no better way of finding the quality of the competition and how successful they are than by sampling it. For example, if you plan to launch a restaurant or catering business, you need to check out rival establishments for the following:

• How good is the food?
• Is the wine list special?
• Is the service up to scratch?

Also, you should find out your rival's unique selling point, and whether you could match it. If you are well known in the area, ask your friends to help out.

If you do your marketing research fully enough, you can organise your business in a way that gives you a clear advantage afterwards. You can even play detective and go on a stakeout to observe how busy your rivals' premises are, and subtly question customers about what they are looking for in this kind of business.

You can also investigate the performance of your rival companies by tracking down their annual accounts at Companies House. Although the data are likely to be at least a year old, you can source turnover and profit and loss details, which will give you an idea of how successful each business is. If your rivals are having problems, try to

CONTACT

Companies House
www.companies
house.gov.uk
☎0303 1234 500

find out why this is so. It could be simply that they are not very good, or that there are simply too many companies offering this service in the area, or that the service isn't in demand.

TRUSTEDPLACES AND THE CUSTOMER FOCUS

Company: trustedplaces
Owners: Sokratis Papafloratos and Walid Al Saqqaf

Sokratis Papafloratos and **Walid Al Saqqaf** gave up their jobs to set up the social networking website Trustedplaces.com in 2006, inspired by the realisation that many of their friends were walking events guides. 'We thought that if could we bring all those friends together in one place, all of a sudden we would have access to hundreds of people's knowledge,' says Papafloratos.

'We did things like going to Starbucks and spending the day there, buying strangers coffee and asking them about some ideas that we had. They were kind of impromptu focus groups,' Papafloratos continues. The success of the focus groups was such that so far, the company hasn't spent any money on advertising since starting up.

! TOP TIPS
THREE FACTS ABOUT MARKET RESEARCH

! It's one thing recognising the importance of market research and quite another carrying it out properly

! Of those companies that do conduct research, many simply don't approach it in the right way.

! This can be just as dangerous as not doing any research at all, as it produces inaccurate results, which can lead to the wrong business decisions being made and false confidence on the part of the entrepreneur

YOUNG GUNS AND THE MASTERPLAN

Not too many £1 million businesses startup on as little as a £1,500 overdraft, but that's what brothers Dominic and Alex Lyon did when they launched music management company Young Guns. A crucial element in them not requiring any more was that their business plan was right on the button, and benefited from the careful thought that the pair put into it over a long period of time.

Having both graduated from prestigious music colleges, the brothers were frustrated at the lack of options for musicians once they'd finished their education. So they came up with the idea of launching a music management company that pools existing acts as well as creating new groups, packages them up, then promotes them to record companies, as well as for corporate events.

But the pair were kicking around the idea for the best part of a decade before it actually got off the ground. "We spent 10-years developing the business plan, thinking, researching and obsessively chatting about it," explains Dominic, who was at that time working as an account manager in the advertising industry.

Eventually, they felt confident enough. So in 2005, the brothers finally took the plunge. It seems the time and effort spent on the business plan has really paid off.

! TOP TIPS

COMPARATIVE RESEARCH

Several special industry sector reports have been regularly published by independent research companies such as Mintel and Keynote, which have been producing reports for more than 35 years. The reports will cost you hundreds and tend to be written from a certain perspective, which may not be your own. However, you can carry out desk research yourself, gathering together reports and comparing statistics. Ask your local library for Keynote and Mintel reports, and use the index to search for the relevant sectors.

Finally, there's always room for some background reading either through the local papers, or by visiting the public library. Check out whether your rivals make the most of free editorial coverage, and whether you could dream up a newsworthy item to interest a news editor. Some pubs and restaurants, for example, thrive by being media-friendly. Could you dream up some publicity stunts of your own?

Primary research

Primary research is research that you can conduct yourself or commission someone else to do for you, instead of using information that is already published. You can carry out research into your market and competition using the internet as mentioned previously, or through direct contact with your potential customers. The latter falls into two broad types: quantitative research, which focuses on a broad cross-section and produces a numerical result, such as '36% of the target audience think this', which can be useful figures to show a potential investor; and qualitative research, which is more in-depth, often using a smaller, but representative, sample, and discovers not only what people do, but why they buy a certain product, how they feel about it and how they would like to see it improved.

An example of qualitative research is a focus group. You gather a small number of people who represent a cross-section of your target market for a discussion with an assigned leader to assess their opinions of the product or service you will be offering. If this can include giving the focus group members first-hand experience of that product or service, their opinions will be better informed. To entice people to attend a focus group, you will need to give them some kind of inducement, such as a small payment or gift. A simple direct survey of your target audience (the bigger sample, the better) is an example of quantitative research, where you either send questions out to a database (either by post or through email), go doorstepping or ask people in the street.

Michael Warren, former director general of the Market Research Society (MRS) and now a freelance researcher and consultant, emphasises that it is misleading to suggest that one kind of research suits certain goods and services better than others. 'Qualitative and quantitative research are complementary to each other, and should be used together,' he advises. 'Qualitative research, in particular, can be used to give a greater understanding of the figures.' The key to success for both qualitative and quantitative research, though, is the kind of questions asked and how they are put across. So a properly devised questionnaire can be an invaluable marketing tool, as long as you avoid the common pitfalls. A good market research agency with experience in your sector can help with this, because you need to take care in drawing up the questions. Alternatively, you can consult marketing guides for advice, but bear in mind that this is something of a skill and getting it wrong can mean you would have wasted any effort you put into doing the research.

Simon Wieremiej, spokesperson for the British Market Research Association (BMRA), says questions such as 'Would you buy this product?' can give misleading answers. 'The answer might be 'Yes', but they could mean that they would pay £1 whereas the price might actually be £10,' he explains. So avoid closed questions with yes/ no answers, as you're likely get more information by eliciting a fuller response. Warren is equally cautious. 'In sectors such as fast-moving consumer goods, where market researchers are trying to explore the image of one client's products against those of its rivals, it is usual for respondents to be asked about other products, some of which they may never have used,' he says. 'You might ask them about a range of variables, including smoothness, price, levels of satisfaction, but you have to be careful about what you compare the product to. Asking people how a new car, say, compares to a Rolls-Royce really gets up respondents' noses because they have probably never driven a Rolls.'

Secondary research

Secondary research is information others have acquired and already published which you may find relevant, for example the BERR startup statistics mentioned above.

Access to this secondary market research data may be yours for the asking and cost you only an email, letter, phone call, or perhaps a nominal fee for copying and postage. There are many websites, sponsored by a variety of organisations, which provide you with the business information you will need at the beginning, a jump-off place for more in-depth research for your business and marketing plans. For

CONTACT

Marketing
Research Society
www.mrs.org.uk
☎020 7490 4911

ACTION POINT
KEY STEPS TO DOING YOUR OWN RESEARCH

Whichever type of primary research you decide to undertake, there are a number of factors you should bear in mind before you start.

KISS (keep it simple, stupid!): Long-winded questionnaires are likely to put respondents off, and will distort the response – the only respondents may be those with nothing better to do that day, which may not be your target market. 'Telling them that a survey will take five minutes is likely to get a better response than one lasting 25 minutes,' says Warren. 'If it does last longer than that, it is bad for the industry and not good for your product image.'

Choose a representative sample: It's no good working hard on a producing a good questionnaire, if you present it to the wrong people, so you need to make sure that your 'sample' represents a cross-section of your potential customers.

Circulate the questionnaire appropriately: Via the internet is usually the best way to do this,.

Offer a prize draw for completed questionnaires: Remember that a low response rate will distort figures, and often people need an incentive to complete questionnaires, because they take up valuable time.

Respect confidentiality: The Marketing Research Society's code of conduct specifies that respondents should not be misled over what they are being asked about. Do not use their responses for follow-up sales once you are trading.

example, websites of trade associations, government departments and market research firms (which will usually charge for general market profiles and more specific information). Spending time researching the relevant media now will pay dividends later.

Many industries have an active trade association that serves as a vital source of industry-specific information. Such associations regularly publish directories for their members, and the better ones include statistical information that tracks industry sales, profits, ratios, economic trends and other valuable data. Find out about and contact possible associations, and visit their websites to see what information is available. When in doubt, call or email the industry association offices and communicate with the managers.

Industry-specific business magazines can offer a wealth of information on your proposed venture and your market. Aside from the major general-interest business publications, such as *Business Week* and *The Economist*, many specialty publications look at specific industries.

Tim Berry and Doug Wilson's book *On Target: The Book On Marketing Plans* advise 'specialism is an important trend in the publishing and internet businesses. Dingbats and Widgets may be boring to the general public, but they are exciting to Dingbat and Widget manufacturers who read about them regularly in their specialised magazines. The titles are an important medium for industry-specific advertising, which is important to readers as well as advertisers. The editorial staff of these magazines have to fill the space between the adverts. They do that by publishing as much industry-specific information as they can find, including statistics, forecasts and industry profiles. Consulting these magazines or websites can sometimes produce a great deal of business and market forecasting, along with key economic information.'

If you don't know which magazines focus on your business area, the best place to start looking is on the internet. For traditional printed directories, several good reference sources list magazines, journals and other publications. They also offer indexes to published articles which you can use to search for the exact references you need. These will be kept in the reference section of most libraries. Once you have identified the right magazines, contact the editorial departments using their website, phone number and published contact information. Use the indexes to identify useful published information. When you find an index listing for an article that forecasts your industry or talks about industry economics or trends, jot down basic information on the publication and ask your local library if it has a copy or contact the title directly. Many business magazines will send back issues free, or allow you to go into their offices and consult them there.

Lastly, special industry sector reports are regularly published by independent research companies such as Mintel and Keynote, which

> **Industry-specific business magazines can offer a wealth of information on your proposed venture and your market**

have been producing reports for more than 35 years. The reports are very expensive and tend to be written from a certain perspective, which may not be your own. However, you can access Keynote and Mintel reports in your local library and carry out desk research yourself by using the index to search for the relevant sectors.

Market research agencies

Sharing the cost of the survey with other organisations can save money.

For many startups, the costs of using an agency may be prohibitive, and good ones are likely to start at four figures, according to Michael Warren. But those costs should be set against the real benefits to your business of getting right the product, the retail layout or new

KIRSTY'S STORY
Focus groups were really useful

To refine her product, **Kirsty McGregor**, founder of parenting website Entertainthekids. com, decided to arrange around nine special preview evenings attended by childcare experts to get feedback on her website, to make sure it was right for her target market.

'We spent days on end collating address lists, stuffing envelopes, and sticking stamps to send out a 7,000 mailing inviting those who work with children (nurseries, kids clubs, childminders, football clubs, primary teachers, tutors, etc) to our preview evenings. There were some good ideas voiced by the attendees, many of which we incorporated into the site prior to the launch.

'It was incredibly nerve-racking. I'm normally so confident, and have such a strong belief in the site. But just prior to every preview evening start time I got so nervous. Would anyone show up? What would they think of it? Would they tell us something that we hadn't realised that would make the site useless, or certainly not as good an idea as we thought it was? Your self-confidence plummets, so you have to pull yourself up by the bootstraps, smile and wait to see what happens.

'On the whole they have been very positive, although we had a real wobble one evening when at 6.30pm, the start time, no one had arrived. Thankfully that wasn't the case by 6.40pm.'

restaurant. Good market research should pay for itself and, as with anything, there are also ways to keep costs down.

First, shop around. The BMRA offers a free helpline and a free service through its website to help you select a market research agency. Contact three or four, outline what you need, then compare prices and service. A good agency should have detailed proposals about ways to carry out the research and should also be happy for you to contact existing or former customers for testimonials. Sharing the cost of the survey with other organisations, who have their questions included in the same questionnaire, can also help to cut costs.

When approaching an agency, be clear from the outset about what you want to discover, whether it is testing a new product during development, or gauging customer needs and people's responses to different products. Going to a market research agency with a definitive set of objectives, and a good sense of how you will use research results to improve your business, can make the agency's task much simpler.

Understanding your competition

As mentioned previously, finding out about your competition is a key part of the market research you need to carry out before starting up. But collecting information isn't enough, it's also vital that you gain an in-depth understanding of your potential competitors. It's important to know whom you will be competing with for your potential customers' time and money. What are their strengths and weaknesses? How are they positioned in the market? A good competitive analysis varies according to what industry you are looking at and your specific marketing plan and situation, but there are some common themes.

Begin by thinking about the general nature of the competition in your type of business, and how and why customers seem to choose one provider over another:

- Price or billing rates
- Reputation

" *It's important to know whom you will be competing with for your potential customers' time and money* **"**

- Image and visibility
- Are brand names important?
- How influential is word of mouth in providing long-term satisfied customers?

For example, competition in the restaurant business might depend on reputation and trends in one part of the market and on location and parking in another. Alternatively, for the internet and internet service providers, speed of connection and response rates to problems might be important. Meanwhile, a purchase decision for a car may be based on style, or speed or reputation for reliability. For many professional service practices, the nature of competition depends on word of mouth because advertising is not completely accepted and, therefore, not as influential. Is there price competition between accountants, doctors and lawyers?

Next, think about the factors that make the most difference for your business and why:

- How do people choose travel agencies or florists for weddings?
- Why does someone hire one gardener over another?
- Why would a customer choose Starbucks over the local coffee house?
- Why select a Dell computer instead of one from HP or Gateway?

This type of information is invaluable in understanding the nature of competition. Compare your potential product or service in the light of those factors of competition. For example:

- If you are planning to open a travel agency, will your agency offer better airline ticketing than others, or perhaps be located next to a major university and cater to student traffic? Are existing travel agents offering good service, better selection or better computer connections?
- The computer you plan to sell is faster and better, or perhaps comes in fruity colours. Do existing computer agents offer better price or service than you have planned?

! TOP TIPS

WHERE TO FIND KEY MARKET INFORMATION

! The internet

! Trade associations

! Government departments

! Local libraries for reference directories

! Industry magazines

! General interest business titles

! Market research firms

In other words, you should know how you plan to position yourself in the market. Why would people buy your product or services instead of the others offered in the same general categories? What benefits will you offer at what price, to whom, and how will your mix compare to others? Think about specific kinds of benefits, features and market groups, comparing where you think you can show the difference. Describe each of your potential major competitors in terms of those same factors. This may include their size, the market share they command, their comparative product quality, their growth, available capital and resources, image, marketing strategy, target markets, or whatever else you consider important. Make sure you specifically describe the strengths and weaknesses of each competitor, and compare them to your own plans in terms of service, pricing, reputation, management, financial position, brand awareness, business development, technology, or other factors that you feel are important. Consider the segments of the market in which competitors operate and their strategy. How much are they likely to affect your business, and what threats and opportunities do they represent?

As indicated earlier, you can find an amazing wealth of market data on the internet. The hard part, of course, is sorting through it and knowing what to keep. Access to competitive information is variable, depending on where you are and the nature of the competition. Competitors that are publicly traded may have a significant amount of information available, as regular financial reporting is a requirement of every serious stock market in the world. Wherever your target is listed for public trading, it has to report data. Competitive information may be limited in situations where your competitors are privately held. If possible, you may want to play the role of a potential customer and gain information from that perspective. Industry associations, industry publications, media coverage, information from the financial community, and their own marketing materials and websites may be good resources to identify these factors and 'rate' the performance and position of each competitor.

SIX CONTINTENTS AND THE TARGETED APPROACH

For the Six Continents pub company, a change in the make up of drinkers led to it developing a new bar concept–All Bar One. Now it's hard to imagine a city centre in the UK without one. It's a spectacular business success story, but what are the reasons behind it and what can you learn from it?

'The first All Bar One opened in December 1994. It was a time of major change in the British pub market, following the gentle, long-term decline of traditional pub goers,' explains **Bob Cartwright**, communications director for Six Continents. With the traditional customer base of predominately male, blue-collar pub drinkers shrinking, pub companies such as Six Continents realised they had to attract new types of customers–women, in particular.

'Shifting social attitudes were changing the role of women at this time. They were taking around 80% of new jobs in knowledge-based businesses and there was a dramatic shift in the age at which they were marrying and having children,' explains Cartwright. These young, women professionals, combined with an ever-expanding group of professional men, had formed a new pub-going market the existing pubs weren't catering for. 'We needed female-friendly pubs that young professionals of both sexes would want to visit.' So Six Continents developed All Bar One.

For a start, the buildings broke the traditional pub mould, with spacious saloons and large windows instead of the usual frosted glass frontage. 'This was so people could walk past and see immediately whether it was the sort of place they would feel comfortable in,' says Cartwright. Behind the bar, things changed as well. 'Beer had always been the traditional pub drink. We decided to have a large choice of wine, displayed very clearly and available to buy by the glass or bottle,' explains Cartwright. 'We also compiled a large [food] menu that would be attractive to both men and women.' In short, everything about All Bar One was designed with its target market in mind–a lesson that small businesses would do well to take on board.

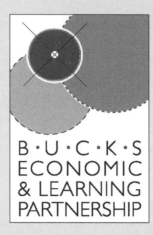

B·U·C·K·S
ECONOMIC
& LEARNING
PARTNERSHIP

Buckinghamshire is the Entrepreneurial Heart of Britain, a place where more entrepreneurs start-up and build more businesses than other parts of Europe.
With an economy worth around £10.9b, it is bigger than many nations.

As well as the very high number of start up businesses, it is home to international companies such as GE Healthcare, Pinewood and Shepperton Studios, Johnson and Johnson and Goodrich Power Systems, all drawn here by the fantastic natural environment, education, and housing, plus the highly skilled workforce and easy access to London, Europe, and the rest of the world. We are home to the Silverstone race circuit and Stoke Mandeville Hospital, both of which are world renowned global brands.

Forming part of the single largest growth area in the UK, Buckinghamshire welcomes budding entrepreneurs and small businesses looking for a supportive environment. Aylesbury itself is home to the new Peter Jones National Enterprise Academy.   There is a wide choice of premises including managed workspace in the new Innovation Centres in Aylesbury and High Wycombe where hands on support is available to guide hungry and innovative businesses to success.

This truly is one of the best places in which to live, work, and develop a business.

Buckinghamshire

the
Entrepreneurial
Heart of
Britain™

Contact us:

Bucks Economic and Learning Partnership, Friars Court, Friarage Passage, Aylesbury, HP20 2SJ.

Tel. 01296 383808, email lauren@belp.co.uk or visit www.belp.co.uk for further information and advice.

WRITING A BUSINESS PLAN AND FINANCE ISSUES

WHAT'S IN THIS CHAPTER

- By this point you should have carried out the relevant research into the viability of your proposed venture, including having examined your market and looking at customers and competition. With all these data to hand, and convinced that your company will be a success, you now need to start planning the business properly. The best way to do this is to prepare a business plan, which will prove valuable not only in securing any necessary funding, but also in helping you run the company after launch. This can be one of the most daunting aspects of starting up a business, because so much can ride on it. However, if you approach it carefully and logically, and clearly understand each key element, you will have little to worry about. Read on for a definitive guide to drawing up your business plan and the various types of finance it could help secure…

Why write a business plan?

Having a well-researched and logical business plan will not only get your venture off the ground, but also keep it on track when it is up and running. In the first instance, unless you have a strong plan, you are unlikely to secure any funds and your idea could fall at the first hurdle. Your plan will serve as a structured form of communication to your investors, whether it's the government's Business Link service, the banks or even family and friends, and it will provide reassurance as well as a means for everyone, yourself included, to measure your business's performance.

> **It's vital to establish just how much you intend to spend and when**

A business plan will help you to prioritise what exactly needs to be achieved and by when. Do you need to find premises for your business before you hire staff? Should you be talking to wholesalers before your product has been finished? In the current climate, it's also important to outline what strategy you have in place for getting your venture through the recession – perhaps you consider it recession-proof, or you have done your research and have started in a sector where companies are growing, or you have strong measures to control expenditure. The answers will be different for each business, but it certainly helps if they are clear in your mind. 'If objectives are clearly flagged up, they are more likely to be achieved,' says **Tim Berry**, president of business planning software company Palo Alto.

By using your business plan to prioritise key tasks, you can also use it to plan your cashflow. It's vital to establish just how much you intend to spend and when. Whether it's to buy stock, order uniforms, lease equipment etc., unless your finances match your requirements at the right moment, your business could stall.

Clearly, compiling a business plan should be at the top of your 'to do' list. If you are in a partnership or part of a potential management team, then decide early on who will write the plan, and then the same individual should be assigned the task of making the business stick to it. How far ahead to plan will again depend on your own aims and the type of business, but a year, broken down month by month, will be a minimum.

PRIDE VALLEY FOODS
AND THE CAREFUL PLAN

Company: Pride Valley Foods
Owner-manager: Hossain Rezaei

Pride Valley Foods was founded in 1990 by **Hossain Rezaei**. The firm supplies speciality breads to some of the biggest suppliers in the country, including Tesco and Marks & Spencer. Based in Seaham, County Durham, the business now employs 250 staff and has, on average, doubled in size every year. Rezaei attributes his success to research and planning.

After researching the market, Rezaei planned his company's growth, for which he used the Tick Tree method. In this method, each of the steps must be completed on time and within budget. Starting from the first branch on the tree, Rezaei borrowed a small amount and built the business gradually. He illustrates his approach with a household example. If you want to decorate a room in your house, you plan a timetable outlining each of the steps. The first step is to remove the furniture, then you may need another person to help you move it and perhaps need somewhere to move it to. You may need to budget for removal costs, such as £50 to hire a van and the time it will take to move the furniture. Only then can you move on to the next stage. With business, the figures are larger but the principle is the same.

'You have to borrow £10,000 and then deliver what you said you would do. When you have done that you can go back and borrow more. A lot of people fail because they go straight to step two or three and they haven't got the track record, the experience or the market knowledge,' Rezaei says.

Rezaei's careful planning also ensured that when Pride Valley's factory was destroyed by fire and insurers initially refused to pay out on the policy, Rezaei kept the business running. While keeping sight of his original plan, Rezaei moved back to old premises, handed customers over to competitors and returned to his backers with an emergency plan. Within six months, his business was back on track because Rezaei had planned a series of steps to get back to his original plan.

Rezaei believes that any business will succeed or fail on the basis of the three Cs – capital, character and capability. What he didn't add to the list was careful planning – but this has undoubtedly been the key to the success of Pride Valley Foods.

Once you've established responsibility and a timeframe, you need to decide on certain criteria, on which your business's success will be determined and how these can be achieved. For instance, it could be hitting a given number of sales by a set date through an aggressive marketing campaign, or expanding to three more product lines through extensive market research. Whatever these achievement criteria turn out to be, you need to think hard about them without making too many assumptions. Consider your business failing in two or three years' time and try to imagine the reasons it might do so.

Preparing data for your business plan

This section will describe the key data you will need to compile before you start, some of which you will be able to get from your market research, discussed in the previous chapter.

The legal structure of your startup

While, understandably, the focus of most entrepreneurs is on their 'idea', it is vital that the operational and logistical requirements are not neglected. For example, decisions regarding whether you intend to trade as a sole trader, partnership or limited company are very important. Prior to deciding, enlist the help of a local accountant or your local Business Link office. (The options available to you are discussed in Chapter 5.0). Similarly, you should understand and cover issues such as your potential VAT (value-added tax) obligations, registering a trademark or trade name and drafting employment contracts.

Managing the numbers

Whether you like figures or not, having a thorough understanding of 'the numbers' that will impact on your business is a crucial component to running a successful business, particularly at the planning stage. At the outset, it will be important to understand:

- Your startup costs
- Your funding requirements
- Your cashflow forecast for the following months.

Your startup costs

Your startup costs include how much it will actually cost to get your business up and running: what you will need to pay out before the launch date, such as legal and administrative fees that may be involved in registering your company, and any marketing, ranging from pre-launch advertising to the design of your logo and stationery. There's also the cost of renting premises if you are not working from home and any stock or equipment you may need, such as general office and IT items, to specialist tools that may be required for your particular business. You will also need to consider how much money you will need during the early months, once you are up and running – this is known as your cash reserve and covers you initially when you are likely to be making a loss. How much your cash reserve will be depends on how quickly you can start to bring revenue into the company, so you need to consider carefully how long it will take until you reach the break-even point (see below) and move into profit. Here's an example of typical startup costs and how you can itemise them:

Initial expenses (legal costs, stationery, sales literature, logo and branding design)	£2,500
Money in the bank as reserve for early losses	£16,500
Startup stock or raw materials (if required)	£900
Other short-term assets (leasehold improvements, fixtures, signage, etc.)	£700
Long-term or fixed assets (land, machinery, IT equipment, etc.)	£10,000
Total startup requirements	£45,000

Your funding requirements

To get your business off the ground, you will most likely need financial help to cover some of the startup costs outlined above. Your business plan will be a vital tool for convincing lenders to support your company. So, you will need to have carefully worked out how much money you need to borrow, and explain your reasoning behind the figure. It's important to remember that once you have secured finance, it won't be easy going back to ask for more, so it's vital that you get it right first time. Although it's wise not to overestimate how much funding you need, as it's likely investors will react unkindly to such an approach, you do need to make sure you don't ask for too little, as this will put a lot of pressure on your company. This is when working out the amount of cash you will need in reserve becomes important, and when you are likely to reach the break-even point.

Your break-even point

Your break-even point is the critical milestone at which your new company stops making a loss and is about to move into profit once all the additional expenses have been taken into account – estimating as accurately as you can when you will reach this point is an expected part of you business plan. Before you can work this out you need to formulate your startup costs and monthly running costs, taking into account any repayments on loans, salaries, etc. You then need to build in your sales projections of how many products, or how much demand you will have for your service, per month. By comparing your projected monthly revenues against your total monthly costs, you should be able to come up with a point at which you start to move into profit, that is, your break-even point.

Calculating the break-even point will give you an excellent idea of the costs involved in your business and the level of sales you will need to generate, which will in turn affect your overall business strategy. How much business you have to generate (either number of products or units of service) in a given time to break even can be calculated using the equation below:

Total revenue per month = Total costs per month
Unit sale price × Unit sales = Total monthly fixed costs + (Unit variable cost × Unit sales)
(Unit sale price × Unit sales) – (Unit variable cost × Unit sales) = Total fixed costs
(Unit sale price – Unit variable cost) × Unit sales = Total fixed costs
Unit sales per month = $\dfrac{\text{Total fixed costs}}{\text{Unit sale price} - \text{Unit variable cost}}$

Once you know how much you need to sell in one month to break even, you can work out from your sales projections how long it will take for your business to reach this point. You can also see in the table the elements of the equation that you need to change to reach the break-even point sooner if you want to.

Your cashflow forecast for the following months

Estimating the amount and origin of cash coming into your business, together with how much is being paid out and where it's going during any given period is a vital part of good business management. This is known as a cashflow forecast and it's also what many lenders or investors will be looking for before they decide to invest in your business. This makes it a key part of your business plan. Once your business is established, it's usual to produce cashflow forecasts for a quarter or even a year in advance. However, during the early stages of your business, it's probably wiser to do this more frequently – say a month in advance. When formulating a cashflow forecast, it's critical that you don't overestimate your incoming cash. You will find it easier to get an accurate indication of your outgoings as you should be able to itemise them, as described above. The problem is, you are unlikely to be able to accurately identify how much money is going to be coming in, as you can only estimate how much business you will generate each month. This means it's vital to err on the side of caution, keeping your forecast on the conservative side.

Identifying the right people

Along with financial predictions, the people entrusted with putting your plan into action will be subject to particular scrutiny by potential financiers. Regardless of the entrepreneur's/founder's skill set, he or she will invariably need help. While many non-core activities can be outsourced, certain functions, such as sales, will need full-time attention. You should outline the various skills required to run the business, price them into the model, and also identify any gaps and prospective candidates to fill them.

Clearly defining and articulating the customer benefits

Many entrepreneurs fail to clearly articulate the benefits of their new venture. As a result, the term 'elevator pitch' was introduced into modern lexicons as a proposed solution to this. An elevator pitch is your idea, supported by your business model, company solution, marketing strategy and competition, all stated in the length of time it takes for a short elevator ride. This simple idea encourages entrepreneurs to think carefully about the language they use when describing their new venture (particularly technological ones). It also reminds you to remain customer-focused and ensure that you concentrate on describing the benefits.

Getting a mentor

Many startup entrepreneurs are paranoid that their idea will be stolen and behave secretively prior to launch. Often the idea is closely guarded and only discussed with close confidantes. However, your confidantes (often family or friends) may find it difficult to pose sufficiently rigorous questions to you, because they don't want to offend you or they lack the relevant experience or judgement to critically analyse your new venture. Hence, an idea with serious flaws, which could have been rectified early on in the process, can move ahead only for the wheels to come off at the most important phase. It is highly recommended that you engage an independent mentor or plan reviewer at an early stage. This person can help hone your idea before you present to financiers or bankers.

Key elements of your business plan

The business plan should give a concise description of what your company will sell or the service it will offer, the buyers you will be selling to and how you will be filling a gap in the market, by touching on pricing and existing competition. So it should be prepared to a high standard, be verifiable (meaning that you need to be able to back up your statements with facts) and with no jargon or general position statements. It should offer the reader a combination of clear description and analysis, including a realistic SWOT (strengths, weaknesses, opportunities and threats; see page 116) test of each area. This will demonstrate to investors that you are realistic about your company's prospects. So ensure that you have a full appreciation of the risks, and you know how to grab your market share – all of which, of course, should have been covered in your market research. For your own benefit as well, it must contain details of how exactly you intend to meet your key objectives, as well as sales forecasts, target dates and who, apart from yourself, is to be responsible for this.

Then comes the boring, but just as necessary part – a financial analysis that shows clearly how much finance you need and where you plan to source it from (see the section on Raising finance, page 129), a summary of startup costs, break-even point and cashflow forecast (as described above), plus profit and loss and balance sheet projections.

The key to all this will be striking a balance between coveringyour business in enough detail, and keeping the plan clear and to the point for it to be useful to refer to time and time again rather than just sitting on a shelf gathering dust once you've begun trading.

The key features of your plan are first described below in brief and then explained in more detail later in the chapter.

The length

The length of a business plan depends on individual circumstances. It should be long enough to cover the subject adequately and short enough to maintain interest. Unless your business requires several million pounds of venture capital and is highly complex, the business plan should be no longer than 15 pages. The British Venture Capital Association (BVCA), the members of which you may well be pitching your plan to, recommends erring on the side of brevity. If investors are interested, they can always call to ask for additional information.

Contact

British Venture
Capital Association
www.bvca.co.uk

The look

The plan should look professional. Ensure there are no grammar or spelling mistakes. Use graphs and charts where appropriate and titles and subtitles to divide different subject matters. Although the aim is to make the plan look good, do avoid expensive stationery, as this could suggest unnecessary waste and extravagance.

> **Although the aim is to make the plan look good, do avoid expensive stationery**

The company

The business plan should detail all the important aspects of your company, viz., the market and customers, the products/services, the strength of the management team – and if there are any gaps in talent, identify how you will fill them. The plan should also explain how products will be made or services provided. Realistic financial projections should be outlined and you should provide different scenarios for sales, costs and cashflows for both the long and short term.

'What if's and ways out

A number of possible scenarios should be presented, along with how your company would cope in different situations. These 'What if?' questions will show how your business will react to or counter the effects of an unexpected drop in sales or an increase in costs. The business plan should also detail potential exit strategies.

The executive summary and mission statement

The last thing to be written is the first part of the business plan: the executive summary. This is the most important section and summarises in two pages what you have written in detail in the following 10–15 pages. This is where, among other things, you lay down the company's mission statement – a few sentences encapsulating what the business does for what types of client, your aims for the company and what gives it its competitive edge. That is, the mission statement should combine the business's current situation with your aspirations. As with the main part of the business plan, the executive summary

! TOP TIPS
CHAPTERS TO INCLUDE IN YOUR BUSINESS PLAN

! Executive summary (including mission statement)

! Products and services (detail on your offer)

! The market (customer and competitor analysis)

! The proposition (why customers will buy from you)

! Marketing strategy (how you will get your message across)

! Sales strategy (how you plan to convert interest into sales)

! Financial data (sales forecast, cost base, profit estimates)

! Management and personnel (profiles of key people behind the business)

! SWOT analysis (strengths, weaknesses, opportunities, threats)

! Ownership and legal structure (shareholders and whether limited, partnership or sole trader)

! Summary (brief overview and roundup)

should be clearly written and powerfully persuasive, yet it should balance sales talk with realism in order to be convincing. It should be no more than 1,000 words and should also state your company's legal status. Both these are discussed in more detail later in the chapter.

Forecasting your sales
Preparing a sales forecast

Developing your sales forecast isn't as hard as most people imagine. Think of your sales forecast as an educated guess. It requires good working knowledge of your business but is much more of an art than a science. Remember that even if you don't have business training, you can guess your own business's sales better than any expert device, statistical analysis or mathematical routine. Experience counts more than any other factor.

> " Sales should close the deals that marketing opens "

A business plan should usually project sales by month for the next year, and annual sales for the following three years. This doesn't mean businesses shouldn't plan for a longer term than just three years, it simply means that the detail of monthly forecasts doesn't pay off beyond a year, except in special cases. It also means that the detail in the yearly forecasts probably doesn't make sense beyond three years. It does mean, of course, that you still plan your business for five, 10, and even 15-year time frames, but you just don't do it within the detailed context of business plan financials. Break your sales down into manageable parts, and then forecast these different elements. Estimate the figures based on line of sales, month by month, then add up the sales lines and add up the months, presenting your estimate graphically in a table or chart; remember that you still need to explain them. A complete business plan will usually include some discussion of your sales forecast, sales strategy, sales programmes and related information. The text, tables, and charts together will provide some visual variety and ease of use. Remember to position the tables and charts near the text covering the related topics.

Drawing up a sales strategy

> **Make sure you discuss important assumptions in enough detail, and that you explain the background sufficiently**

Near the sales forecast you should describe your sales strategy, which should deal with how and when to close sales prospects, how to compensate sales people, how to optimise order processing and database management, and how to manoeuvre price, delivery and conditions. It should answer questions such as:

- How will you sell? Through retail, wholesale, discount, mail order or over the phone, for example.
- Will you maintain a sales force?
- How will you train your sales people, and how will they be compensated?

Your business plan text should summarise and highlight the numbers you have entered in the sales forecast table. Make sure you discuss important assumptions in enough detail, and that you explain the background sufficiently. Try to anticipate the questions your readers will ask. Include whatever information you think will be relevant and that your readers will need. Details are critical to implementation and your business plan should include specific information related to sales programmes.

- How is this strategy to be implemented?
- Do you have concrete and specific plans?
- How will implementation be measured?

Business plans are about results, and generating results depends in part on how specific you are in the plan. For anything related to a

MARKETING VERSUS SALES STRATEGY

Don't confuse sales strategy with your marketing strategy. Sales should close the deals that marketing opens. To understand the difference between marketing and sales strategies, think of marketing as the broader effort of generating sales leads on a large scale, and sales as the efforts to bring those sales leads into the system as individual sales transactions. Marketing aims to build the business's image, customer awareness and propensity to buy, while sales involves getting the order.

sale that is supposed to happen, include it here and list the person responsible, dates required and budgets. All this will make your business plan more real.

SWOT analysis

SWOT analysis is a method of describing your future company in terms of those factors that will have the most impact on the business. Strengths and weaknesses are internal factors, such as the quality of your product or the skills of your management, whereas opportunities and threats are external factors, which may include the development of a whole new market (opportunity), the arrival of a clutch of new competitors, the impact of the recession (threat) or the eventual economic recovery (opportunity). SWOT is an easy, understandable way of identifying key issues and communicating them to others. To make things even simpler to grasp, the typical SWOT analysis is done on a four-cell grid:

> **SWOT is an easy, understandable way of identifying key issues and communicating them to others**

Strengths	Weaknesses
Opportunities	**Threats**

Sometimes it helps to start without the grid and list any issues at all that might affect the business – internal or external, real or perceived. Then, when the flow starts to dry up, organise the chosen items into the SWOT categories. Here's a guide to help you complete the categories.

Strengths

In the first box list all the strengths of your company:

- Why should you succeed?
- What will you do well?
- Why will customers do business with you?
- What distinct advantages does your company offer?

> **The important consideration is honesty**

The important consideration is honesty. Avoid being too modest or too optimistic. Any SWOT analysis is essentially subjective, but try for a third-party viewpoint: what strengths does the outsider see? A jump-start trick, especially for a group SWOT session is to begin by brainstorming adjectives that characterise your business, writing them down as quickly as people say them, and then using those words to construct a more considered profile of your company's strengths. If you are the sole proprietor or the prime mover in the business, try starting with a list of your own positive personal characteristics.

Weaknesses

A weakness is something that could seriously impede your company's performance – a limitation or deficiency in resource, skills or capabilities. These could be factors that you will be able to address on launch. For example, a weakness could be a lack of awareness in the marketplace compared with your competition, which means you will need to promote your company heavily to raise its profile, ideally before you launch the business or immediately after. Also, although you may list your personal knowledge of the market as a strength, the fact that the company will initially be heavily reliant on you could be seen as a weakness. If you can spot the key weaknesses of your proposed venture now, you can address them in time for the launch, and it shows investors that all-important element of realism in your approach. So don't try to disguise weaknesses, simply acknowledge them and ensure you have a strategy in place to tackle them.

Opportunities

Under opportunities think about where the openings are for your business, or the customer needs not being met by your competitors. You will probably start with marketing issues, presumably because your business fills a niche or can compete effectively, but do include all the possibilities. For instance, think of the interesting trends in your business sector – in terms of not only markets but also in technology changes, the legislative and regulatory environment and social patterns.

Threats

Threats are key impediments that your company will face on launch. What are the more apparent obstacles in your way, both actual and potential? Obvious candidates would include the economic downturn, a sudden rush of bad debts or a slack sales period leading to cashflow problems. But try to think further than that:

- What is your competition doing that could take business away from you or stunt your company's growth?
- How might your competitors react to any moves you make?
- What trends do you see that could wipe you out or make your service or product obsolete?
- Might technology changes threaten your products or services?
- What happens if a key customer goes under before paying a sizeable invoice?

It's important to include a couple of worst-case scenarios. Weighing threats against opportunities is not a reason to indulge in pessimism, but rather a question of considering how possible damage may be overcome, bypassed or restricted.

> " It's important to include a couple of worst-case scenarios... to consider how possible damage may be overcome "

Using SWOT data

"

A SWOT analysis helps identify the critical issues in any situation and organises them in a way that enables you to come up with a sound strategic approach "

Once you have the results of your own SWOT analysis and at least one (but preferably more) from another source, combine them on the grid. Then sort each category first by relative importance. Then re-sort them in terms of reality – this an interesting exercise, which might well require some soul-searching. For example, ask yourself what evidence you really have for saying that customers will choose your product over your competitors'. Finally trim the categories to around no more than five or six items each per category, homing in on the really critical issues. You can use this as the basis for some strategic planning. This cut-down SWOT summary and a description of your sound strategic approach to address the points listed should appear in your business plan. This will cover how you plan to:

- Build on the strengths
- Minimise the weaknesses
- Seize the opportunities
- Counter the threats.

USING SWOT ANALYSIS TO CLARIFY YOUR BUSINESS GOALS

After a SWOT analysis you might see things in terms of answers to these four questions:

- How can strengths be used to take advantage of opportunities?
- How can strengths be used to avoid or defuse threats?
- How can weaknesses be overcome to take advantage of opportunities?
- How can weaknesses be overcome to counteract or minimise threats?
- Remember to try to be objective at all times when writing your strategy approach.

ACTION POINT

FOUR KEY RECOMMENDATIONS FOR A FLAWLESS SWOT ANALYSIS

Be comprehensive: This means picking up small details. A minor weakness could be too few filing cabinets, while a major threat could be a decline in the value of sterling following an election. Of course, this could also be an key opportunity if there was a rise in currency value instead.

Be prepared: Put real effort into background preparation and gathering information. Be self-critical, but don't be too defensive. SWOT analysis is there to stimulate ideas and not stifle them.

Include others: SWOT works well in group sessions. To get a real brainstorm going you need more than four people, but to keep it manageable limit numbers to around 10.

Test your analysis: Ask an outsider (your accountant, perhaps, or family member) to conduct the same exercise and compare their views with your findings. The more people who look at your SWOT analysis, the more ideas you are likely to get.

The people

Anyone who runs a business knows that none of the areas covered by a business plan can be tackled without people. Why then do so many business plans feel that it's sufficient to insert an appendix with the CVs of the managers? This token gesture does not give any feel for how the business will be run, what the potential gaps in expertise may be or what essential skills will be needed in the future. It all comes back to strategic planning versus day-to-day fire-fighting.

If you are launching solo, the people section will initially revolve around your skills and experience. But this model can still help you to draw up a list of the kind of people you will need to meet your projections for the business, either at startup or beyond, which will show that you have a clear understanding of what is required to realise your vision. Here is a model that might help you to analyse the 'people' section of the plan.

> If you are launching solo, the people section will initially revolve around your skills and experience

1. Draw up a table with four columns: (a) people, (b) experience, (c) skills and (d) functions.
2. Make a list of all the people who are involved in your business in column (a) and summarise their experience and skills in columns (b) and (c), so that you can clearly see who you have on board and what they each bring to the business.
3. Make a list of the areas of sector and functional expertise required for the business and see who is ideally placed to fill each of these roles. Are there any functions that can't be undertaken by the people who are within the team and, if so, how do you propose to fill these gaps?
4. Draw up another table showing the business in three years' time. How will the management team be different? What steps will you need to take to both keep existing staff satisfied and recruit new staff of sufficient calibre to deliver your ambitious future plans as described in other sections?

Businesses change over time, and it is unusual for an early-stage company to have a full management team. Generally an entrepreneur will endeavour to fill many roles, some of which they will be particularly unsuited to. Why not explore in the business plan what roles could be performed better by others, such as a finance director, sales director and even the chief executive? How are you going to afford people of sufficient calibre to deliver what you want? Perhaps you will need to raise some further finance to cover this at a later date. One of the most valid reasons for raising equity capital is to pay for people who are good enough to take a company to a higher level, and yet generally entrepreneurs leave such recruitment too late.

The mission statement

An effective mission statement should be able to tell your company story and ideals in less than 30 seconds, and, as such, it can be one of the more challenging elements of your business plan. The readers should be able to gain a clear understanding of what your company's about from the mission statement, so it's vital to think it through very carefully. Essentially, it should only be around three to four sentences long, defining what your company is, what it does, what it stands for and why, and it is often best developed with input from everyone involved in the launch.

It can help to examine other companies' mission statements, but don't be tempted to copy any, because it's vital that the mission statement is original and accurately reflects your business, not someone else's. You should also make sure that you believe in your mission statement, as it will provide the basis for your business going forward, inspiring both you and your future employees to success. Therefore, if it's a lie, it can be demotivational for your employees and put off customers once this becomes apparent.

> **It's vital that the mission statement is original and accurately reflects your business**

MISSION CONTROL: EXAMPLE MISSION STATEMENTS FROM FAMOUS COMPANIES

IBM
'At IBM, we strive to lead in the invention, development and manufacture of the industry's most advanced information technologies, including computer systems, software, storage systems and microelectronics.

We translate these advanced technologies into value for our customers through our professional solutions, services and consulting businesses worldwide.'

Amazon.com
'To be the most customer-centric company in the world, where people can find and discover anything they want to buy online.'

Apple Computers (1984)
'To produce high-quality, low cost, easy-to-use products that incorporate high technology for the individual. We are proving that high technology does not have to be intimidating for non-computer experts.'

Sainsbury's
'Our mission is to be the consumer's first choice for food, delivering products of outstanding quality and great service at a competitive cost through working faster, simpler and together.'

The executive summary

The executive summary presents the highlights of your business plan, and even though it opens the document, it's often the final part to be completed – for obvious reasons. The executive summary is the doorway to your business plan, so it's important to get it right or your target readers will go no further. As a general rule, for a standard plan, the first paragraph should include:

- Business name
- Business location
- What product or service you sell
- The purpose of the plan.

Next, highlight important points, such as projected sales and profits, unit sales, profitability and keys to success. Essentially, you should include the news you don't want anyone to miss. This is a good place to put a 'highlights' chart – a bar graph that shows prospective sales, gross margin and profits before interest and taxes for the next three years – as well as drawing attention to them in the text. As you are starting up, one of the main purposes of your plan is likely to be to secure investment, so say this in your executive summary, and specify how much investment is required and the amount of equity ownership offered in return. It's also a good idea to add highlights of your management team and your competitive edge.

If you are looking for a loan, say so in the executive summary, and specify the amount required (but leave out other details about the loan).

> " Investors are looking to be inspired "

! TOP TIPS

WRITING YOUR PLAN

! Write from the audience's perspective – tell them what they need to know

! Research the market thoroughly – it proves the viability of your business

! Understand the competition – and how you will beat it

! Pay attention to detail – it shows you really care

! Focus on the opportunity – talk it up, but be realistic

! Ensure all key areas are covered – be comprehensive

! Make sure your figures add up – they won't take it seriously otherwise

! Write a killer executive summary – it's the bit that gets them interested

! Get it reviewed – ideally by an experienced independent source

! Implement the plan – don't leave it on a shelf and forget about it

Getting people to read your plan

Although many people work hard to produce business plans that are technically perfect, because they recognise the importance of the document in securing essential finance and other support vital to getting a business off the ground, many business plans still fail. This is because often they need to show more than technical excellence. Remember that potential investors receive lots of business plans and so are looking to be inspired by those that offer more than the ordinary. So while you should include the necessary sales forecast, SWOT analysis and mission statement, here are some tips that could provide the key to unlocking a target reader's interest and encourage them to venture beyond the executive summary.

Research your target reader

> Tell them who you are, how you got into this position of writing the plan, and engagingly unfurl your vision for the business

The more you know about the reader and their requirements, the better equipped you will be to give them what they want – and so get what you want. The bank manager, the equity provider and whoever else you may be pitching your business plan to are likely to all have different needs and concerns, but will probably have one thing in common: they are busy, short of time, impatient and hassled. So spoon feed them. Make their lives easier and they will appreciate it. Once you have excited the finance provider with your vision, give some background about the business. Don't make assumptions about what they know about your potential company, your ambitions and your plan. Tell them who you are, how you got into this position of writing the plan, and engagingly unfurl your vision for the business. In short, put it all in perspective. Frame the plan, and the reader will have some reference points straight away.

Explain your proposition succinctly yet comprehensively

Once your readers know two things – where you came from and where you are going – next comes the crucial bit: can you explain what your value proposition is to your customers in no more than 30 seconds or a few lines of text? If you can, you will be in a very small minority of entrepreneurs – even some of the successful ones have never managed it. Succinctly summarise:

- Who will buy your product or service and why they will buy?
- How many will they buy?
- Why will they continue to buy over time?
- Why will they buy from you rather than someone else?
- In short, what value are you really delivering to your customer?

It can often help to test yourself. For example, bore your friends with your proposition, or if you get the chance, try it out on prospective customers, and once you have it off pat, write it down. It will be one of your most valuable assets. If all this sounds quite simple on paper, remember that many have found it impossible to achieve in practice. But after all the time spent researching your market, working through your sales forecasts, constructing your SWOT analysis and other relevant details and then committing them to paper, you may just crack it. Working on producing a killer executive summary will be well worth the effort, as it could prove decisive in gaining the investment you need to launch your company.

KIRSTY'S STORY

I prepared a fantastic business plan

Co-founder of the website Entertainthekids.com, **Kirsty McGregor** was 10 months into the planning process with five months left before launch when she got a pleasant surprise...

'The process took this long because we still had "day jobs", family life and other commitments, and wanted to give ourselves the best chance of surviving the rocky road that most startups face in their first few years. So we took our time, did lots of research and planning, and used the most professional approach we could.

'Once I had the idea for the site, I discussed it with my brother Ross who was just finishing a degree in e-business. He thought it was great too, but we needed to put some numbers down – I had no idea if it was financially viable. The two biggest costs I thought we would have were the website development itself, and the marketing costs to promote the website address to the general public – or more particularly to our target market of parents and carers. We drew up a shortlist of some website designers and asked them to quote for the work to get a ball-park figure.

'Then we started thinking about marketing. My old employer had an in-house marketing company that I knew well and respected, so we got talking to them.

'We'd pretty much resigned ourselves to the fact that we weren't going to get funding, but thought we'd approach banks just in case. We looked at the likely costs, and I prepared some draft projections. I wrote a fantastic business plan (if I do say so myself) and enclosed three sets of projections, worst case, most likely case and best case, and we submitted it initially to three major banks.' The first two turned her down – however, her luck turned and the third agreed to provide a loan.

ACTION POINT
COMMON BUSINESS PLAN MISTAKES

While including the necessary items in a business plan, make sure you don't commit any of the following common business plan mistakes.

Putting it off: Too many businesses make business plans only when they have no choice in the matter. Unless the bank or the investors want a plan, there is no plan. Don't wait to write your plan until you think you will have enough time. It should play a key role in the development of your business, creating a strategic framework to build your company around, and not just created in response to a specific need, such as securing funding. This is why it is essential to review your plan regularly – it should be an organic document that develops as the business grows and as the influences on it change, such as marketing conditions.

Cashflow casualness: Most people think in terms of profits instead of cash. When you imagine a new business, you think of what it would cost to make the product, what you could sell it for, and what the profits per unit might be. We are trained to think of business as sales minus costs and expenses, which equal profits. Unfortunately, we don't spend the profits in a business. We spend cash. So understanding cashflow is critical. If you have only one table in your business plan, make it the cashflow table.

Idea inflation: Don't overestimate the importance of the idea. You don't need a great idea to start a business; you need time, money, perseverance and common sense. Few successful businesses are based entirely on new ideas. A new idea is harder to sell than an existing one, because people don't understand a new idea and they are often unsure if it will work. Plans don't sell new business ideas to investors, people do. Investors invest in people, not ideas. The plan, although necessary, is only a way to present information.

Fear and dread: Although preparing a business plan can seem daunting, if you approach it carefully and strategically, and have carried out the necessary research into the viability of your business beforehand, there is no need to fear anything – in fact fear and dread could mean you put it off until the last minute and then don't dedicate the time and energy to it that it deserves. There are also plenty of resources available to help you get it right.

Spongy, vague goals: Leave out the vague and the meaningless babble of business phrases (such as 'being the best'), because they are simply hype. Remember that the objective of a plan is to secure results, and for results, you need tracking and follow up. You need specific dates, management responsibilities, budgets and milestones. Then you can follow up. No matter how well thought out or brilliantly presented your business plan may be, it means nothing unless it produces results.

One size doesn't fit all: Tailor your plan to its real business purpose. Business plans can be different things: sales documents to sell an idea for a new business; or detailed action plans, financial plans, marketing plans or even personnel plans. They can be used to start a business, or just run a business better.

Diluted priorities: Remember, strategy is focused. A priority list with three to four items is focused. A priority list with 20 items is certainly not strategic, and rarely, if ever, effective. The more items on the list, the less the importance of each.

Hockey-stick shaped growth projections: Sales grow slowly at first, but then shoot up boldly with huge growth rates, as soon as 'something' happens. Have projections that are conservative, so you can defend them. When in doubt, be less optimistic.

Presenting your plan

When the business plan has been prepared and it has received input from a financial adviser, the next step is to put it in front of investors. If you are using a business angel network, which match young businesses with private investors, there should be plenty of advice on offer as they will know exactly what a business angel is looking for. Local agencies such as Business Link can provide advice on how to structure and present your plan. Try to also run through the plan with any business contacts that you have, as they may spot something that you hadn't noticed. Asking friends and family to help can also be useful.

At this point, you may send just a copy of the executive summary. This has the advantage of saving costs and increasing the chances of receiving attention. Response times to the business plan will vary, but can take as little as a week. If the answer is 'No', you should find out the reasons why and then consider incorporating those ideas into a revised business plan, changing and strengthening the management team or carrying out further market research before approaching other potential investors.

And remember, the business plan is a living document. Don't think of it as a fixed route and be prepared to adapt it to suit your audience. Even if you are in an established business, you must be prepared

CONTACT

Business Link
www.businesslink.
gov.uk
☎0845 600 9 006

to adapt the plan as your market or customer base changes or if disaster strikes.

Raising finance

If the primary function of your plan is to raise finance, you must clearly state how much money you need and why, based on the details you are presenting. Although banks remain the most common source of initial finance, it pays to bear in mind all the options available, and adapt your plan accordingly. For example, you may arrange finance in return for a stake in your business – known as 'equity' – rather than it simply securing a loan. In such a case, you need to include how big a stake of your company you are prepared to forfeit for the amount of funding you need. The range of finance options open to you are described below.

Debt finance

Debt finance is simply borrowing money to buy the things you need to launch your business, and then paying it back in some way. Although many small companies are now financed by the founders themselves, when people think about raising money, their first port of call is generally the bank, from which a loan is the most typical form of debt financing. Generally it has to be repaid at an agreed interest rate and within a specified period of time. The interest rate can either be variable or fixed.

Typically the loan is secured against an asset. This means that if the business fails to repay the loan, the lender has the right to claim the asset. An asset could be a house or other premises or some equipment owned by the business. If you are unwilling to put personal possessions like your house on the line and your company has insufficient assets, a bank is unlikely to lend you money. Often a bank will also expect some financial commitment from you personally, such as a percentage of the amount you are requesting. As the loan is secured, the cost is usually less than other more risky types of borrowing. However, a bank loan also locks companies into a payment schedule, which may cause cashflow problems for small businesses. You will have to show how the money will be repaid, and details from your business plan should help.

The straightjacket of making a set payment at what may be a fixed interest rate can also cause a lot of problems for fast-growing companies that consume capital very fast. For these reasons, loans are more suited to tried-and-tested business models that offer good prospects for profitability.

Following the credit crunch, banks have become very risk averse, making securing finance from them more difficult, particularly if you are launching a startup and have no track record of running a company. That's not to say, however, that it isn't available. Banks are still providing finance, but the terms are likely to be tougher, such as higher interest rates. This makes it more important than ever to shop around for the best deal, as it could save you money in the long term.

You can also use a financial broker to suggest the best terms on offer for the type of finance that your business needs. This can save you time and money, and can also increase your chances of getting a loan by presenting your proposal in the best way to the most appropriate lenders. Before enlisting the help of a broker, however, find out what they are going to charge you.

With loans harder to come by, there could be a tendency to be so relieved you've secured one that you rush into it. However, try to negotiate the best terms you can, as this can have a direct impact on the health of your business once you launch. Aside from discussing obvious issues, such as the due date of the loan and the interest rate, you also need to establish the amount of the loan fees. It's important to make sure that you will have the flexibility to pay off your loan earlier than the due date and, if possible, try to avoid any penalty for early settlement. Try to negotiate for a grace period for your payment schedule and check to make sure that late payment charges are fair. Make sure you have scrutinised the small print before you put pen to

CONTACT

National Association of Commercial Financial Brokers www.nacfb.org

There is a vast range of different debt financing tools and each business should find the one that is right for them

paper. It can help to ask an expert, such as a solicitor, to review the terms.

As shown in the box, there is a vast range of different debt financing tools and each business should find the one that is right for them. Using them creatively and wisely can help to reduce the reliance on a bank. So, if your business needs some working capital, but the amount fluctuates, an overdraft is probably best for you. The interest rate is agreed in advance and you only pay interest for the time and amount that you are overdrawn. But if your business needs longer-term finance, in particular for a specific purchase or planned expenditure, you should look to take a loan that can be repaid over a set period. There are many reasons why debt finance could suit your business – it is accessible, flexible and tailored. Debt finance will be the first option for most small businesses, and whether it is loans, overdrafts, leasing or invoice discounting, the company is borrowing against reserves rather than giving someone ownership of shares. One key reason that most businesses will borrow money rather than

DIFFERENT TYPES OF DEBT FINANCE

Debt finance can also take the form of an overdraft, term loan, leasing, factoring and invoice discounting.

- An overdraft is generally used to fund working cashflow rather than capital expenditure, and is repayable on demand, while exceeding the agreed limits can be expensive.
- Increasingly banks are offering term loans to small businesses as an alternative to using an overdraft facility. In particular, it allows the banks to impose a regular repayment schedule over a fixed period of time and to see the amount of credit gradually reducing.
- Leasing, which is a way of borrowing to buy specific equipment or machinery, is also gaining popularity.
- Factoring and invoice discounting is where the small business borrows against sales as a means of freeing up cash. Invoice discounting involves a company loaning you a large percentage of the money for each invoice as soon as it is raised, which is then repaid plus a commission fee when payment is received from your customer within a specified time period. Under factoring, the company will also chase the debt for you, for a slightly larger commission payment.

Each method provides a way around cashflow problems for new or small companies, and they can prove particularly useful for those businesses that have a large outlay for each job or if they use a lot of suppliers.

sell shares in their business is that debt finance is usually available from organisations in smaller amounts than equity, and unless the company is very large it will be too small for formal equity.

Asset-based lending

With traditional bank loans being particularly difficult to come by at the moment, offering the assets of your business as security may help to persuade reluctant lenders. This is called asset-based lending, and has been slowly growing in popularity for some time now, and certainly long before the recession hit. Under the system, a bank will lend on items with high sell-on values, such as stock, machinery, premises, invoices, even brands or trademarks. The borrower usually has access to a revolving credit facility, where there's an upper limit, and the amount loaned changes as it does with an overdraft. Lenders retain security over the assets for the length of the contract.

To get the most from asset-based lending, it helps if your business is asset-rich, which could cause problems for startups. However, if you have machinery or property to use as assets you can expect advances of up to 80% of their value. For stock and raw materials, this reduces to 30%–70%. Typically, the annual cost of borrowing on a revolving credit facility is around 1.75%–3% above the Bank of England base rate, plus an annual and/or closing fee of around 0.5%–1.5% of the total borrowed.

Before agreeing to an asset-based loan, which could take up to six weeks to secure, a lender may consult a specialist valuer. As part of the assessment process, an in-depth evaluation of your business will be carried out, in which your proposed assets will be valued and cashflow and budget projections reviewed.

Equity finance

Equity finance is where you give up a stake in your business in return for money. Many small businesses actually use equity finance without even

> **The big advantage of equity finance is that it never has to be repaid and there is no interest rate paid on the money**

realising it. As Bank of England figures show, some 61% of businesses are launched with either personal capital or that of friends and relatives. That can be an equity arrangement where friends and family take a stake in the business in return for their funds. The big advantage of equity finance is that it never has to be repaid and there is no interest rate paid on the money. Equity investments are true 'risk capital', as there is no guarantee of the investor getting their money back. The investment is not tied to any particular assets that can be redeemed from the business and, should the business fail, an equity investor is less likely to get their original investment back than other investors.

The return from an equity investment can be generated either through a sale of the shares once the company has grown or through dividends, a discretionary payout to shareholders if the business does well. However, the reason that firms will give you cash in this form is that they will take a share of the business in return, therefore gaining some influence over it. Formal equity finance is available through a number of different sources, such as business angels, venture capitalists (see box) or the stock markets. Each varies in the amount of money available and the process of completing the deal.

However, because all equity investors are prepared to put up risk capital in return for a share in a growth business, if your business cannot support growth rates of at least 20% a year, you may not be able to attract equity funding. It is this control and the prospect of a high return if your business is successful that attracts this type of investor. It is also these factors that many owner-managers are wary of – they are reluctant to give up control of their company. Those

THE MONEY LENDERS

Business angels are usually individuals who invest in companies they think have the potential to make them money, and are typically looking to write a cheque for a minimum of around £25,000 – any smaller amounts are not usually appropriate because the fixed costs are too large. Venture capitalists are organisations set up to invest in companies, and prefer to deal in figures higher than business angels.

businesses that have fast growth potential, such as IT or internet companies, are often reluctant to give away equity as it is likely they will need further cash injections as they grow, which would further dilute their stake in the business.

However, you can gain more than just money from the deal. Companies also sell the equity for 'valuable consideration' (or expert advice) – in return they will usually get expert help, as investors are keen to make sure the business is a success. And many companies are giving up effective control if they rely on an overdraft as a major source of finance, as paying back the loan can heavily influence how the business is run.

Attracting equity investment

Although you are more likely to secure finance from a lender to fund your startup, if you have a particularly innovative idea that has rapid growth potential, and are prepared to give up some control of your business, it could be worth looking for equity finance.

First you have to track down the relevant individuals or organisations. The way to find a business angel is to use a business angel network, which specialises in selecting suitable companies to present to their members. You should be able to get details of angel networks in your area from your local government's Business Link office. A good source of venture capitalists is the British Venture Capital Association (BVCA), which has a full list of members on its website (see contact box), along with details of what they're looking for in businesses. It's also possible to get introductions via accountants, lawyers, and corporate finance and business advisers. It's also worth looking out for events that match investors to businesses, as well as 'investment-readiness' programmes run by venture capitalists themselves, which provide tips on how companies should prepare for equity investment.

Once you have identified potential equity investor targets, don't pin your hopes on securing finance from them, because, although you have the potential of raising far more than from a lender, only a fraction of the proposals that business angels and venture capitalists receive any interest at all – let alone any actual funding. And under

> **Explore the many different options that are available and investigate each one so that you can find the right finance to suit your purpose**

the prevailing economic circumstances, equity finance is even more difficult to attract, as investors simply have less to invest. This means that to stand any chance of success, you need a very strong business proposition, along with a business plan that describes it clearly and thoroughly.

To gain the interest of investors, you will need to give details about how they will benefit from financing your operation. As many will be looking to see a return on their investment within a set period – say around three to five years – suggest a potential exit strategy and what they can expect to make. As with lenders, it's wise to point out how you plan to get through the current tough trading conditions and outline how you plan to take advantage when economic recovery begins. Some equity investors specialise in certain sectors, location, business stage and finance range, so it pays to do your homework before pitching to an investor, as you may be wasting your time if they generally don't deal with startups, your chosen business area, or with companies in your part of the country.

The strength of your management team will play an important part in helping you to secure equity investment. Investors will be looking for personal qualities. If neither you nor your team, if you have one, has run a business before, then focus on the skills you bring to the table and why you are confident of success. They will also, ideally, want to see that you have taken the time to build key contacts in your sector and will be looking for commitment from you to put in the necessary hours, as well as investing some of your own money.

Another key consideration is that you need to decide well in advance how much control of your company you are prepared to give up. You need to retain a big enough share for you to be motivated to make your company a success.

CONTACT

British Business Angels Association
www.bbaa.org.uk
☎020 7089 2305

British Venture Capital Association
www.bvca.co.uk

Government help

With the aim of spurring banks on to start lending more to businesses, the government has introduced a new scheme called the Enterprise

Finance Guarantee (EFG) as part of its new Solutions for Business range of initiatives. Essentially, the government is pledging to underwrite bank loans to businesses it considers viable, in order to reduce the risk involved on the part of lenders. Up to £1bn of guarantees will be provided for £1.3bn of lending, expressly to new and small businesses. The good news is that there are already a number of lenders that have joined the scheme, and they are currently offering loans ranging from £1,000 to £1m covering repayment periods of between three months to 10 years. To find out which lenders are involved, visit the Department of Business, Enterprise and Regulatory Reform website. The scheme is available for companies with a turnover of under £25m.

CONTACT

Enterprise Finance
Guarantee
www.businesslink.
gov.uk/realhelp

Department
of Business,
Enterprise and
Regulatory Reform
www.berr.gov.uk

Other ways to fund your business

Your own money

This is one of the most common ways of funding a business and if you have the money readily available it can be beneficial. There is no waiting around and virtually no red tape involved. However, if something goes wrong and you have nothing to fall back on, you could face a severe knock-on effect. Your business's fate is in your own hands.

The four Fs

The four Fs are: founder, family, friends and foolhardies. If your own money is not quite enough, you may choose to seek help and next-stage funding from friends and family. Those involved may ask for something in exchange, such as a stake in the company, but this is up to your own discretion. Written guarantees and/or legal documentation may also have to be drawn up.

Whatever you do, make sure that you plan for every eventuality. Unfortunately, most people don't enter a business partnership thinking about what can go wrong, but just like a marriage, divorce can happen to anyone and at any time.

Start-Up Business Insurance Planning

Like it or not from the day you start trading you are exposed to risks associated with operating a business. Some of these risks you accept as part of being in business, and some of these risks you can transfer to an insurance company.

An essential part of putting together your new business plan is to identify the insurance that you will require. This process consists basically of two elements.

1. Identifying the risks that could affect your business and identifying those you wish to transfer to an insurer.
2. Identifying any insurance that may be a legal requirement for the business.

The risks facing your business can be broken down into straightforward classes for consideration.

- Property Damage and the effects of loss or destruction of physical assets of the business and the consequential loss arising from the loss of the assets. Fire, theft, vandalism etc.
- Liability and the legal responsibility upon the business with regards to injury to members of the public and employees, and any liability arising out of work undertaken whether this be the physical production of a product, a service rendered or professional advice given.
- Motor Insurance, any specialist requirements for insurance for cars and commercial vehicles, noting that with small businesses you will need to review the class of use under any private motor insurance.

Having identified the risks for which you wish to insure, an insurance professional such as a broker can assist you in this, you are then able to assess the annual cost of the insurance to the business. For many, these costs may be a lot lower than you anticipate; there is fierce competition in the small and medium sized business insurance market with many providers offering a low cost solution for small business insurance packages.

Blackfriars Insurance Brokers Ltd has been established for over 25 years and offers a complete range of business insurance services which are all based on our desire to offer a comprehensive insurance solution at highly competitive premiums.

Visit us at www.blackfriarsgroup.co.uk or call on 01270 767327.

Take your business idea for a road test with this popular online service

VentureNavigator (www.venturenavigator.co.uk), an online business support service seeking to improve the success rate of businesses is going from strength-to-strength

The easy to use service already has thousands of users including growing companies, start-ups, and entrepreneurs. By signing up you receive impartial assessments, tailored feedback and advice on key business issues.

Originally the result of a collaborative project led by the University of Essex, VentureNavigator helps you take a strategic look at your business plan, your strengths, weaknesses and what you should do next. Available 24 hours a day, you won't have to leave your desk or your day job to find out whether your idea is based on a winning concept!

Former BBC Dragon's Den member Doug Richard says: *"This is an invaluable service because it doesn't focus on a simple or narrow interpretation of what a business needs to succeed. It's able to examine and assist with a broad range of requirements including managerial, financial, cultural and administrative factors, all of which a business needs to develop, grow and ultimately thrive."*

VentureNavigator's easy to use online assessments cover a range of sectors and issues, including General Business Viability, Investment Readiness and Management Skills. Once you've completed an assessment, VentureNavigator recommends carefully chosen resources including articles and media clips that provide guidance on topics specific to your business, saving you the hassle of sifting through masses of printed and online materials.

The popular 'Community' area enables members to post questions relating to their own businesses and get advice from the other members, including directors, investors, lawyers, accountants, marketing specialists and entrepreneurs of all types. This combined pool of expertise means a question will receive answers from a diverse and multi-faceted group of business people.

VentureNavigator is live now at www.venturenavigator.co.uk and sign-up and use is free.

SETTING UP

WHAT'S IN THIS CHAPTER

- There are essentially three legal or accounting structures recognised for starting a business. You can be a sole trader, team up to form a partnership or operate a limited company. Before you launch, you need to decide which is the best structure for you, then go through the necessary processes to officially register your business. If a partnership or limited company is for you, you are also likely to need to open a business bank account, and the relationship with your bank manager could be crucial to your success. Read on to find out the pros and cons of the various business options, how to set up each one and the best way to deal with your bank...

Limited company

There are two types of limited company – those that are publicly traded on the stock market (known as a public limited company or 'plc') and those that are privately owned (identified by the abbreviation 'Ltd' at the end of their name). Most small- to medium-sized startups don't start life on the stock exchange, so this chapter will focus on limited companies that are privately owned.

A limited or limited liability company is very different from a sole trader business. Registering and running a limited company requires more legal administration than a sole trader business or a partnership. However, if you are a sole trader or partner, you can be held personally liable for your business, which means that any outstanding debts can be met from your personal assets. In a limited company, it is the business itself that shoulders the liability as opposed to the individuals who run it. This is because a limited company is a separate legal entity to the company directors (discussed below). Profits and losses belong to the company, and the business can continue regardless of the death, resignation or bankruptcy of the shareholders or people who run it.

Limited companies pay corporation tax on their profits and company directors are taxed as employees in the same way as any other people who work for the company. Your personal financial risk is restricted to how much you have invested in the company and any guarantees you gave when raising finance for the business. However, if the company fails and you have not carried out your duties as a company director, you could be liable for debts, as well as being disqualified from acting as a director in another company.

Before you can start trading, you need to officially register your limited company, decide on the company officers and choose a name for your business. Then, once you've filed the correct documents with Companies House, you are ready to start trading. Here's a guide to each step.

> " In a limited company, it is the business itself that shoulders the liability as opposed to the individuals who run it "

CONTACT

Companies House
www.companies
house.gov.uk

Registering your company

Doing it yourself versus taking help

Although you can register a limited company yourself, unless you've done it before you may need to engage the services of a solicitor, accountant, chartered secretary or a company formation agent. Formation agents, such as the National Business Register (see also Introduction), use their own software that works directly with the Companies House systems. If you want to register your company electronically (most are registered this way) you will need to have the specific Companies House electronic interface – hence the need for a formation agent. However, you can still deliver the physical documents directly to Companies House without the need of a formation agent or specific electronic interface.

Fees for formation agents can be up to £200 depending on the level of service you require. A key advantage of using a formation agent is the advice they can give you on the compiling of the necessary documents and the right structure for your business. Companies House does not provide this service when registering, so if you are unfamiliar with the process it's advisable to get help to avoid errors. Going through the registration process yourself can be time-consuming, especially if you make a mistake. In addition Companies House staff will not advise you about specific matters, such as the content of the required memorandum and articles (more about these later). Alternatively, you could also get assistance from an online registration company. The standard service usually costs £80–£100 including fees, but since some documentation needs to be posted, registration takes three to eight days. This option is usually cheaper than using a formation agent, although you won't receive the same level of personal service.

Finally, you can buy an 'off the shelf' company, receiving a ready-made limited company that has designated company officers listed on the paperwork. You simply transfer your name, and the names of any other company directors, to the company once you receive your documentation. The process can be completed on the same

> " Formation agents can give you good advice on the compiling of the necessary registration documents and the right structure for your business "

Contact

National Business Register
www.start.biz/home
☎0870 700 8787

day, and many accountancy firms have several ready-made limited companies that they can sell to you. This is the quickest option, and with the exception of registering the company yourself, can often be the cheapest too.

Recent developments in the registration process

It has never been easier to register a limited company due to recent key developments, according to **Simon Harrison** at Complete Formations, one of the UK's leading online company registration agents. 'While accountants and solicitors still play a role in register-ing companies, particularly for their corporate clients, their involve-ment in incorporations for individuals has undoubtedly reduced,' he explains. 'A typical modern scenario might be where a private individual uses an accountant for advice on what type of company to incorporate, based on an assessment of tax position and plans for the future. The individual might then go away to form the company themselves through a formation agent and save themselves money in the process.'

The costs of incorporating a company have also reduced due in part to greater competition between formation agents, and their development of more efficient internal systems, which have automated some of the manual tasks. 'Examples of this include batch printing of incorporation documents and providing more controls and guidance over what customers can and should enter on the online registration forms,' says Harrison. 'This, in turn, results in less support costs dealing with repetitive issues. It is now possible to purchase an electronic company formation for as little as £24.99 plus VAT.'

Another significant change in the way in which companies are registered today is the manner in which the eventual directors, secretary (if the option is taken to have one) and the subscribers are appointed. 'Previously, accountants, solicitors and company formation agents typically used nominees to act as the shareholder and company officers at the time a company was incorporated,' says Harrison. 'Once the company was successfully formed, the purchaser's officers would be appointed and the nominees would resign. This

> "A significant change in the way companies are registered today is the manner in which the eventual directors, secretary and the subscribers are appointed"

practice often caused issues when the purchasers then went to open a company bank account and the nominees were still shown on the Companies House register, which might not have yet been updated to reflect the new ownership and management appointments.

'With the exception of ready-made companies, where the use of nominees is still commonplace, the expectation for most companies incorporated today is that the first appointees will be those which the purchaser requests. This does mean that more time must be spent by the purchaser at the pre-formation stage, entering details of their directors and shareholders. Once the company has been set up, however, there is not then the requirement for this task to be undertaken in order to take ownership of the business.'

The necessary documents

If you get professional help to register your company, which will save time and avoid errors, you are unlikely to be dealing directly with these documents; however, it's still useful to know them. When registering a limited company, four documents must be provided to Companies House. These are described in the box below.

1. Memorandum of Association

This document sets out:

- The company's name
- Where the company's registered office is located in England, Wales or Scotland
- What the company will do. This can be as simple as: 'to conduct business as a general commercial company'.

2. Articles of Association

In this document you set out the rules for running your company. You must state how shares will be allocated and transferred, how the directors, the secretary and your meetings will be governed. The standard document used is Table A of the Companies Act. However,

> **"When registering a limited company, four documents must be provided to Companies House "**

if you choose an amended version of Table A, you must submit this version when registering. Once your company is incorporated you can only make changes if the holders of 75% of the voting rights in your company agree, so it pays to get this right at the outset.

3. Form 10

This document gives details of the first director or directors, company secretary and the address of the registered office. Company directors must also give their name, address, date of birth, occupation and details of other directorships held in the past five years. Companies based in Northern Ireland should use Form 21.

4. Form 12

This document is the statutory declaration of compliance with all the legal requirements of the incorporation of a company. It must be signed by one of the company directors or the secretary named on Form 10 or the solicitor forming the company. The signing of the document must be witnessed by a solicitor, a commissioner for oaths, a justice of the peace, or a notary public. Companies based in Northern Ireland should use Form 23. Form 12 must not be signed and dated before any of the other documents are completed, signed and dated.

Obtaining the documents

Form 10 and Form 12 can be obtained for free from the Companies House website. The Memorandum and Articles of Association can be obtained from legal stationers, accountants, solicitors or company formation agents. They cost around £20–£30.

Cost of submitting the documents

The standard fee to register a limited company is £20, but a same-day service costs £50. If the registration documents are filed using the Companies House software filing service, the fee is £15 for standard and £30 for same-day registration. However, to file electronically you must either purchase the suitable software, develop your own or go through an agent.

Company officers

If you set up a limited private company, you appoint company officers, who are simply the formally named directors and company secretary, as stated in the Articles of Association described previously. Usually, as the founder of the company, you would be one of the directors, along with the people with whom you may have launched the company. One of the directors could also be appointed company secretary, although this could be someone who is not a director. All companies used to have to appoint a company secretary, but this is no longer the case. It is a legal requirement for company officers to be in place at all times and for their names and current addresses to be written on the registration documents. If there is a change in company officers, you must inform Companies House straightaway. All private limited companies must have at least one director. The following sections provide a rundown of the official roles of your company officers.

> " It is a legal requirement for company officers to be in place at all times and for their names and current addresses to be written on the registration documents "

Directors

Company directors must manage the company's affairs in accordance with its Articles of Association and the law. At least one director must be a natural person (i.e. an individual). The post does not require any formal qualifications, but you cannot become a company director if:

- You are an undischarged bankrupt or disqualified by a court from holding a directorship
- You are under 16.

Company directors have a responsibility to make sure that certain documents reach the registrar at Companies House. These are:

- Accounts
- Annual returns
- Notice of change of directors or secretaries
- Notice of change of registered office.

Directors who fail to deliver these documents on time can be prosecuted and are subject to fines of up to £5,000 for each offence. An average 1,000 directors are prosecuted each year for failing to deliver accounts and returns to the registrar on time. So unless you are particularly knowledgeable about company facts and figures, it's a good idea to appoint an accountant to help you prepare these documents. Your accountant will also advise you on the necessary information you need to keep hold of, and prepare, such as invoices, receipts, etc.

Company Secretary

The duties of a company secretary are not specified by law, but are usually contained within an employment contract. For private limited companies, the secretary is not required to have any special qualifications, but this is not the case if you decide to change your company to a public limited company. The main duties of a company secretary are to:

- Maintain the statutory registers, which means updating the details on the business held at Companies House when necessary. For example, if you relocate or appoint or lose a director
- Ensure statutory forms are filed promptly
- Provide members and auditors with notice of meetings
- Send the registrar copies of resolutions and agreements
- Send a copy of the accounts to every member of the company
- Keep or arrange minutes of meetings.

With limited companies now no longer needing to appoint a company secretary by law, few will probably do so when launching, with the administrative duties being covered by the directors. These do not take up much time at all. In fact, once your company has launched, there is unlikely to be much to do on this front for a couple of years at least, barring submitting accounts and annual returns and recording the content of director meetings, unless you relocate or change directors over this period. Your accountant will help with accounts and returns, and can also offer general advice on the official roles of company officers, as can your solicitor.

Sole trader

Sole trading is defined as when an individual is the only owner of the business and has complete control over the way it is run. The law makes no distinction between the business and a sole trader. As mentioned in the previous section, this unlimited liability means that any business debt can be met from the owner's personal wealth if the business fails, and the business usually ceases on the owner's retirement or death.

> **Sole traders pretty much drive the UK economy**

A sole trading business is usually small in size, with a low turn-over, and few, if any, employees. If you want to literally go it alone in business – remember you won't actually be alone! A massive 71% of all British businesses have no employees, according to Department for Business, Enterprise and Regulatory Reform figures (BERR Directorate Analytical Unit – Enterprise Directorate: Small and Medium Enterprise Statistics for the UK and Regions). (There are an estimated 3.7 million active businesses in the UK, according to the latest government statistics, and more than 2.3 million of these are class zero businesses – that is without employees.) So you could say that sole traders pretty much drive the UK economy. The popularity of this type of business reflects the ease with which you can start sole trading: registration is straightforward, record keeping is simple and you get to keep all the profits after tax. Starting small by sole trading is a way to test your chosen market, and many companies are born this way; however, there are pitfalls.

Most sole traders operate in the service sector, such as photography, plumbing, hairdressing, shops, real estate agencies and bed and breakfast hotels. Some 24% of the UK's 2.3 million class zero businesses are in the construction sector, with 18% in business-related services (BERR Directorate Analytical Unit – Enterprise Directorate: Small and Medium Enterprise Statistics for the UK and Regions).

Getting down to business

You need to fulfil certain legal requirements before you can open for business. If you are going to trade under a name different from your own personal name, you must display the business name or names of the owners and an address where documents can be served on all business stationery and at your premises. So you will need to design letterheads, business cards and signage accordingly.

Issues regarding business name

A business's name is a lot more than just a name and the whole of the next chapter will cover this in detail. Here we deal with the legal issues concerning business names.

It is not compulsory to register a business name, but you can do so with the National Business Register. You need to be careful about choosing a name, because an incorrect name can cause trouble. Certain words and expressions such as 'international', 'federation' and 'registered' are restricted under the Business Names Act 1985 and the Company and Business Names Regulations 1995. Companies House and the National Business Register have lists of these words and details of how to obtain approval to use them. In addition, your business name cannot be the same or too similar to that of another business, trademark or company. If it does conflict, you could face legal action from its owner. Check phone books, trade journals and magazines to ensure against clashes, and you can run free name checks against all these via the National Business Register, as well as the limited companies names index at Companies House. To be absolutely sure that you can use a name, contact a solicitor to perform the checks or register your name with the National Business Register, which will then do the checks for you and ensure no one copies it in the future or passes it off as their own.

Registering with HMRC

You must register as self-employed with Her Majesty's Revenue and Customs (HMRC) within three months of starting up or you will have to pay a fine. The three-month limit starts from the last day of your first month of trading.

Legal issues

A sole trader business is simple to set up legally, although certain trades may need a licence. These include nightclubs, taxi and car hire, restaurants, pet shops, indoor sports venues, adult shops, street trading, hotels, pet kennels, nursing homes, waste management, weapons sales and money lending. You can get a licence from the relevant local authority for most of these. To make sure you are on the right side of the law, refer to the relevant Acts of Parliament.

> **To make sure you are on the right side of the law, refer to the relevant Acts of Parliament**

- The Trade Descriptions Act 1972 – it is a criminal offence to knowingly make false or misleading claims – verbal or written – about goods or services you offer. This covers areas such as ingredients, place of manufacture and customer testimonials, as well as associating yourself with a brand without being entitled to.
- The Sale of Goods Act 1979 – this dictates that the goods you sell must be of satisfactory quality, match your promises of performance and be as you describe them.
- The Supply of Goods and Services Act 1982 – this commits you to undertake the services you offer with reasonable care, skill, time and cost.
- The Data Protection Act 1984 – this directs you to register the source, nature and purpose of any personal data you keep about individuals, except data used for internal administration such as the payroll. Registration forms are available at post offices.
- The Consumer Protection Act 1987 – this holds you liable if you supply a faulty product causing damage or injury, unless you can show that not enough was known about its dangers at the time of

supply. To protect yourself under this Act, offer an estimate first and a written quote only when you have properly assessed costs.

- The Price Marking Order 1991 – this makes it compulsory to put the price of goods offered for sale in writing.

You should also consider any legislation relating to environmental and health and safety requirements, as well as checking the planning and building regulations relating to your premises. Local authorities and the Department for Business, Enterprise and Regulatory Return should be the first ports of call for this.

CONTACT

National Business Register
www.start.biz/
home
☎0870 700 8787

The Department
for Business,
Enterprise and
Regulatory Reform
www.berr.gov.uk

Tax and sole traders

As a sole trader, your profits are taxed like any other income by HMRC, and as you are self-employed, your tax will be self-assessed. The amount you owe is calculated after business expenses and personal allowances have been deducted. Your income will fall under tax Schedule D, and as you will be paying income tax twice a year, it makes sense to put money aside. As a self-employed person, many of your business expenses can be deducted from your taxable income, such as overheads on your premises, travel, delivery costs and trade association subscriptions, but you will have to pay capital gains tax if you sell or give away any assets. You will also be paying National Insurance Contributions (NICs).

WHO IS AN E-TRADER?

You are an e-trader if you:

- Sell goods that were bought with the intention of re-selling them
- Sell items you made yourself for a profit
- Sell or buy on behalf of others for financial gain
- Receive payment for a service.

If you do any of the above, then you must register as self-employed with HMRC within the three-month deadline mentioned earlier. With regards to eBay, it is extremely unwise to delay registering, as HMRC carries out checks on online auction sites to root out members who process a high number of transactions.

ACTION POINT

KEY THINGS TO DO AFTER SETTING UP AS A SOLE TRADER

Once you've set up as a sole trader there are a few other things to consider that will help you and your new business.

Banking: You can operate your sole trading business from your personal bank account. You must, however, be able to distinguish your personal spending from that of your business for tax purposes. You can also run separate bank accounts and major banks are keen to get you on board for the future custom you may bring. Shop around for a bank that best suits your needs.

Insurance: Ensure your business will keep working even when you are not by insuring it. As a sole trader, unless you employ staff or make alternative arrangements, your business will come to a standstill if you fall ill, have an accident or go on holiday. So shop around for health and medical insurance tailored to small businesses with self-employed owners. Check to see if subsidised insurance schemes are offered by your trade association or local chamber of commerce. You should also consider taking out disability insurance to cover you for time off through illness or injury. But check the qualifying period – some policies with lower premiums won't pay out until after an excess period of three months.

Pensions: Although putting aside money for the future may be hard for you right now, a pension plan is well worth considering. And not just for the financial security it will offer you in retirement – investing in a pension scheme can be tax-beneficial too. Everyone in the UK can get a basic state pension if they have built up a record of NICs for a quarter of their working life. But only those with a record of NICs for nine-tenths of their working lives are entitled to a full state pension, so self-employed people need to make further arrangements. Sole traders should also contribute to a private pension scheme. Many pension schemes on the market are designed for the self-employed, and several of these allow you to pay a lump sum, take a break from payments for a year or even make withdrawals.

Taking on staff: As a sole trader you might want to take on employees to help with your growing business. There are no restrictions on staff numbers, but you will have to deduct pay-as-you-earn (PAYE) tax from wages and pay it to HMRC each month. You will also need to make some summaries for employees and HMRC annually, as well as when a staff member leaves your employment. As a sole trading employer you will be responsible for your employees' Class 1 NICs and your employer contributions. These are calculated as a percentage of an employee's wage. See also Chapter 9 for more details about this. You will also need to consider statutory sick pay, equal opportunities and health and safety conditions, as well as employment terms and contracts. And remember that if you have taken over a business, you must uphold employees' existing terms of employment.

If your income rises above a certain level (currently £68,000), you will have to apply for value-added tax (VAT) registration. This means you will be collecting VAT from your customers and paying it to HMRC less the VAT you have paid out in the course of conducting your business. You can talk to your local HMRC offices for advice, Make an appointment and explain the details of your business plan and ask them exactly what you need to do. They will provide you with advice, relevant leaflets and a selection of forms – such as VAT registration – which you should complete before beginning trading. This is vitally important. If you start off with all the necessary information, it will make the bookkeeping process much easier. It also helps to have a contact within the local offices whom you can call should you run into any difficulties. Bookkeeping is covered in more detail in Chapter 9.

The increase in popularity of online businesses had led to an increasing number of people setting up part-time businesses for additional income to their main job. As a result, many are unsure what they have to declare for tax purposes and at what point they should register as self-employed. HMRC rules stipulate that all e-traders must be registered with it so that their income can be taxed.

Business partnerships

Collaboratively owned or acquired firms are probably more successful and grow faster, and in certain important sectors, such as hi-tech, collaborative ventures may actually predominate. This is when two or more people combine to form a business unit. Each partner receives a percentage of the return of the business, depending upon how much they invested. As with sole traders, all partners are also responsible for all the debts incurred by the business. This doesn't only apply to debts you have incurred as a partner but to those of any partner. This means in a partnership you need to pay particular care to the conduct of your fellow partners, because creditors will take your personal assets to pay off debts incurred by any of the others if necessary.

When considering what format the business should take, partnerships need extra attention. One of the most fundamental issues

> One of the fundamental issues is to draw up a partnership agreement

CONTACT

Prince's Trust
www.princes-trust.
org.uk

is to draw up a partnership agreement. 'We require all business partnerships to visit a solicitor (through our pro bono legal advice set up) and have a legal partnership agreement in place before we can finalise funding,' says **Elaine Thatcher**, business support manager for the Prince's Trust in London.

Such an agreement forces partners to think about issues such as the structure and roles of each person involved, as well as the likely exit routes for the partners, according to **Thelma Quince**, who recently completed a study into 390 businesses in East Anglia. This can ensure that there is a mechanism for valuing and buying one partner's shares. 'It is a bit like a marriage and divorce. No one wants to think about the fact that it could go wrong,' says Quince. But partners can address the issues in less confrontational ways by asking what each partner wants to do when they are bored of the business. One of the common factors with collaborations that weren't successful in Quince's study was mutual respect. 'If you lose confidence in the competence of your partner and start to worry about whether they can do the job, that can be fatal,' she warns. A number of threads ran through the accounts co-owners in the study gave as to why collaboration had failed (see box below). Quince found that mostly the collaboration failed when personal, individualistic or selfish goals started to take precedence over the collaborative, shared goals. 'One partner attempted to take control and focused on personal gain rather than long-term growth of the business,' was one comment.

According to Quince, partnerships can be highly successful, but a high proportion of co-owning teams are likely to experience conflict leading to the departure of one or more of the original owning team. When this happens it can have severe effects not only on the business, but on partners' personal lives. Quince's research revealed that in 42% of the firms founded collaboratively by people who were not related or married to each other, the original owning team had fragmented, leaving only one of the original co-owners. Meanwhile, 41% of the 106 co-owners taking part in the study reported that they had prior experience of an unsuccessful collaborative relationship.

WHY PARTNERSHIPS FAIL

The reasons that collaborations don't work include:

- Differences in personal values
- Differences in personal objectives
- Differences in objectives and visions for the firm
- Loss of respect for the competence of the other
- Failure to communicate effectively
- Failure to reward effort justly
- Loss of trust in the other
- The price of conflict.

In their accounts of failed relationships the co-owners described three main adverse effects of the conflict. Only three claimed the conflict had not adversely effected themselves or their business, with just two of these feeling that, in the long term, the outcome of the conflict had actually been beneficial. Most, however, told a very different story. For nearly 40%, partner conflict had hit their businesses badly in a number of ways, including: lost revenue, which in eight cases sunk the firm; poor morale among employees; suspicion and lack of cooperation between co-owners; and even personal effects on partners, such as financial loss, lack of self-worth and marriage break-ups.

So although many partnerships work, they can be prone to conflict, which anyone thinking of starting up this kind of business must bear in mind. Meanwhile, a carefully constructed partnership agreement can help increase the chances of a harmonious and successful long-term relationship between partners.

The consequences of conflict

As further evidence of the need to approach partnerships with caution, here are personal comments on the fallout from partner disharmony

HOLROYD HOWE AND THE JOINT EFFORT

Company: Holroyd Howe Independent
Owner-managers: Rick Holroyd and Nick Howe

Being a successful entrepreneur is often viewed as essentially a solo experience, with the hard decisions, particularly in the formative days of a business, agonised over by the man or woman at the top. The idea of forming a partnership is often dismissed by budding owners-managers. Even those that take the plunge with a co-founder can find that ideas and personalities clash to the point of breakdown.

However, Holroyd Howe Independent is a business that could be used as a living and breathing example of how partnerships can, and do, work. Founders **Rick Holroyd** and **Nick Howe**'s eponymous firm is well on its way to becoming the premier independent contract caterer in the UK.

Holroyd freely admits that he probably could not have done it without Howe, underlining the joint effort that has gone into building the venture. 'I don't think that either of us would've wanted to embark upon setting up the business alone, that's probably been one of the strengths of the business,' Holroyd explains. 'It was always my intention to start with someone else because I probably wasn't the full ticket in terms of running all aspects of the business. It was important to have someone who complemented me in terms of skills.'

Holroyd rejects the idea that compromise has played a vital role in their relationship, insisting that the duo arrive at the best approach after discussion, rather than fudging the issue. 'It's amazing how the vision has been almost identical,' he says. 'But the way we see things are at the opposite ends of the spectrum – we're very different characters.

'It's very important to put your individual views to one side. Every decision we've made has been for the good of the business, and not for ourselves individually. We've seen startups that have lasted six months or a year and I think it's because egos get in the way – you can't afford to let that happen.'

by a number of people who contributed to Thelma Quince's study of 390 businesses in East Anglia:

- 'Disharmony at board level led to unnecessary risk and confusion of direction'
- 'Challenged my reason to go on'
- 'Staff morale declined'
- 'The board was unable to make decisions about things that mattered – views were too diverse. Performance suffered through

PROS AND CONS OF PARTNERSHIPS

These are the advantages and disadvantages of collaboration cited by almost all of the 106 co-owners in Thelma Quince's East Anglian study.

Why you should collaborate...

- Being able to share the burden
- Having access to more skills, knowledge and experience
- Better, more effective decision-making
- Being able to look at problems from different perspectives

And why you shouldn't

(These were the most important disadvantages of collaboration seen by the co-owners in Quince's study.)

- Less autonomy and not always getting your own way
- Differences in personal aims and objectives for the firm
- Decision-making can be slower
- Collaboration often means a loss of spontaneity

! TOP TIPS

FOR A SUCCESSFUL PARTNERSHIP, CO-OWNERS NEED TO:

- ! Have the same shared visions, aspirations and objectives for their firm
- ! Have similar or compatible personal values
- ! Have clearly defined responsibilities and roles
- ! Have complementary skills and knowledge
- ! Have mutual respect for the other's competence
- ! Have mutual trust in the other and for the other's honesty
- ! Be good at working as a team
- ! Be tolerant of the other's weaknesses

inertia and the company became loss making. The team collapsed and this came close to causing the collapse of the company'

- 'It caused an early sale of the company at the wrong time and at a disadvantageous price'
- 'The additional financial commitment was difficult to sustain'
- 'My marriage broke up shortly after the break up of the company'

From the owners who had once collaborated, but now found themselves in sole ownership came other stories of attempted suicides, nervous breakdowns, divorce, attempted assaults and one sad case of attempted murder.

Banking on success

> **There are many factors to consider when choosing a bank**

Whether you decide to be a sole trader, set up a partnership or run a private limited company, you will need a good relationship with your bank. And although it has never been easier to switch banks, taking time to decide on the right one (and bank manager) for you at the outset can save problems later that could adversely affect your business. If you are a sole trader you can keep a personal account, but need to make it clear what incomings and outgoings relate to your business. If you launch a partnership or limited company, you will need to set up business bank accounts.

> **You need a manager who will understand your business and one whom you can trust**

There are many factors to consider when choosing a bank. Interest rates and charges will obviously play their part, but it's also essential to look at the quality of service you will receive from your bank manager. After all, this is the person who you will deal with on a regular basis and the person you will need to approach for funding. So you need a manager who will understand your business and one whom you can trust.

When looking at banks, don't hesitate to ask to speak to the manager who will be dealing with your account, and when you do, make sure your needs are met.

To help you find the right bank manager, Allied Irish Bank (GB) has put together a list of questions that you should be asking:

- Do you really understand my business and industry?
  Every industry has slightly different needs and you want to be sure your bank understands what's important in your industry.

- How long have you been in your job?
  Ideally, you don't want to keep having to build relationships with different bank managers; continuity is key.

- Can I reach you whenever I need to? Or will I speak to someone working in a call centre whom I have never met?
  There is no substitute for having a contact who intimately understands your business and what you want to achieve. Not so easy to do over the telephone.

- Are you able to make a quick decision when I need one?
  We all know that if you really need to extend your overdraft for a short period you need a quick decision. Having to jump through lots of 'hoops' just eats up your valuable time, and few businesses can afford that.

- Will I have one point of contact who understands who I am and, as importantly, knows about my business?
  The Model-T Ford approach to service is no longer good enough– one colour does not suit everyone.

- Can I speak to companies you currently work with in a similar industry for a reference?
  There is no substitute for third-party endorsement. All banks say they deliver great service, but do they really? You need to find out.

- Will you provide more general business advice when I need it?
  Getting the basics such as a cheque account, credit card, etc is simple, but businesses require far more. They want a bank that will deliver much more value.

- How are you rated in the industry?
  Have they won any awards recently, for instance? Again, third-party endorsement can be a powerful method with which to judge the success of an organisation.

- Do you have the name of a company in your patch that you helped to grow?

Most businesses have similar aspirations–to grow and to improve profitability. Banks play a major role in helping to turn ambition into reality. You need to know that the bank you select can help you achieve your business objectives.

Remember, when it comes to choosing a bank, the more questions you ask, the more likely it is that you will enjoy a long and fruitful relationship.

What banks offer businesses

Before you start comparing different business bank accounts, it's worth knowing what products and services they may offer, what they involve, and deciding on the ones that are most critical to your business.

Bank facilities

- Deposits: paying in cash and cheques
- Withdrawals: taking out cash through an ATM or at a branch
- Payment by cheque: use of a business chequebook, which can sometimes be personalised with your company logo
- Automatic money transfers: direct debits and direct credits
- Night safe: for depositing money when the bank is closed
- Balance enquiry and statements: for keeping track of your finances
- Payment cards
  - Company debit card: this will debit an amount immediately from your business account. In most cases the transactions are free and there is no annual fee.
  - Company credit card: a charge card (such as Barclaycard or MasterCard) that can be issued to key members of staff. Repayment is made monthly from your business current account (usually interest-free credit). There is usually a fee per transaction, an annual fee or both.

- Borrowing
  - Overdraft and loan facilities: short-term financing, subject to an application procedure. May also provide access to the government-backed Small Firm Loan Guarantee scheme.
  - Asset finance: leasing and hire purchase facilities to enable you to buy equipment
  - Factoring and invoice discounting: short-term borrowing against the value of unpaid invoices
  - Commercial mortgage: funding to help buy a business. Often up to 80% of the purchase can be financed by the bank.

See Chapter 4.0 for a detailed discussion about ways to borrow money or arrange funding.

Other features

- Deposit accounts: a lot of banks have business deposit accounts with higher interest than a current account for any reserve funds your business may have.
- Merchant services: if you want to accept credit and debit card payments from customers, you will need a merchant account. This is provided by a bank but to get one you will often need two years' trading history and audited accounts. Once set up, you will be charged an annual fee plus a percentage of every transaction.
- Insurance: larger banks often offer their customers insurance cover for business interruption, health, loan repayment and more.
- Support: most of the larger banks offer resources and support to help you run your business. For example, you may be assigned a relationship manager who will offer business advice. The bank may also provide seminars, educational literature or bookkeeping software.
- Introductory offers: many banks offer special introductory offers to startups. This is usually a period of free banking for 12–24 months.

CONTACT

British Bankers'
Association
www.bba.org.uk

The British Bankers' Association's Business Account Finder offers independent advice on what various banks offer small businesses.

Dealing with banks in a downturn

It was less than careful lending by banks and other financial institutions that caused the credit crunch and the ensuing economic downturn in 2008, so it's logical that they will be a lot more cautious when handling their customers, whether they are individuals or businesses.

Before the boom finally collapsed in 2008 and the recession began, banks couldn't lend enough money, and that included overdraft facilities for new businesses. But the credit crunch has sent shockwaves through the finance industry that haven't been seen since the Great Depression of the 1930s – in fact, many commentators have suggested that the current recession could actually be worse. With some of the more established institutions going out of business or having to be propped up by the state, fear has gripped the banking community, resulting in a highly risk averse approach. In the wake of such a massive turnaround, it's no surprise that businesses' relationships with their banks have been affected.

Many companies have found that their banks have become more stringent with respect to existing overdraft and loan arrangements. In some instances, agreements have been tightened putting additional financial pressure on companies, and in extreme cases overdraft facilities have been withdrawn and loans called in. This has resulted in a number of businesses simply not having the cash reserves to continue trading – and it's the younger and smaller operations that have been hit the hardest.

If you are starting up, of course, you probably don't have an existing relationship with a bank. What this means for you is that banks will require stronger assurances than previously of the viability of your business simply to secure a business bank account, never mind a loan. So a well-thought out business plan and professional approach are more important than ever (see Chapter 4.0 for more on this).

You may also find it difficult to secure as large an overdraft as previously, while bank loans are likely to be far more difficult to come by. However, the good news is that if you do get an overdraft or loan, the current low interest rates mean that your monthly charges or re-payments are likely to be lower than they were previously. But you should also be prepared for your bank to tighten any agreements, particularly if the recession deepens.

If you are offered a bank account along with an overdraft facility, you can be confident that your business idea has a good chance of success and that you have put together a strong business plan, which will stand you in good stead when looking for more finance, should you need it. Banks and other lenders are still open for business, but are only tending to invest in those businesses that they consider to have an excellent chance of success.

As banks are still actively looking for new business customers, it remains important for you to shop around and find the one with the best offer for your company. Then, to get the most out of your relationship, it's more important than ever to handle your bank manager with care and respect, as described in the following Action Point.

ACTION POINT
MANAGING YOUR BANK MANAGER

Although it is important to ensure you have a bank and a bank manager capable of giving you what you want, it is a two-way relationship and there are a number of things you can do to get the most out of it, as **Christopher Jenkins**, managing director of Wingrave Yeats, a leading London accountancy and management consulting firm, points out.

Keep business and personal accounts apart: It's not always a good idea to keep your business account at the same bank as your personal account. Resist the temptation of the one-stop borrowing concept. You don't invest without spreading risk, so don't borrow without doing the same.

Keep your bank regularly informed: Don't go and see the bank only when you need something – no one likes to be constantly confronted with tales of doom and gloom, or even worse, thinly veiled gestures of optimism. Get in contact or make an appointment to visit when you have good news and when you don't need to borrow more money. Get them excited about your business, enthuse about it and go away without asking them for more cash. Equally, if you are having any problems that could affect your ability to make a loan payment or stay within your overdraft limit, give your bank manager plenty of warning. You will find your bank far more receptive and willing to help you out of your predicament if you let them know of any issues as far in advance as possible.

Be professional: Make sure any figures or information you present is correct and consistent with the story you told last month. Remember that everything goes on file and will come up again – often when you least expect it. Don't let your accountants/financial advisers do it all for you, but don't go anywhere without them. Bankers can spot a report that has been written by a professional but signed off in your name. They want to know that you as the borrower understand and believe what you are telling them. However, don't try to forecast for the bank without professional help. A profits and losses forecast and cashflow estimate that hasn't been reconciled to a balance sheet and which would show negative debtors in year two will not go down well with a banker.

Consider what the bank wants to see: If you don't feed your bank regular information, it can only resort to what can be gleaned from your account. Bankers examine average balance calculations from your statements and also highs and lows on the account. 'Hardcore borrowing' (where the account is constantly up against the limit) makes them twitchy, but they appreciate wide swings from full utilisation of the facility to occasional credit balances. They also compare your company statistics with comparable industry standards. So look at the trend of your own account before you present it to them, and have prepared answers in your mind to the questions they are bound to ask.

Lending usually comes with covenants, which are certain financial limits that your company must adhere to. For example, not allowing particular balance sheet items or ratios to fall below or go over an agreed figure. It is easy to monitor these covenants and rather than letting the bank do so, include a calculation in your monthly management accounts that you send it.

Manage your total borrowings: Be careful with your capital expenditure. Try out asset finance (leasing and hire purchase facilities to help you to buy equipment, leasing and rental deals rather than outright purchase of equipment and technology goods. While they may look expensive, they are 'off-balance sheet financing', which does wonders for your covenant calculations. Also consider other forms of maintaining cashflow, such as using a factoring company to collect and manage your invoices.

At all times, try to minimise the bank's perception of risk in lending to you, and increase its confidence and enthusiasm to lend by promising no more than you know you can achieve. Understand what they can and can't offer and then structure your request so that it's watertight in banking terms.

DESIGN AND PRINT CENTRE AND THE UNEXPECTED BONUS

Company: Design and Print Centre
Owner-manager: David Miller

Building a strong relationship with his business bank has helped **David Miller** through the tough couple of years of starting Design and Print Centre. Although launching a design and communications agency into a crowded marketplace, a strong business plan, incorporating the benefits of working virtually from a cost and billing perspective, helped secure the necessary investment.

Managing to attract an unsecured loan for £40,000 to launch his business from Lloyd's Bank, meant that Miller and his fellow directors did not have to secure their homes or any other personal assets against the borrowing, Miller was determined to run a tight ship to avoid further borrowing that might need securing.

'This was difficult initially as cash was tight, but if we were approaching our agreed overdraft limit I simply told my bank business adviser, who was prepared to let us exceed it for a limited period if necessary,' he explained. 'Keeping him informed was key.'

What's more, regular meetings with his bank manager meant that his adviser understood his business and its market. 'This led him to putting us in touch with some of his clients who might be able to use our services, which I never expected,' said Miller.

IP Strategy – What's Yours?

Technical innovations, brands and designs, collectively referred to as "intellectual property" or "IP", are important assets for any business. Intellectual property rights, if exercised correctly, provide a business with the opportunity to gain exclusivity in their IP, allowing them to maximise the return on their investment in creating the IP.

Some intellectual property rights come into existence automatically. One example is copyright. Stronger, 'registered' rights, such as patents, registered trade marks and registered designs, need to be actively sought. Especially in the case of patents, it is vital that the protection is sought before the technical innovation to be protected is made public.

For small companies in particular, securing appropriate protection for their IP can be critical, as adequate IP protection is more often than not a prerequisite for the investment needed to succeed. It must be appreciated, however, that there can be significant costs associated with obtaining intellectual property protection, so any IP strategy must strike a balance between these costs and the commercial value of owning the IP. Thought needs to be given not only to what to protect and how but also to when and where protection should be sought.

It must also not be forgotten that your competitors may well have their own IP rights. It is important to be aware of the impact that rights of others could have; at worst, halting your activities completely. Prudent businesses will have in place strategies for dealing with this. Such strategies might include watching the IP filing activity of known competitors. This may allow a business to work around competitor's patents or other rights and/or to consider whether they might be vulnerable to attack. Watching a competitor's IP filing activity can also provide useful intelligence for their development work.

Every small business should develop an IP strategy at the earliest opportunity, as part of their overall business strategy, and update the strategy regularly as their business grows.

Stephen Carter
Mewburn Ellis LLP
33 Gutter Lane
London EC2V 8AS
Tel: 020 7776 5300
e-mail: stephen.carter@mewburn.com
www.mewburn.com

PATENTS • TRADE MARKS • DESIGNS • COPYRIGHT

FINDING A NAME AND CREATING A BRAND

WHAT'S IN THIS CHAPTER

- Choosing a business name is one of the first and most important things that you will do when starting a business. There's a lot more to it than simply going for something you like, from practical reasons of recognition to legal factors. and before you submit a business plan to anyone, you should get it right. Read on for tips and examples that should help you choose the right name for your business…

What's in a name?

In a rational world, a company with a strong product, service, or niche idea could expect to make a healthy profit. However, it takes more than that to get across to customers the benefit of using your business instead of your competitor's. The name is the first thing that any potential buyer is going to encounter about your business and, in this respect, is more important than your sales pitch or even your end product. You might have the best idea in the world, but if people are going elsewhere because your competition 'looks' more attractive, then no one will ever know.

As the name is the entry point to your business and, superficially, the only differentiator between you and your competitors, customers will make instant judgements on where they want to buy from. Therefore, it's essential that you strike the right tone with your business's name. However, in today's world, you also need to take it one step further – successful companies do not just have good names, they develop a brand. And, in time, brands can literally sell themselves. Company branding specialist, **Jim Fowle**, of Red Mullet Design, says: 'When starting a company, your brand is of vital importance. Branding is not just a memorable logo, but also an effective, memorable name that can really help people remember you. This can be portrayed strongly visually as well. In the initial stages, we find it's good to envisage your name and branding, making sure it's recognisable, simple and reflects your business.'

It's easier said than done. You want not just to stand out from your competition, but you also need to be taken seriously. When you are choosing a business name it's essential to remember that this is a name that you will have to say dozens of times each day and it is something you will be known by. Make sure that you like how it sounds and how it looks before committing. 'Initially, in the early stages, the best option is to be experimental,' suggests Fowle. 'Sometimes it's easy to get too clever and lose sight of what you are trying to achieve. It is about getting the balance of a good name and having good branding at the same time. This encapsulates the perfect package.'

> " The right business name can offer a real advantage in the battle for customers "

> " Names should be snappy, original and instantly informative as to what your business does "

THERE ARE ESSENTIALLY THREE KINDS OF BUSINESS NAME:

Descriptive – these describe what the business does, or may be named after the owner. For example: Design and Print Centre.
Pros: Provides information about your business or who runs it
Cons: Can lack creativity and be less memorable

Associative – these aim to create positive associations in customers' minds. For example: Ocean Fish Bar.
Pros: Can help to generate a positive image of your company
Cons: If not original or creative, they can come across as clichéd

Abstract – these may have no meaning at all, and could be just words joined together. For example: Shoon (shoe shop).
Pros: Easier to be original and can attract attention
Cons: Provide no information about the company

It's tempting to incorporate your own name into your business' moniker but remember it won't add any information about the company. A safe and trustworthy method is to link your business's name to the area in which you operate – customers associate such firms with strong local roots and a friendly approach to the public. Therefore, the Acton Sandwich Shop or Govan Records would be perceived to be well-established, reputable businesses. Humour or a nice play on words is an effective way to stand out from the crowd. While a fish and chip shop called Your Plaice or Mine or a hairdressers named Hair Today, Gone Tomorrow would elicit predictable groans from passers-by, puns can be used for good effect, as long as they are not overly cheesy or digress from what image you are trying to convey for your firm. Ideally, names should be snappy, original and instantly informative as to what your business does.

What you can and can't call your business

Words or expressions deemed to be offensive are not allowed by Companies House. You will have to exercise your own judgement as to what such words include, but chances are that swear words or phrases generally considered insulting will not be not permitted. There are also phrases that are deemed to be 'sensitive' and you will have to gain permission to use them. These phrases can be classified into five main groups, and include words that:

- Suggest your business is of national importance, such as British, Scottish, national or international
- Depict a special status or authority such as association, chamber of commerce, council
- Describe a particular function, such as a charity or trust
- Refer to a specialised activity, such as surveyor or chemist
- Give the impression that your business is connected to the government or the Royal Family.

Limited companies

If you are starting a limited company, your company name must end with Limited (or Ltd). Also, this word must not appear anywhere else in your name, so 'Limited Ltd' is not allowed. Once you have chosen your name and made sure that it complies with the rules, you can apply to have it registered at Companies House.

CONTACT

Companies House
www.companies
house.gov.uk

Sole traders

If you are a sole trader, you can trade under your name and/or your business partner's name if you have one. However, this is not obligatory and you can be far more creative if you wish. Sole traders,

! TOP TIPS
YOUR BUSINESS NAME CHECKLIST

When you choose a name for your business, make sure it:

! Is not already taken

! Has no negative connotations

! Reflects what your business stands for

! Is appropriate and appealing to your audience

! Has the potential to be memorable

! Won't be able to limit your business in any way

! Has a meaning that can be transferred overseas if necessary

! Is easy to say and spell

! Can be owned and protected as your trademark

! Can be registered as an internet URL or web address

(Source: More Th>n Business)

however, are not allowed to use Ltd or plc (private limited company) in their name, as it describes the business incorrectly. Sole traders don't have to register their business's name with Companies House.

Checking for originality

The Companies House website is one good way to check if the name you have chosen isn't already being used – just go to the CheckSURE website and see what's available before choosing a business name. However, as stated above, sole traders do not have to register with Companies House, so they will not show up on this search. So you should also check local phone books and business directories and run some internet searches on your chosen name. If you find there is a sole trader on the other side of the country who is using your name, then this may not be a problem, but if the company is local or national then you will have to choose again.

You also need to check if your proposed name isn't too similar to a name that someone else has registered as a trademark. The easiest way to do this is via the Intellectual Property Office website – such simple checks now will save you time and money later.

If you are setting up your own website, checking out available domain names is also well worth your time. Many companies pick a different name for their website than the name they use to do business. But this isn't the best scenario if your company is going to be web-based. See the section on domain names below for more details.

CONTACT

CheckSURE
www.checksure.biz

Intellectual
Property Office
www.ipo.gov.uk

A great name is good marketing

The small business insurance company More Th>n Business conducted a survey into the impact of business names on potential customers. First, the company asked for nominations for the most creative company name, with entries coming not only from the companies themselves, but also their customers, giving a clear indication of just how much attention a great company name can attract. Once a list of the best names had been compiled, they were then tested on the general public. Three-quarters of those surveyed admitted to being influenced by a catchy name, while 58% said it would make them remember the business. In fact, they were found to be most important to the younger people, with three-quarters of 18–24-year-olds stating they would notice and remember a shop with a humorous name. 'Our research confirms what the UK's most creative business owners already knew – that the right business name can offer a real advantage in the battle for customers,' says **Mike Bowman**, head of insurance at More Th>n Business. 'With over

> **A creative name plays a huge role in setting a small business apart and getting it noticed**

400,000 new startups each year, it is becoming increasingly difficult for business owners to settle on a catchy yet original name, but the research shows that it's definitely worth putting in the time and effort to get the right name.'

Citing the great marketing potential of a good, creative business name, Bowman, adds: 'A creative name plays a huge role in setting a small business apart and getting it noticed. Small businesses and independent high street retailers may not have massive marketing budgets, but this doesn't mean there is a lack of creative flair.' More Th>n Business awarded the title of most creative British business name to Aisle Alter Hymn, a wedding shop for gay and lesbian couples in South Shields, Tyne & Wear. However, remember that you don't have to use a pun to achieve a memorable name, but if you are in an industry where it's hard to market your unique selling point, it may just

ACTION POINT
WHERE TO START LOOKING FOR A NAME

Get friends and family together for a brainstorm: It helps to canvass opinion and your nearest and dearest is as good a place to start as any, according to small business insurance company More Th>n Business.

Examine what competitors are called: Do you think the names of your competitors work? By checking them out you should know the standard you are up against, and although you can't copy any and would be ill-advised to choose a similar name, you may be inspired by good ones.

Think of good business names that stand out in your mind: Beyond your competitors, you can also get inspiration from famous companies without directly copying them.

Use the internet, phone book, magazines and business directories to research: You can pretty much carry out all necessary investigation from home using handy sources of information.

Choose at least 10 names: Then you can whittle these down to a shortlist of three or four by checking which of your possible names are available – remember that many will already be taken. Once you have your shortlist of available names, use family and friends in the elimination process and make sure each of the names generated stands up to the checklist on page 171.

help you stand out from the crowd, as William the Concreter would probably agree.

The top 20 creative business names

Here's a rundown of the best business names in the UK, as found in the survey by small business insurer More Th>n Business:

1. Aisle Alter Hymn (UK's first wedding shop for gay, lesbian and heterosexual couples in South Shields, Tyne & Wear)
2. Battersea Cods Home (fish and chip shop in Sheffield, South Yorkshire)
3. Mad Hakkers (hairdressers in Leven, Fife)
4. Mr Bit (window cleaners in Derby and Coventry, West Midlands)
5. Only Foods and Sauces (takeaway in Walsall, West Midlands)
6. Spruce Springclean (window cleaners in West Byfleet, Surrey)
7. Tree Wise Men (tree surgeons in Wallington, Surrey)
8. Vinyl Resting Place (second-hand records shop in Croydon, Surrey)
9. Walter Wall (carpet sales in Exeter, Devon)
10. Plaice Station (fish and chip shop in Manchester)
11. William the Concreter (concrete suppliers in Hastings)
12. Carter, Whey and Tippet (refuse collection service in London)
13. Dustin Often (cleaning service in Leicester)
14. C Thru Cleaning (cleaning service in Middlesex)
15. Give Us A Break (window fitters in Leicester)
16. R Soles (Bootmaker in London)
17. Floral and Hardy (gardeners in Hayes, Kent)
18. Sarnie Schwarzenegger's (sandwich shop in Liverpool)
19. Abra-Kebab-Ra (kebab shop in Dublin)
20. Wok This Way (Chinese takeaway in Glasgow)

There are also some other serious contenders, including north-east entertainers Amps and Decks and arborists Tree Amigos, and Pimp my Pet, Fishcoteque, Pain in the Glass, Junk and Disorderly, Curl up and Dye, Spice Boys, Bubble n Chic and The Head Gardener. Can you guess what these businesses do?

Your domain name

> " There is no standard in the length of a domain, but the rule of thumb is the shorter the better "

Today, the vast majority of companies need a website, and the name you choose for your web address is just as important as your main registered name. That's because your website should lie at the heart of your marketing strategy, and attract as many customers as possible. If it is isn't doing this, you are missing out on a major online marketing opportunity, particularly at a time when more and more people are using the internet to research the businesses they want to buy from. Of course, if your business exists solely online, your web address could be your registered company name as well, but sometimes it can be useful to have a separate registered name – in which case it's back to the start of this chapter for you.

Just like your registered name, your domain name should describe the nature of your business or reflect your main one to create brand awareness and encourage repeat hits – that is the number of times a customer clicks onto your website – and online sales. It is the central ingredient for successful online marketing and, if appropriate to the market, your name could be spread without you even having to do anything. Names can include letters, numbers and hyphens, so there are a several ways to distinguish yourself from the competition. For example, if your company is called John Smith Printers and the .com and .co.uk names are already taken, think of an alternative. This could be perhaps jsprinters.com or jsprint.com. Although johnsmith-printers.com would be the obvious choice in this case, often the shorter the web address the better, as it can be easier to remember and be keyed in more quickly, while still reflecting the company and what it does.

You don't always need a name that directly states what you do. Having a unrelated catchy name can sometimes work to your advantage. Take Amazon.com, for example. The name is not directly linked to the products the company sells. However, Amazon has built a reputable brand around a totally new name that stands out from the crowd.

CREASE LIGHTNING AND THE NAME GAME

Arguably, there's no better way to attract a potential customer's attention than putting a smile on their face. Make someone laugh and they'll automatically have positive associations with your company, and if the amusing name also cleverly says what you do, you could be on to a winner. **Judy White** runs a one-woman ironing and laundry business in Bristol and won an award from *Yellow Pages* for the name of her company Crease Lightning, which was inspired by the popular song from the musical *Grease*. 'I came up with the name because I am a massive *Grease* fan,' she says. 'I even wear my hair like Olivia Newton John does in the movie.'

Not everyone takes the naming of their business to such extremes, but the clever thing about Crease Lightning is that it's not just amusing, it also reminds people of a popular movie that's both funny and entertaining. Although humour is a good trick for getting your business noticed and loved even before anyone has even bought anything from you, it only works if its appropriate and positive. There is a funeral directors in Twickenham, south-west London, called Wake and Paine, but presumably that's simply the names of the proprietors, as humour is certainly not the right route to take when naming such a business. The professions from legal to architectural also need a more serious approach, as often do many tradesmen, especially builders, who need to engender a feeling of trust. So remember that humour is not for everyone.

What makes a successful domain name?

Before attempting to buy any domain name, you need to think about:

- How easy is it to recall the name?
- What about the visual appearance of the name, and how it will appear on any documentation you produce? (The name needs to be there along with your main registered name (if it's different) and all you other contact details.)
- How will this affect your personal business email address, which, of course, is a key way for people to contact you.

> **If you keep your domain name short, simple and catchy, it can be found, accessed and remembered more easily**

As your domain name needs to make an instant impression on the customer, keep it short, recognisable and consistent with the brand you plan to establish.

If in doubt, remember the acronym RAIL:

Recall: How easy is it to recall the name?

Aesthetics: How does the name look and how will it appear on business cards and company literature?

Impressions: First impressions are crucial, so choose your name carefully

Length: Web addresses are limited to the 26 letters of the English alphabet, 10 numerals and a hyphen – 37 characters in all. When picking a name, less is more. A short name is preferable to a long one.

> **When choosing a name it is vital to consider the email address you will have as well**

Lesley Cowley, operations director at Nominet, the internet registry for .uk domain names, confirms the length of name is crucial in customer retention. 'There is no standard in the length of a domain, but the rule of thumb is the shorter the better,' he says. As it is becoming increasingly difficult for customers to find what they are looking for, your name will also have to be easily picked out by search engines, which is an increasingly popular route people take to locate a specific website or a selection that offer the service required. If you keep your domain name short, simple and catchy, it can be found, accessed and remembered more easily.

As briefly touched on earlier, another key consideration when selecting a name is your email address, which should be memorable and descriptive. It is a means by which you are remembered, contacted and will gain repeat hits or sales, not just a name.

Choosing a domain ending

Once you have chosen a domain name you will have to think about the ending. Will it be .com, .org, .net or something more unusual?

DOMAIN NAMES AND SEARCH OPTIMISATION

There are companies you can pay to make your business more attractive to search engines, and they provide a service called web optimisation or search engine optimisation. But this can be expensive and, these days, it's not really possible to fool search engines like it was in the past, so be wary of companies that offer a foolproof service, as websites that are spotted by search engines as trying to use underhand means to jump up the rankings are blacklisted – a marketing catastrophe. Some companies offer a kosher service, which will involve them helping you to track down keywords and phrases that your potential customers would use to locate your service, and then cleverly build them into the content of your site, perhaps donating a page each to the main keywords and phrases. Your domain name can help here too, as it will be a little more attractive to search engines if it is descriptive – although this is only a minor factor compared with keyword association.

Ultimately, search engines want to be sure that when someone searches for a particular service, they deliver relevant company websites. So if your company has lots of appropriate content about what you do, including perhaps advice and other relevant information, and is full of the necessary keywords, then this will help greatly.

This depends on many factors, including the nature of your business, whether you are national, international or both, and what is important to you and your customer base. The suffix .com is the broadest option, but as **Nick Saalfeld**, group editor of CompuServe UK, says, if you can't register .com, then simply go elsewhere. 'You have two big choices, .com and .co.uk,' he explains. 'These are the most desirable. However, with the uptake of alternative names, such as .net and .uk, .com is slowly becoming less desirable.'

Whatever the experts say, though, the best and most highly regarded name is still .com. It is globally and universally recognised, so if you can register it, as well as .co.uk, do it sooner rather than later. Even if you don't use the UK name, by registering it you will keep others from copying your name and it will protect you from the competition. In theory, the more names you own, then the better the chance you have of maintaining that brand as yours and yours alone. Unfortunately, today – with websites launching pretty much at the same rate as companies, and with some businesses having more than one website to perhaps target a specific sector – the short

> "The best and most highly regarded name is still .com"

names are becoming scarce and fading fast. This means it's even more important to think as creatively as possible when deciding on both your main company name and that of your web address.

'A British company should aim to own .co.uk and .com addresses, both of which imply a corporate entity, with .co.uk specifically identifying you as British,' says Saalfeld.

Throughout this chapter, you will notice an emphasis on the originality of your domain name. Obviously this is to avoid confusion with other companies, and because you can't register exactly the same name as another business. However, you may find that the company that has registered the name you want doesn't actually do anything like what your business does. If that is the case, then it's probably because its function is to register and sell domain names. As more companies go online, the demand for particular words or phrases is only going to increase. And cashing in on that demand are the clever people who have already snapped up the popular domains to sell for a profit later on.

Registering a domain name

> As with every business agreement you enter into do read the small print

CONTACT

Nominet
www.nominet.org.uk

Anyone can register a domain name as long it hasn't been used already. Nominet encourages companies and individuals to register a domain via an internet service provider – or ISP, the majority of whom are Nominet UK members and can register on your behalf. Once you have registered with an ISP, they will submit the application to Nominet, ensuring a more thorough and secure process. However, contractual terms, charges and service levels of ISPs vary greatly, so it's worth shopping around to find the best deal. Some companies offer domain registration, while others include free webspace and email addresses or more specialist options. As with every business agreement you enter into, do read the small print, and ask to see copies of the terms and conditions for domain name registration and clarify your right to move across to another ISP if you are unhappy. Besides ISPs, there are around 6,000 companies who have domain registration facilities.

Once you have decided upon which company is going to register your domain name, the process is generally swift and painless. First, you will be asked to pay a fee to secure your domain. Second, the company will send you a template of your registered domain name to the network information centre (NIC). Each country has its own NIC, which is where all the details of registered domains are held. Third, if your registration is accepted, the company you have chosen will set up a domain name system (DNS) entry. Essentially, this means assigning your name to a name server that collates and keeps all registered names, so that your domain can be found on the internet. The process takes between two and three days. Once these stages are complete, you will be live on the internet and can use your name.

Cost of registering a domain

As mentioned above, there are a variety of packages on offer when it comes to registering a domain name for your business. Some are cheaper than others and it often depends on what other services are included, such as whether you go for simple registration or choose any additional support services. Nominet's Cowley has seen a great deal of variation in the cost of domain names – from free of charge to £200 for .co.uk names – but this depends on levels of service and support. Prices will vary, depending on what your business needs, but there is an average price you will pay for single domain name registration, which is around £10.

If you ask many companies how much they paid for their domain name, many will say £5, perhaps £15 or a little more. But if you thought that the name you had chosen was absolutely key to your business, perhaps because you only planned to trade online, and found that it was being sold, just how much would you be prepared to pay? Would you go as far as spending £560,000? That price tag doesn't cover the cost of creating the website, nor does it include the cost of web hosting. For a cool half million, all you get is a domain name – a highly popular one, of course, but, that's right, just a name. And the domain

> **"If you ask many companies how much they paid for their domain name, many will say £5, perhaps £15 or a little more"**

CONTACT

123-reg.co.uk
www.123-reg.co.uk

name in question, according to web hosting site 123-reg.co.uk, is cruises.co.uk. Apparently, it was bought by website cruise.co.uk, and is going to be used to host 'the UK's largest cruise community'.

So what about the most expensive domain name ever purchased? Well poker.com has got to be up there, which allegedly went for a around US$20m, according to **Melissa Chang**, the president of Pure Incubation, a US internet incubator company based in Massachusetts. On her personal blog website www.16thletter.com, she says: 'The domain was for sale by moniker.com at a silent auction in Amsterdam, but I can't find a confirmation of who bought it or

THE WORLD'S MOST EXPENSIVE DOMAIN NAMES

The most expensive .com domain names:

poker.com ($20m)
sex.com ($12m)
porn.com ($9.5m)
business.com ($7.5m)
diamond.com ($7.5m)
beer.com ($7m)
casino.com ($5.5m)
korea.com ($5m)
asseenontv.com ($5.1m)
seo.com ($5m)
shop.com ($3.5m)
altavista.com ($3.3m)
loans.com ($3m)
vodka.com ($3m)
creditcheck.com ($3m)
wine.com ($2.9m)
creditcards.com ($2.75m)
Pizza.com ($2.6m)
autos.com ($2.2m)
computer.com ($2.2m)
express.com ($1.8m)
seniors.com ($1.5m)

tandberg.com ($1.5m)
cameras.com ($1.5m)
vip.com ($1.4m)
scores.com ($1.18m)
chinese.com ($1.12m)
invest.com ($1.015m)
topix.com ($1m)
wallstreet.com ($1m)
rock.com ($1m)
guy.com ($1m)
(Source: www.16thletter.com)

The most expensive non .com name:
poker.de ($957,937)

The top five most expensive .co.uk domain names:

1. Cruises.co.uk (£560,000)
2. Recycle.co.uk (£150,000)
3. Ink.co.uk (£130,425)
4. Mobile.co.uk (£120,000)
5. Taste.co.uk (£110,000)
(Source: www.brandrepublic.com)

[exactly] how much it went for. Rumours are more than $20 million.' This provides an example of how prized domain names are and the lengths companies will go to keep their purchases under wraps. And there are lots of alleged examples that similarly dwarf the official .co.uk domain name purchase record (see box), proving just how important a name can be.

EASYJET AND THE SIMPLE APPROACH

Company: easyJet
Owner-e Stelios Haji-Ioannou

Startups.co.uk has several interesting video interviews with successful entrepreneurs, and one of the shortest and most interesting is the owner of easyJet's account of where the name of his company came from.

In classic abstract style, **Stelios Haji-Ioannou** called his company Stelmar, which was an amalgamation of Stelios Maritime. The reason he wanted to incorporate his name was to stamp his own personal credentials on the company. 'I wanted to achieve something specific and for it to be known as Stelios' company and not my father's,' he says. In the same vein, Stelair was the working title for the airline he planned to set up, once again trying to involve his name in the business. But then he changed his mind. 'I decided that I shouldn't be so self-centred,' he says. 'And it was also difficult to pronounce... I also decided that the brand had to be extendable over several industries.' There were also considerations of longevity behind his decision to call this business easyJet, as well as consideration for his shareholders. 'I'd like to think that the more mature easyJet companies can carry on independent of me,' he says. 'I think people would still like to fly easyJet, whether I'm in charge or not.'

7.0

PRODUCT PREPARATION

WHAT'S IN THIS CHAPTER

■ Once you have decided on the business you want to run, carried out the necessary research into its viability and put together your business plan, perhaps also having secured early-stage finance, it's time to make sure you have the necessary elements in place to be able to launch effectively. Depending on your business, this can range from finding the right premises to recruiting staff, looking at key issues such as pricing and insurance along the way. Read on to find out the areas you need to consider addressing before you are ready for the off. This is the largest section of the book, because there's a lot to cover…

Searching for the right premises

Finding the appropriate home for your business can be time consuming and, once you've found the right place, it can be a key expense for your company. It can, however, cost you very little if you can simply rent a desk in another company's premises, or it can take up hardly any of your time in searching for the right space if you decide to work from home. So before you do anything else, decide the kind of premises you will need to launch your business. If your business dictates that you are going to need dedicated premises to operate from, knowing the type of property you need – office, workshop, shop, etc. – is merely the beginning. You also need to consider the location and available transport links, and then ask yourself questions such as how important common areas are to you and what standard of facilities you need, such as bathroom, storage, meeting room, kitchen, delivery access and so on.

Determining what you need

One overriding factor dominates the priorities of startup businesses looking for premises, and that's cost. There is usually an overwhelming temptation to go for the cheapest property, but this is often a mistake that can take decades to rectify – and even bring a promising business to its knees. Ironically, some people swing too far in the other direction, committing themselves to a heavy initial outlay because they believe image is vital – and image doesn't come cheap. So finding the right premises is the real secret. That can, and will, vary enormously according to the type of business. But there are some general rules that apply to any operation.

> **One overriding factor dominates looking for premises, and that's cost**

Location

Location is an important consideration for all new businesses. A key factor when deciding where to locate your business is whether you need passing trade or will customers come looking for you. Rents fall quickly within yards of main roads. Offices are even more flexible, particularly if most business is done on the phone. Manufacturing and storage relies heavily on access, so think about how vans and lorries will deliver and collect goods. Nearby parking can be important, but as traffic restrictions tighten, public transport may be even more so.

If you are starting up a retail shop, it's crucial to get the location right, as it will determine your business activity, and can also define your image. Should you head straight for the high street and aim to directly attract customers as they walk past, or should you locate on the edge of town or just off the main shopping avenue, because there are better parking facilities? Alternatively, should you head out of town altogether and follow the larger stores into a retail park, but pay more rent? When deciding, consider what sort of shop you are and the kind of customers you are going to be targeting, then research possible locations in terms of how accessible it is to your target market, how much competition exists there and how much it will cost you. For example, if you run a sandwich bar or café, are the customers in the high street the ones who will buy takeaway snacks? Will they be able to afford your prices? What is the footfall or number of passers-by that walk in or past your shop? How visible is your store next to your competitors, and how easy is your business to get to?

> **We studied what kind of people were shopping in the area**

Size

Size is another crucial factor. Health and safety laws provide basic guidance on how much space is needed per office desk or manufacturing process, but it will pay you to allow for growth. After all, the whole point of business is to expand, so try to be flexible. Although

PEOPLE AND PERFECT PLACE

Company: People
Owner-manager: Jo-Anne Bayliss

Jo-Anne Bayliss, joint founder of People, a fashion shop in Kings Heath, Birmingham, knows all about researching the ideal location for your business. She believes that knowledge of the area is crucial. 'We had lived in the area for four years and were seconds from the location,' she explains. 'We also knew that this area contained a lot of creative and young people, and that they would buy our products. This stretch of road also contains several gift shops, there is an existing customer base and shopping here saves a trip into town, even though this street is only a five-minute walk into Kings Heath high street.'

When researching their location Bayliss and her co-founders used several methods and techniques. 'The library was very useful and told us how many people lived in the area, where people were employed and what was going to be built in the near future, for example,' she says. 'We also carried out a questionnaire in the street, asked friends, studied what kind of people were shopping in the area, as well as counting them as they passed by. What's more, we consulted a business adviser who gave us more information on the area, such as bus routes and that Kings Heath is the second busiest area in the city.'

you may think this will cost more, bear in mind that today's outgoings must be balanced against the prospects of tomorrow's earnings.

Growth

Almost every small business aims to become a big business, but this prospect can be choked from birth if the wrong decisions are made. Building in flexibility at the start can be important. Can a building be physically altered internally, such as knocking down walls, extending outwards or upwards? Is there spare land next door for expansion? It can be important to make agreements with landlords from the outset about what will be allowed and how much extra will be charged on top of the cost of rebuilding or alteration. Demand for office space has declined during the downturn, which should give you some room to negotiate with the landlord over what alterations you can make and any additional fees. Planning rules must also be considered, as

> " Building in flexibility at the start can be important "

> **It is crucial to consider restrictions on potential alterations in how premises may be used**

local authorities are not always open to discussion about the future of premises. They may have rigid rules about increasing density of development, or buildings may be in a conservation area or near housing, in which case it will be much more difficult to consider changes. Even where no physical changes are required, you must consider restrictions on potential alterations in how premises may be used. Lease conditions and planning rules are usually quite specific about what goes on within a building. For example, you can't change a shop to an office, or vice versa, without permission from the local authority and landlord. In fact, even switching from one type of shop

IGLU.COM AND THE INCUBATOR SAVIOUR

Company: Iglu.com
Owner-managers: Richard Downs and Emmanuelle Drouot

Richard Downs started to put together his business plan for Iglu.com while a fulltime MBA student at London Business School (LBS). The original plan was based on selling property on the internet, but was quickly focused on the holiday ski market to take advantage of the correlation between skiers and internet users, as well as the fragmented nature of the market. Having met his partner, **Emmanuelle Drouot**, Iglu.com needed to be ready in time for launch at the impending Ski Show. As the countdown began, the company was lucky enough to find a home in the newly created LBS incubator, which provides basic office facilities for startup companies. This gave them the time to focus on the business rather than hunting for suitable office space. The website was completed at 2am on the morning of the show, explains Downs, who notes that even half a week spent looking for office space would have been disastrous. 'If we had missed the ski season, we would have been marginalised. The market opportunity would not be there,' he says, noting that a 12-month delay would have seen competitors steal the top slot.

The space offered by LBS is scaleable and is charged by the number of people. This makes the incubator relatively inexpensive for companies of two or three, but relatively expensive for larger groups. 'If a company is successful and grows, there is an economic impetus to move out,' says Downs. Iglu.com, which currently consists of a team of eight, is preparing to do just that as it has outgrown its original needs. The company is moving as a private tenant to another part of the building and hopes to keep a close association with the incubator and be on hand to provide advice to other startups. 'The other benefit is the network – being in an area with people in the same industry to throw around ideas,' says Downs.

to another can sometimes fall foul of planning restrictions. So you will need to cover all the options and regulations before signing on the dotted line.

Other factors to consider

On top of your company's specific requirements, there are some other issues you will need to consider before making a final decision on the premises to go for.

Use of premises

Most leases overflow with restrictions on how buildings can be used. This is partly to protect the landlord's investment by, for instance, preventing dangerous or noisy activities. There may also be covenants from the original ground landlord on types of business activity, as well as local planning restrictions. Sub-letting is commonly denied without the permission of the landlord. If a lease contains too many of these caveats, it can restrict your ability to pass on the lease to another tenant when you want to move on.

Redecoration and repair

Designating when, where, and how often redecoration and repair should take place, and who should do it can be a crucial factor, particularly for older premises, where hefty costs may be involved. Furthermore, many modern leases load most of these onto tenants, and landlords usually demand power to carry out the work at your expense if it is not done on time and to a required standard. Tenants also face what are called dilapidations schedules at the end of their lease term, where the landlord can demand payment where premises haven't been kept in good condition.

Alterations

Structural changes and extensions are usually restricted. Internal changes require negotiation and may need clearing when the lease ends.

> **If a lease contains too many caveats, it can restrict your ability to pass on the lease to another tenant**

A tradition has grown up in the UK for long leases. At one time, these ran for as long as a century, but the term has gradually been eroded to between 10 and 15 years. These generally apply to new buildings or those in high-demand city centres. Much shorter terms can be found – or negotiated – nowadays, as landlords are adjusting to conditions where tenants are unwilling to commit themselves for such long periods. Three to five years is generally considered a good compromise between a landlord seeking security of investment and small businesses unsure of their future. For financial reasons, a landlord may prefer to maintain the lease length at 10 years, but allow a break clause. This effectively means the tenant can leave after, say, three or five years. On the other hand, it also means that the landlord can demand this break even when a tenant does not want to move, causing expense and disruption.

Security of tenure

Many businesses may feel more secure with longer leases. They are usually assured of this by the 1954 Landlord and Tenant Act, which gives them the right to a new lease when the existing one expires. But sometimes these restrictions do not apply. Serviced premises are one example, along with a sub-lease situation or older buildings in temporary use pending redevelopment. Others may seek the freedom to get out of their commitment. Watch out for restrictions on sub-letting or assigning a lease, which are common, as landlords usually like to keep control of who is using their buildings. Be aware that this may involve you paying someone a premium to take on the responsibility for a lease. One crucial factor when taking on an assignment, which means paying a fee to the existing leaseholder to take over their lease, is whether that lease is subject to an archaic rule called 'privity of contract'. Until the law was changed in 1996, a tenant remained responsible for rent and other charges even after assignment of the lease to a new tenant.

Alternatives

There are options outside renting premises through a traditional lease.

- Serviced offices – serviced offices are becoming common as more investors plough into this growing sector. This involves a contract rather than a lease, running for terms ranging from a few hours to several months. The charges may appear high compared with usual rents, but include all services such as heating, lighting, security and business rates. Offices sometimes come complete with furniture and carpets.
- Serviced industry – the serviced industry sector is growing as landlords find it more difficult to attract tenants to older industrial space. The same terms apply as serviced offices, with an all-in monthly charge for rent and services.

Before you start the search

Having decided on the building details, there are a few things to bear in mind before you should start your search. Although landlords used to give few choices, today's business environment is less certain and the market has responded by providing a range of options to suit. Consider your business's financial model, and decide on your growth plans and the amount of money you want to spend. This will give you guidance on the services you want the landlord to include in the package, those you wish to pay for and the length of the lease term that suits you best. So before you start your research, calculate your budget, including one-off costs for items such as furniture and IT equipment, as well as ongoing costs such rates and service charges. Remember again that the current economic climate means that landlords are far more open to negotiating rates than they have been for a number of years, so be prepared to haggle as it could save your business valuable funds both now and in the future.

Before you secure the space

There are many ways to find potentially appropriate units – through commercial agents, online searches, local newspapers and even just

CONTACT

Where to go for further help:
Royal Institution of Chartered Surveyors (RICS): information Centre
☎020 7334 3838/3842/3819

Rent Review and Lease Renewal Helpline:
☎020 7334 3806

Dispute Resolution Service
Surveyor Court, Westwood Way, Coventry, CV4 8JE
☎020 7222 7000/01203 694757

Commercial Property Leases in England & Wales: Code of Practice.
Available from the RICS Bookshop;
☎020 7222 7000; or by mail order from: RICS Books, Mail Order Department, Surveyor Court, Westwood Way, Coventry, CV4
www.rics.org.uk

walking around. Then comes the really important stage – the viewings. At this stage try think about questions that go beyond the obvious:

- Can you control the room's temperature?
- Is the building well maintained and watertight?

Once you've found the property that meets all your criteria (including, of course, your budget):

- Check out the landlord before you agree to take the space
- Talk to other tenants in the building to establish their reputation, and ask for a copy of their 'customer service charter', as you need to know how responsive they will be if anything goes wrong. If they don't have one, take that as a warning sign!
- Clarify what the monthly payment covers (for example rent only, or are some utilities included)
- Confirm what services the landlord is contractually obliged to give.

Before signing the first offer that you are presented with, try to negotiate, because you may be able to achieve a rent-free period, for example. Lastly, rethink the whole process to help you finally decide if this is the right space for your business and for your customers. This will be your last chance to change your mind without it potentially costing you money, so ask yourself these key questions:

- Are you sure you can afford both the direct and indirect costs?
- Are you happy with the landlord?
- Do you understand the deal and what you are committing to?

Once you've done your homework and you feel confident that you are getting a fair deal, you should move to secure the space.

Getting the right help

The cost, time and plethora of potential problems means buying, leasing and selling property can absorb huge amounts of your time, and at worst, lead to bankruptcy before you are even off the ground. So it's advisable to take specialist advice from a chartered surveyor or a valuer. Just as lawyers know the law, surveyors know bricks and mortar. There are different types of surveyor and valuer who can help.

- One group are effectively agents and know all about availability, rents and prices. It may be worth employing one to find the right space.
- Building surveyors specialise in the nitty-gritty of construction. They can organise a new-build or inspect existing buildings for potential faults. Another skill lies in analysing the average 40-page lease a landlord will expect. Or they can take over negotiations on rent reviews, rating appeals and planning applications. Use an expert with letters after their name. Professional organisations award these, such as the Royal Institution of Chartered Surveyors (RICS). Ask in advance how much it will all cost. Then, after taking a deep breath, consider how quickly such fees will be saved in making the right choice or winning a cut in the asking rent.

Equipping your office

Once you've chosen your premises and completed the formalities, the next step will be preparing your workspace for business, making sure that it has the necessary equipment to allow you to be able to run your company. It's also important to think carefully about the layout, as this will directly affect your ability to operate. Office or workspace-making can be as rewarding as home-making, but you are likely to have only a limited amount of time to do this as you will start paying rent from the moment you've signed the contract, so it can also be just as stressful.

If you are manufacturing a product, then your workspace is likely to be your workshop, so you will need to get all the necessary equipment installed and make sure that you adhere to statutory health and safety guidelines. Your industry association should point you in the right direction for your specific requirements. If you simply have an office – and if you have a workshop you may also have an area

CONTACT

Health and Safety
Executive
www.hse.gov.uk

set aside for this purpose – think carefully about the equipment you will need to keep your business running smoothly, from technology such as telephones and IT to desks and chairs. Health and safety should also be a priority, particularly if you are employing people, and the Health and Safety Executive will be able to provide you with the necessary guidelines – the last thing you want in the early stages of starting your business is to find yourself liable for damages following a workplace accident involving one of your staff (or customers for that matter). (Guidance on insuring your business is covered later in this chapter.)

If you will be dealing with customers face to face, it's vital to make sure that your office reflects the values of your business and doesn't deter customers. So put some careful thought into décor – having spent time and effort thinking about the vision and values of your company for your business plan, your premises should reflect them. Of course, if you are opening a shop or a restaurant, for example, this is one of the most important facets of your business. This also involves key elements such as signage, which must be consistent with your brand image and logo, and must complement your marketing materials. Positioning is also vital here, particularly if you are looking to attract custom to your premises.

You may do some of the décor preparation yourself, as well as installing some of the equipment. However, to ensure your premises looks professional, it could well be worth using decorators, builders and office installation companies. If you will be doing this, plan this well in advance, as you will not only pay for the work, but also for any delay in getting your business up and running. Recommendations from friends and other businesses, and reputable trade federations, are a good way of sourcing the best companies in your area.

To prevent overspending or misjudging the equipment you will need, think carefully about this well in advance and make a comprehensive list of the items you will need. Then consider the best places to source what you need. Be as economical as you can, but go for quality as well. Decide for which items you need go for the 'Rolls Royce' option, because, say, they directly determine the quality of product or service you offer, and for which you can choose the 'Volkswagen' – reliable. Always look for good value and never be tempted to go for poor quality, as this is likely to end up being a false economy, with an item letting you down at a crucial time. Check out what can be bought second hand and whether there are special online markets or exchanges for your particular sector.

Security is an area you shouldn't look to cut back on. If your premises doesn't look impenetrable, it'll just attract thieves. For recommendations on what precautions to take, call your local police station. The police will usually come and survey your premises, and will probably also recommend a good local security company to do the work for you – and testimonials don't come better than that.

Finally, although it may sound obvious, don't overlook utilities, such as heating, lighting and water. Effective air conditioning, for example, can help make your working environment more pleasant throughout the year.

Building the right team

As well as finding the right premises, staffing is a key area that small businesses can focus on, explains **Nick Shrager**, a member of the National Council of the Institute of Business Advisors. 'It's all about customer retention,' he says. 'If staff make the customers feel welcome, they'll come back – and it's six times easier to sell to an existing customer than to a new one.'

You may feel that you can start and run a small business all by yourself. But there usually will be some areas you can't handle – we're not all salespeople, for example. The first thing is to identify what skills and experience your company needs to grow and make it a success. Then you can start to work out who you need to recruit for a successful launch and what your requirements will be in the short and long term. Of course, you also need to honestly assess what you can reasonably manage without the expertise of others by relying on your own resources. This is something you should have addressed in your business plan (see Chapter 4), along with defining the exact nature of your product or service and its marketplace, and how to recognise the problems of that market. All of this will help you to decide what additional people and skills you may require. It will also show you where your strengths lie.

> "It's vital to be honest about your strengths and weaknesses"

'It's vital to be strictly honest about your strengths and weaknesses,' agrees **Brial Steel** of Business Link Berkshire and Wiltshire. 'And it should be an ongoing process, continuous improvement comes through continuous monitoring.' Practically speaking, you can learn to market your own product – after all you are the expert on it – and you can run the office and develop new custom. But if, for example, on

---

GUIDELINES ON EQUAL OPPORTUNITIES LEGISLATION

Throughout the recruitment process, you should be fully aware of equal opportunities legislation. This means understanding how discrimination can occur – even unintentionally – during the recruitment process.

Some job advertisements may discourage particular groups from even applying for the vacancy. For example, an advertisement calling for 'vibrant' or 'thrusting' personnel is implicitly ageist as it will deter older candidates who will associate these words with youthfulness. Also, untrained interviewers can form very subjective opinions on the basis of entirely irrelevant criteria – such as background or appearance.

Unlawful discrimination

You are not allowed to express a preference in terms of the gender, age or race or colour of the candidate, as this is discrimination.

Genuine occupational qualification

You are only allowed to state a preference for a man or woman if you can produce a genuine occupational qualification (GOQ) saying why it must be a man or woman. For example, if you need a man for cleaning male toilets. Ideally, as your company grows, you should monitor the applications received to make sure that they attract applicants from a cross-section of society, with sufficient numbers from diverse groups and sections. Also, the entire selection process should be monitored to ensure that selection occurs on the basis of criteria related to the job requirements – and nothing else.

top of this you are spending far too much time struggling to balance the books, it's probably time to pay someone else to do this, most likely on a part-time basis.

Finding the right people

If you get the recruitment process right, you virtually eliminate the risk of hiring the wrong person for the job. On the other hand, getting the process wrong means that you won't attract applications from suitable candidates and will be much less able to spot them during the selection process. Recruitment is not just carried out to meet immediate vacancies, but should be seen as part of an overall organisational strategy for sourcing personnel. Once you fill one vacancy, you should be left with a list of candidates who you would consider for the same or other vacancies in the future. This makes the process much easier the next time round.

A recruitment exercise exposes your company to a wide section of the public. These people could be current or potential clients, customers or suppliers. What's more, people talk. If a job applicant has had an unfavourable experience with your company, you can be sure that they will tell others about it. Hence it's vital that the recruitment process creates a positive impression of your company while at the same time you are able to find the right person you have decided you need to launch your business effectively.

> **Recruitment shouldn't just cover immediate vacancies, but should be seen as part of an overall organisational strategy for sourcing personnel**

The job profile

Define the role (job profile) and the person required (person specification) as accurately as you can in order to attract the right people. It also helps if you have a clear idea of the kind of person you need and the actual work involved. When listing skill requirements, only mention those actually related to the position. Similarly, when stating prior experience needs, think about how much is strictly necessary for the candidate to do the job well. You may ideally want your new employee to be an office whizz and highly trained in all things, but consider the competencies they actually need for the position offered.

The advertisement

Once you have prepared a profile, draw up a clear but brief recruitment advertisement. This should include:

- The job requirements
- The criteria for applicants
- The salary package
- The length of the contract
- A short description of your organisation
- The job location
- The application procedure (do people apply in writing, by phone, or fill in an application form?).

Where you advertise will depend on the type of position offered. Surveys show that specialist and trade publications work best for managerial and professional posts. Meanwhile, advertisements for skilled workers give best results when placed in the local press. The internet as a recruitment tool is also becoming more and more popular, and can be very cost-effective, so it will pay for you to research the online options available. Some trade magazines, for example, will offer to put your vacancy online as part of the recruitment advertisement package. There is more on where to place your advertisement later in this chapter.

Where to look for staff

When you've drawn up the profile of the person you are looking for and written a draft of the advertisement, there are four main routes to making contact. Each has its pros and cons.

Local newspaper

Everyone looking for a job knows the day the job pages come out. It's the one day that is guaranteed to be a big seller for a local paper as everyone from national to one-man-band companies vie to attract new staff. It isn't the cheapest form of recruitment, but you are guaranteed to get a sizeable response. Most locals told startups. co.uk that smaller companies didn't need to put an advertisement in for more than one week to get a more than adequate choice of applicants.

Prices vary from region to region, but the procedure is largely the same. You fax or email through the text of your advert (over the phone there is too much risk of misspelling), and the recruitment classified desk will call you back to discuss options. If you've never placed an advertisement before, don't worry, they will go through with you how big the advertisement should be and how long it should appear to attract a certain response, and then calculate the cost. The simplest advertisements might be charged by lineage, for example £17 per line plus VAT, where each line will fit three or four words. You wouldn't be able to say a great deal or have a company logo, but it would get the message across. So typically, a small advertisement in a local paper will cost in the region of £300. Many local papers are part of a wider syndicate, so you might also be able to get your advertisement in more than one paper. For example, some local papers have a more business-orientated journal, which can be helpful if you are looking to reach that market. This is again something the classified department will be able to help you with.

Pros: This is possibly the best way to access your region, as the local paper on job day is still the first port of call for many people.

Cons: This is not a very targeted approach, as the paper goes to everyone and unless you make your advertisement specific, you might have to wade through lots of unsuitable applicants.

Check with your local newsagent which paper people buy for jobs in your area and which day is job day – it's usually Thursday.

Job centres

The Employment Service has over 1,000 job centres nationwide that can help you find people for a whole range of positions and sectors, either locally or nationwide in some cases. It doesn't cost anything to post a vacancy with them and you can benefit from support both before and after the position is filled. Services offered by Jobcentre Plus include advice on recruitment methods and procedures, information about the local labour market such as employment levels, availability of candidates and wage rates, and advice on any difficulties or barriers to filling your vacancies. It is also important to file any other details, such as whether a driving licence will be required to avoid wasting your and your candidates' time later on. The details of the job are entered into a computer system that job seekers can either access themselves or through a consultant. If you then agree your expectations with your contact at the job centre, they can let you know when there are enough suitable applicants.

You can now create, view and update your jobs yourself through Employer Direct online. You can also email your vacancies at any time.

Pros: You can use the job centre as a base for interviews and the consultants are always on hand to help. It is also free.

Cons: It can be a time-consuming process as you are relying on people coming into the job centre to see your advertisements.

Online recruitment

You don't have to be an online company to think about recruiting online. Often if you place a newspaper advertisement with a local paper, they will have a package to post your advertisement on an affiliated website. But there are also dedicated websites: Monster. co.uk, Stepstone and easyJobs are some of the ones available, where both potential employees and employers can search online. The idea is that you save time by cutting out the middleman, using the website instead. With Monster, for example, you can potentially deal with the whole process online. You log on, post your vacancy

CONTACT

Employer Direct Online
www. jobcentre
plus.gov.uk/key
employerdirect;
vacancies@job
centre; gsi.gov.uk
Fax: 0845 601 2004

CONTACT

Gojobsite
www.gojobsite.
co.uk
☎0870 774 8710

Monster
www.monster.co.uk
☎0800 169 5015

Stepstone
www.stepstone.
co.uk
☎020 8762 6700
easyJobs.com
www.easyjobs.
co.uk

and pay for it using your credit card. For a small business, you will probably choose the one-off option, which costs £270 and will post your advertisement for up to 60 days.

Pros: Once you are registered you can control the job advertisements yourself, taking them down when you have enough applicants. There is also the added bonus of a team on hand to help you out with any problems. Moreover, you can reach a much wider audience, nationally and possible Europe-wide, without going through agents.

Cons: People are unlikely to see the job as easily as they might in a newspaper when scanning the advertisements. Websites rely on people searching.

Recruitment agency

There are a lot of recognisable high-street recruitment agencies, including Select, Travail, Manpower, Hays and Reed, which can pro-vide you with both part-time and permanent staff. In theory, they all deal with every level of company, from small operations to national businesses. There are also many industry-specific recruitment agen-cies. With most agencies you can choose how to contact them initially – by phone, email or in person at your local branch. You will then need to provide details of what type of staff you are looking for and the kind of salary you plan to pay. Agency staff will advise you on the current employment rates if you are not sure, or indeed if your estimate is over or under the odds. It is also likely that you will have to undergo some kind of credit check just so the agency knows you can pay the bill.

If you don't have premises, you can hold your interviews at the agency, but they will need to come and view your offices to check they are suitable for the potential employee. It also helps for them to see the culture of your company, the people and environment to help match the applicants. Once you have agreed exactly what the job description is and what the conditions and the salary are, you will have to sign an agreement. This just ensures that the candidate is getting the job they have applied for. But it is important from your point of view that you have the position clearly defined at this stage to avoid difficulties later. This is also important when the agency fee is

CONTACT

Hays
www. haysworks. com

Manpower
www.manpower. co.uk
reed.co.uk
www.reed.co.uk

Select
www.select.co.uk

Travail
www.travail.co.uk
(all websites have nearest branch finders)

set. They may take a percentage of the candidate's annual salary, say 20%. However, the amount will vary according to the level the person is coming in at and how hard they were to find.

After you have recruited someone, there will probably be a period during which the fee is refundable – but only a few months. So it is in your interests not only to choose carefully but also to work with the agency to ensure you and your new staff member is happy in the first three months. That way, it will be money well spent not wasted.

Pros: If the agency wants your fee, it is in their interests to find you someone good, therefore you should receive decent support and guidance.

Cons: As part of the process your finances and premises will be investigated and questioned if not up to standard.

The response

All applications to job advertisements should be replied to. Remember they could well be or know clients. The sooner the response, the better, as this shows your company is efficient and interacts well with the public. Remember too that all applications – even unsolicited ones – are confidential.

The criteria

Even if the response to your advertisement is overwhelming, don't eliminate candidates on the basis of certain self-selected criteria such as geographical proximity to your office. You could easily miss the application from your ideal employee. Instead, use a checklist of *essential* criteria, based on the job profile and person specifications you compiled earlier. It's surprisingly easy to let personal prejudice slip in, so it's best to be aware of this possibility at all times.

Stay objective. You could try using a points system to screen applications based on every core skill requirement spotted. This lends a broad and more objective method to the process.

ACTION POINT

MAKE SURE YOU HAVE THE PEOPLE AND THE SKILLS TO LAUNCH SUCCESSFULLY

Identify the skills your company needs to succeed: Carefully look at the various functions required for the successful running of your business from administration to sales and marketing.

Assess which of these you and your existing workforce can realistically cover: If you already have staff on board, honestly assess who can handle the various functions and the skills necessary.

Work out the skills gaps: Make a list of the remaining functions to gauge where help is needed.

Decide on how many people you will need to take on: Look at the functions and skills needed and assess how many people will be required to plug the gaps and whether they'll be recruited on a freelance, part-time or full-time basis.

Kick-off the recruitment process: Draw up the necessary job descriptions and decide how to reach the people you need.

Once you are an employer

Part of the process of building your team is recognising your obligations as an employer. This involves making sure that you are up to speed on all the relevant employer legislation, so that you avoid any legal problems – which can be quite severe – and treat your staff fairly. Gaining a reputation for being a good employer will pay dividends in the long run as it will help you attract the best talent. Here are some pointers (for more details, contact the Department for Business, Enterprise and Regulatory Reform).

Equal opportunities

Just as when you are recruiting, your workforce should be treated equally, regardless of colour, race, nationality, ethnic or national origin, sex, age or marital status. Also you shouldn't discriminate against a disabled person because of their disability either directly or by failing to make 'reasonable adjustments' for a disabled person. For free information about equality at work, contact ACAS Equality Direct (see contacts below).

Terms and conditions of employment

Within the first two months of their employment, an employee must receive a written statement of main employment information, covering main terms and conditions, including pay, holidays, details of notice and disciplinary procedures.

Transfer of an undertaking

Employees' terms and conditions are preserved when a business (or part of one) transfers to a new employer.

Fair and unfair dismissal

If an employee has at least one year's service, they have the right to complain of general unfair dismissal.

Unions

Employees have the right to belong or not belong to a union, and the right not to be refused employment on the grounds of trade union membership or non-membership.

PERIOD OF NOTICE

- For continuous employment of more than one month, but less than two years, one week's notice of termination of employment must be given unless a longer period is stated in the employment contract.
- After two years or more, at least two weeks' notice must be given.
- After two years employment, one additional week's notice for each further complete year is required.
- After 12 years continuous employment, a minimum of 12 weeks' notice is required.
- An employee is required to give his or her employer at least one week's notice that they are leaving if employed continuously for one month.
- This minimum is unaffected by longer service, but you may ask for longer in their contract.

Redundancy

If you have fewer than 20 employees, you are under no obligation to notify any staff about redundancy. However, failure to do so could result in a claim being made for unfair dismissal. Companies with 20–99 employees must give at least 30 days' notification, while those with more than 99 employees need to provide at least 90 days' notification. What's more, an employer who proposes to make at least 20 employees redundant at one establishment over a period of 90 days or less is required to consult either representatives of a recognised independent trade union or other elected representatives of the affected employees.

Illegal workers

You can face a criminal prosecution if you employ illegal workers and haven't made certain checks on new employees, such as seeing a P45, P60 or payslip showing a National Insurance (NI) number – or one of a range of other specified documents. Copies need to be retained in most cases.

National minimum wage

All employers must adhere to the UK minimum wage, which is £5.73 an hour (£4.77 an hour for 18–21-year-olds).

Pay and tax

You must inform Her Majesty's Revenue & Customs (HMRC) when you take on your first employee. HMRC will set up a PAYE (pay as you earn) scheme and send you a new employer's starter pack. You should complete a P45 form for each employee or complete a P46, making the necessary tax deductions and send them in monthly. All employees must be given itemised pay statements showing deductions. National Insurance is payable for employees aged 16 or over earning more than £110 per week (as of April 2009).

Statutory sick pay

If an employee is sick for less than four consecutive days, no action is needed. If the employee is sick for more than four days, and is entitled to statutory sick pay (SSP), you are obliged to pay it in the same way as wages and keep records of payments made and dates of sickness absence. If the employee is sick for more than four days, and not entitled to SSP, the employee may claim state incapacity benefit instead.

Statutory maternity pay

Employees can claim statutory maternity pay (SMP) if on the 15th week before their baby is due they have been employed by you for more than 26 weeks. They can choose to take SMP from the 11th week before the baby is born. Employees must tell you at least 28 days before they intend to stop work, and you should get them to make this request in writing. They must also provide you with evidence of when their baby is due. This is normally on the maternity certificate MATB1. The earliest that this certificate may be issued by their doctor or midwife is 20 weeks before the week in which their baby is due. You should receive this no later than three weeks after the date their SMP begins.

Hours

Working hours are limited to an average of 48 hours a week, although workers can choose to work more if they want to. Night-workers' hours are limited to an average of eight hours work in a 24-hour period, and they have a right to receive free health assessments. All employees have a right to 11 hours' rest a day, a day off each week, and an in-work rest break if the working day is longer than six hours.

Insurance

If you employ staff you must take out Employer's Liability Insurance and display the necessary certificate.

Health and safety

You must register your business with either the Health and Safety Authority (most factories, workshops, etc.) or the local authority (most offices, shops and catering businesses).

CONTACT

Department
for Business,
Enterprise and
Regulatory Reform
www.berr.gov.uk

ACAS Equality
Direct
☎0845 600 3444

Health and Safety
Authority
www.hse.gov.uk

Finding and dealing with suppliers

Many businesses are built around selling goods, and as such are reliant on getting these items at the best possible prices, so that they can make more profit on a sale. This is where suppliers or wholesalers come in. If you've never dealt with these kind of businesses before, you could be surprised as sometimes it can even be difficult to track down the right one. However, this is a relationship that is worth nurturing, as it is key to the success of your new business.

Finding wholesalers

It's not just large firms who make use of wholesalers, but how do you find them in the first place? Thumbing through your *Yellow Pages* or calling a directory service might yield results, but for the modern small business the lack of wholesaling presence on the internet is a cause of great frustration. Wholesalers tend to stick to traditional tried and tested methods – and this includes attitudes, or a lack of them, towards technology such as the web and email.

Relationships between wholesalers and their customer base are often built up over years of loyal service, so suppliers often rely on word of mouth and local knowledge to attract new clients. You are unlikely to come across attention-grabbing advertising from wholesalers in comparison with large retailers. 'It can be very hard for people new to trading to find wholesaler contact information and thus it makes it hard to shop around,' admits wholesaling specialist **Richard Grady**. 'One of the reasons for this is that very few UK wholesalers have decent websites and even fewer have taken any time to ensure their sites are ranked well in internet search engines. This means that if you are looking for suppliers on the internet, it will take ages and you probably won't have much luck,' he warns.

Luckily, this gap in the market has been belatedly acknowledged with several websites and books that point you in the direction of

> "
> If you are looking for suppliers on the internet, it will take ages and you probably won't have much luck "

your nearest wholesalers. However, entrepreneurs will still have to do most of the legwork in researching the quality of wholesale products and getting the best value for money. Grady has compiled an online resource to accompany his sought-after e-book, *UK-Trader's UK Wholesale Guide*. Visitors to his website (see contact box) can get details on over 700 wholesalers and gain other relevant information. Alternatively, www.thewholesaler.co.uk has a large wholesale directory, with details on products ranging from fireworks to toiletries.

As websites like these may charge you for membership and access, it can be worth sticking to print publications when looking for your wholesalers. Therefore, a quick flick through *The Trader* magazine (monthly at most newsagents) will reveal plenty of wholesale advertisements, as well as a list of contacts.

CONTACT

The UK-Trader
www.theuktrader.
co.uk

The Trader
www.thetrader.
co.uk

Sourcing overseas suppliers

Many companies look abroad to source cheaper products or raw materials. This approach is definitely worth considering, particularly at the moment when every penny counts. The breaking down of global trade barriers also means that this may be necessary to stay competitive.

If you find a willing supplier selling the product you need at the cheapest possible price, you have to consider the following: how far away the country is; whether there might be compromise on levels of regulation and protection; and how well you will be able to communicate with your chosen supplier should any problems arise. Issues of creditworthiness and reliability are even more important when your supplier is based abroad.

As a general rule, developed countries are easier to trade with than developing ones. If your supplier is from a country in the European Union, for instance, many key regulations and standards will be similar to those in the UK. If a country has high volumes of existing trade with the UK, it probably means other businesses have been successful in establishing relationships with traders there. If this is the case, enquire after good suppliers in your target country from other traders in your sector, or go on an overseas trade visit, or attend some foreign-focused trade exhibitions.

In fact, trade shows and expos are among the best places to find new suppliers, but make sure that the event is relevant to your needs, as they can be time-consuming and expensive. To find the appropriate fairs and expos, check out the trade publications associated with your sector, and look online. Websites such as www.exhibitions. co.uk, www.tradeshows.esources.co.uk, www.biztradeshows.com and www.expocentral.com will point you in the right direction. For international tradeshow listings, visit www.FITA.org.

For an overview on international trade, visit the Business Link, while for information on potential suppliers, your local UK Trade and Investment (UKTI) team should be your first port of call. The UKTI website also includes an online test to see whether your company is ready to trade with businesses abroad and tips from international trade advisers. It's also worth trying your supplier country's embassy in the UK – you will find contact details on the Foreign & Commonwealth Office website. Furthermore, contact information for your target country's chambers of commerce can be found on the British Chambers of Commerce (BCC) website. Trade associations for your sector will most likely have information regarding suppliers for your industry too. You should be able to find details of trade associations for your industry sector on the Trade Association Forum website.

Once you find your supplier, make sure you research their reliability. Speak with experienced UK importers or trade associations in your sector so that you have an idea of what to expect. Find out if your supplier has any UK references they can provide and try to visit them, so that you can check out their work and their production systems first hand.

Make sure to carry out financial checks too. If your supplier cannot furnish you with a credit history, your bank's international trade team may be able to carry out a 'status query', which will investigate the company's financial standing for you. But no matter how clean your supplier's bill of financial health, don't sign a long-term contract

CONTACT

Business Link
www.businesslink.
gov.uk

**UK Trade and
Investment**
www.uktradeinvest.
gov.uk

**Foreign &
Commonwealth
Office website**
www.fco.gov.uk

**British Chambers
of Commerce
(BCC) website**
www.british
chambers.org.uk

**Trade Association
Forum**
www.taforum.org

straight off or agree to any advance payments until you have built up a relationship of trust.

Approaching wholesalers

As long as you have proof of trading, which can be as little as a letterhead or business card, you are entitled to deal with a wholesaler. Suppliers need business just as much as you do, so there's little chance you will be turned away. So be confident when approaching them and focus your concerns on getting a good deal for your business. It is important that you actually visit the wholesaler in person because as mentioned above, wholesalers are quite traditional in their practices, and the chances of getting hold of an email address to contact them are slim.

There is, similarly, a limited amount you can do over the telephone. Your supplier will be happy to send you a list of stock and the relevant prices, but to gain a proper understanding of what you are ploughing your wholesaling budget into, it is vital you have a face-to-face meeting.

The time that you actually visit is up to you, but be aware that the busiest time for a wholesaler will be around midday, when shop owners converge to purchase stock for their stores. If you arrive around 4pm, you will have a less frantic search for your goods, as

PHONE BEFORE YOU GO

Do phone ahead before your visit to save yourself from a wasted journey, as it is best to find out in advance if your wholesaler has the goods you require. Stock changes every day at a wholesaler, so lists you receive a week in advance will be out of date by the time you turn up to purchase the items that you need. Many wholesalers also like to assign certain visiting times for customers to look at stock – this is particularly the case with larger and more popular suppliers. Wholesalers with valuable items that require supervised visits will also need you to call ahead. Policies vary according to the supplier, so check out their procedures before you turn up.

this is the wholesaler's quietest period. You will also benefit from more attention from the wholesale staff, as they will have fewer customers to deal with. The downside is that stock you have turned up to buy may have already gone, so, again, it is vital that you call ahead to check on what stock is still available. Striking the right balance is important, so don't be put off if it takes a few visits before you get it right.

Choosing a good wholesaler

As is common when you are starting up a business, for all the calculations and careful planning, sometimes a good or bad gut instinct can serve you best of all. 'Most people will get a feel for whether they are comfortable with an individual quite quickly and this is often very accurate,' explains Grady. 'I would tend to be happier dealing with a large wholesaler with pleasant premises and a friendly atmosphere, although, that said, I have also traded with some very good suppliers that have operated from very unpleasant lock-up units on rough industrial estates!'

> A good wholesaler will take the time to talk to you and listen to your needs

Generally speaking, a good wholesaler will take the time to talk to you and listen to your needs. The more they are prepared to do for you suggests that they are reliable and their stock will not let you down – customer service, after all, is essential to wholesalers who rely heavily on repeated visits from shop owners and small firms. On the other side of the coin, if you turn up to a derelict garage and are confronted by a nervous looking 'wholesaler' who thrusts a box of pickles into your hands before snatching your money and speeding off in his GTi to the sound of wailing police sirens, you should maybe consider looking elsewhere for your supplies in the future. So trust your first impressions. If you are not happy you can always change your wholesaler until you find someone you are comfortable dealing with.

How much should you spend on stock?

Before you set off to visit your wholesaler, make sure you have worked out a budget to suit your business's needs and means. Although the need to budget carefully is essential in almost all aspects of business startups, it is particularly important when it comes to buying stock. Working out how much you need of a certain product and how much money to set aside can be a tricky balance to strike. Purchasing too few supplies to satisfy customer demand or keeping your business running smoothly, means you could end up losing out financially. Buying too much stock also means not only will you have a room full of unsold items, but you will also be hit financially. It's also wise to keep some money back, because if you don't, you might miss a bargain or neglect other essential areas of your business. Of the two scenarios, over-spending is the least preferable, as you won't be able to correct your order next time if your firm suffers serious financial damage. So, when working out your budget, err on the side of caution.

'How much you buy in one go depends on what you are purchasing the stock for,' says Grady. 'If you have a large high-street outlet, then you are going to need to buy far more stock than an individual trading part-time from home. Most wholesalers have fairly low minimum orders, say from £50 to £300, and this means that traders can buy in small quantities initially. This is recommended so that you can check that you can actually sell the products. There is nothing worse than being stuck with a large quantity of stock that you can't sell, especially if you have invested all of your capital into it.

'Wholesalers will expect payment with order unless you have a credit account with them. It is not usually appropriate to finance stock purchases with other finance deals or instalments as the purchases would normally be too regular – every couple of weeks or monthly.'

> **There is nothing worse than being stuck with a large quantity of stock that you can't sell**

WHOLESALER CREDIT ACCOUNTS

As a new startup you shouldn't expect a wholesaler to offer you a credit account with them. You probably will have to make some straightforward purchases with them first. This is generally what wholesalers will expect from you. It may be cheaper to set up a credit account, when you've established yourself with suppliers, than get involved in any finance deals with your bank, and it is best to avoid getting into a never-ending circle of loans and deals to fund your stock purchases.

Don't forget about VAT

Unfortunately, we all have to pay VAT and wholesalers are no different – in fact it is the most common tax you will come across when dealing with your wholesaler. VAT is charged by suppliers of goods and services, and wholesalers certainly fall into the former category. As they are not entitled to any exemptions or a reduced VAT level, wholesalers will charge the standard rate of 15% on your purchase – which was reduced from 17.5% in 2008 to help stimulate business during the recession. What you must be aware of is that many wholesalers price their goods without VAT, so you may be under the impression that you have a brilliant deal when, in fact, you will have a 15% charge slapped on top of it. So the four widescreen televisions you buy for just £1,000 will in fact set you back £1,150.

'From my experience, it's fair to say that many new traders do forget that the prices displayed by wholesalers won't include VAT,' says Grady. 'I know of a couple of people that got very excited at the incredibly low deals on offer and got a shock when they got to the till and found another 15% added to the cost.' Although you are obliged to pay the VAT on these, and indeed any other goods, you are entitled to claim the money back if your firm is VAT registered. Input tax (the VAT you pay on raw goods) can be claimed back as part of the legitimate expenses that your business runs up – if you regularly pay more VAT than you collect you can claim this money back on a monthly basis by filling in a return.

CONTACT

For the most up-to date figure on VAT visit www.hmrc. gov.uk/vat/ vatregistering.htm

New traders often forget that the prices displayed by wholesalers don't include VAT 🙶🙶

To become VAT registered, your firm's turnover must exceed £68,000 a year, although this figure has risen considerably in the past few years. These increases have been aimed at helping new businesses that cannot deal with the burden of filling out continual VAT forms. However, although small firms often grumble about VAT, you can often save money by registering for it and many businesses voluntarily put their name forward even if they are under the threshold. So, if you are VAT registered and you keep in mind the charge when purchasing, you will be able to shape your budget accordingly to ensure that your cashflow is unaffected.

Are you guaranteed?

There are no specific guarantees that wholesalers use, although the goods you buy will usually have a manufacturer's warranty, which will be passed to you from the supplier once the transaction is made. A wholesaler should be happy to replace faulty stock, although, legally, they are not bound to do so, unlike high-street stores. Significantly, the regulations that amended the Sale of Goods Act in 2002 did not cover wholesalers. This means that although shops are duty-bound to give refunds or exchanges for faulty goods, wholesalers are not. 'The regulations only cover business-to-consumer transactions, so wholesalers wouldn't be relevant,' says **Martyn Rapley** of the Department for Business, Enterprise and Regulatory Reform. 'However, the main requirements of the Sale of Goods Act ... are certainly relevant.'

So it's not all bad news if you have, for example, bought 100 solar-powered torches. The original Sale of Goods Act makes it clear that all products sold should be of satisfactory quality and serve the purpose for which they are intended. Most reputable wholesalers offer exchanges or refunds for faulty items, so just because the law now only recognises this right in retailers, this shouldn't damage your chances of getting your money back or getting a decent replacement. However, a word of warning: the new regulations shift the onus of proving the goods were faulty at the time of purchase to the seller – but only in regard to shops. Wholesalers will still be able to demand that you prove the products were inadequate when you first bought them. Also, if you buy untested goods from a clearance warehouse, they will have no warranty at all and you will run the risk of having a damaged bank balance as well as damaged stock.

Buying online

As befits their traditional image, wholesalers generally prefer to do their trading on the floor of a warehouse rather than in cyberspace. Consequently, there are few UK websites dedicated to wholesaling, and even fewer for individual suppliers themselves. However, this is slowly beginning to change and several websites have been created to allow you to purchase goods online, the most common being sites dedicated to selling pallets of items at knockdown prices. 'When buying online, make sure you know exactly what you are purchasing – read the description thoroughly and study any pictures,' says wholesaling specialist Grady. 'If you are not sure, contact the supplier for additional information. Nothing beats a visit to the supplier so that you can see the products before making a purchase. Also, use a credit card to make your payment, that way you have a right of recourse via the credit card company if things go wrong.'

Buying batches or pallets of goods online from wholesalers is different from buying on Amazon, for example, as you may not be entirely sure what you are being sold due to the varied goods on offer in a single purchase. Make sure you have a detailed list of what is on offer and contact the wholesaler if you have any queries. Although it is wise to exercise caution when purchasing online, you can make big savings as internet sales can often be much cheaper, due to lower overheads, than traditional warehouse buying.

> When buying online, make sure you know exactly what you are purchasing

Making a profit

There are several simple steps you can take to make a profit on your wholesale stock.

Cash payments

Simple cash payments may be the most beneficial for your business, as many wholesalers give discounts (see more on this below) to customers who pay upfront in this way. The method of payment, however, depends greatly on the cashflow situation of your company, and it is important not to risk over-stretching your business by making large cash purchases early on. Try to build up the amount of stock from a low level to begin with, to ensure you can sell all of it on and to save valuable funds for the future.

Price matching

Once you have a firm idea of the amount of stock your business can sell on, you can 'price match' wholesalers against each other on large orders. Don't be afraid to ask your supplier to compare prices with someone else for you – wholesalers are generally, contrary to their image, approachable and happy to see your business flourish (as well as keen to keep your custom), and will often knock down their prices to a competitor's level.

Getting discounts

Discounts are given roughly in proportion to the amount of money you spend, much like many other trades that offer such incentives to encourage you to place large orders. Therefore, orders under £200 are generally not going to attract discounts from wholesalers. But don't forget that if you buy goods for the sake of a discount and are left with excess stock and a big hole in your budget you could end up in trouble. So make sure you strike the right balance, meeting your customers' needs without buying too much stock.

! TOP TIPS

DEALING WITH WHOLESALERS

! Get to know the wholesalers that you deal with – this will help you find out when new products are in stock and get the best deals on price

! Don't be afraid to ask one wholesaler to 'price match' another, especially if you are placing a particularly large order

! Don't expect huge discounts unless you are buying in huge quantities

! Startups are unlikely to get an instant credit account. Pay cash up front for a couple of months before requesting credit

! Don't be intimidated – as most suppliers will be more than happy to help you as much as they possibly can

Give it time

Don't be frustrated if you don't see instant profits on your wholesale goods. If you continue to stick to an appropriate budget, shop around for value and strike up a good working relationship with your wholesaler, you should start to see results within a few months. Of course, much of this depends on the size and circumstances of your business, but by sticking to this formula you will be on course to meet the potentially large profits that buying wholesale goods provides.

Insuring your business

Making sure your company is protected against as many disasters as possible could ultimately save it and protect all the time and effort you are likely to put in to making it a success. However, finding the right business insurance can be a difficult and complex process. There is a certain amount of jargon associated with the area, which can put off many small firms. As an entrepreneur you might see your insurance as one of those unavoidable costs – you don't much like it but you will go along with it. However, for many firms it ends up being their life support. You never know if disaster is lurking around the corner, but it is too late to get cover after the incident has happened.

Insurance is also not an area where one size fits all, so don't buy a policy unless you really need to. However, don't fall into the trap of scrimping on costs, as you might find out that you are not covered when the worst happens. Essentially, it is important to understand your own risks, know what the insurance market has to offer and to thoroughly read and understand any policy before committing to it.

Why you need insurance

Aside from legal requirements and demands from customers to have a certain level of liability, you might well think that there is little point to your insurance policy. However, there are many examples of businesses going to the wall following a disaster for which they weren't covered. Similarly there are many instances when a company has bounced back after it looked like it had passed the point of no return, all because it was insured to the very hilt.

You might consider the risks that your business faces to be small or even affordable, but if this is the case, then you are probably underestimating them. The chances of your business being hit by a flood or destroyed by a fire might seem low, but disruption to your work can come from many quarters. For example, a crime in your street could lead the police to cordon off the area for a period of time. Despite not being able to trade, you will still have to pay your staff, rent and other costs, and you could lose a very significant amount of business or incur heavy costs while attempting to maintain it. However, all of this could be prevented with a business continuity insurance deal.

As mentioned earlier, some of your clients might ask about your insurance details before they are prepared to do business with you. Public liability is important for many clients, particularly in the public sector. In a business-to-business setting, an insurance policy acts almost like a credential. By having a high level of cover, you are demonstrating that you are a respectable business, which takes health and safety very seriously, and that you fully understand your own responsibilities. So paying for insurance is far from just dead money, but a way of accessing opportunities that you wouldn't otherwise be able to gain.

Essential cover

There is some insurance that you must have, and this is covered below.

Liability insurance

Nearly all businesses need some level of liability insurance, and employer's liability insurance is the most common one. If you are about to take on staff then you should ensure you have this first. Also, if you are thinking of setting up a limited company then it is a legal requirement, as technically the company is the employer. If any member of your staff is taken ill, suffers injury or dies and this is deemed to be as a result of their work, then you are potentially liable. Therefore, the law states that you must have cover in order to cope with this eventuality. By law, employers must have at least £5m of liability, although many policies offer £10m. There are just under 400 deaths and nearly 30,000 major injuries at work each year in the UK, so you are well advised not to make any savings in this area.

Motor insurance

As any driver knows, motor insurance is a legal requirement, but many come unstuck when using vehicles for work-related activities. You might think that your current insurance covers you, but unless your policy includes work use then you are mistaken. The good news is, however, that this isn't usually expensive and some insurers offer it for free. If you are employing someone who is using their own vehicle for work purposes other than travelling to work, then you have a responsibility to ensure they are fully covered. A work purpose could be as innocent as dropping you off at a meeting – it doesn't matter how minor this seems, they still require business insurance. It is also highly advisable to check with the Driver and Vehicle Licensing Agency (DVLA) that your staff are legally able to drive and take copies of their insurance and MOT documents, as well as their driving licences.

CONTACT

DVLA
www.dvla.gov.uk

Public liability

Public liability insurance, though not compulsory, is something only the most cavalier business would cut back on. It covers you for damage against property or persons that you might encounter during your work. Many clients won't deal with you or can't legally work with you unless you have it, so you might consider it to be obligatory.

Pricing

One of the most important decisions to be made when you start a business is the pricing of your products or services. Customers buying standard products that are available from numerous sources will look for the supplier with the cheapest prices. This makes it difficult, if not impossible, for the small firm to compete with major suppliers who have the advantage of bulk purchasing or mass production. Fortunately, there are niches you can occupy where price is not the most significant consideration, being outweighed in the eyes of the customer by quality, service or uniqueness.

'Small companies often make the mistake of charging very low prices because they feel they must compete on a price-only basis,' warns marketing consultant **Annmarie Hanlon**. 'But there will always be a large company that can afford to drop its prices to squeeze

There are niches you can occupy where price is not the most significant consideration

the small company out. Instead, you should compete on product or service quality. A small company can give an attention to detail which is difficult for a big company dealing with 20,000 customers to achieve.'

Pricing confidence

Having spent five years as a director of the Prince's Youth Business Trust, Hanlon speaks from the experience of being midwife at the birth of numerous businesses. 'There is less confidence in a cheap service than in a more expensive one,' she says. 'Hairdressing is a good example, where there is an idea that if you are paying your hairdresser more you are getting a better hair-do. I know a hairdresser in the Midlands who charges more than anyone else in the area. Customers receive a welcoming neck and shoulder massage on arrival and are given a hot towel to wipe their hands. With these added attentions, a premium price is perceived as appropriate.'

Location and environment

Hanlon points out that location and environment are also important. 'If an establishment in a back street and with no reception area charged the same prices as a lush Mayfair location, its customers would feel they were being ripped off. It's all about ensuring the price is appropriate for the service.'

This is illustrated by what she calls 'the salmon sandwich issue'. She explains: 'If you buy a salmon sandwich from your local sandwich shop to take away in a paper bag you are happy with a price of £1. If you go to a well-known department store, the sandwich is nicely packaged and you have a perception that the quality is better, so

> **To maximise your profits, you will need to think creatively about your pricing structure**

> **Compete on product or service quality. A small company can give an attention to detail which is difficult for a big company**

£1.50 might be acceptable. Then there might be a premium product with finest Scottish smoked salmon and delicious trimmings. For that you might well accept a price of £2.10 because you think it is right for what is being offered. But if the same £2.10 sandwich was being sold for 45p you would wonder what was wrong with it.'

Offer a specialised service

In the retail sector, specialisation can sidestep price competition. Offer a wide selection in a narrow field. Observe what is lacking in an area and not encompassed by the big chains. It's a matter of finding a demand in your area that's not catered for, where your customers will feel they are getting value for money as opposed to cut prices. Family convenience stores that buy from middlemen – wholesalers and cash and carries – cannot match the prices of supermarkets, which buy in vast quantities direct from manufacturers. But their strength can be their location. They usually serve a localised market, such as a housing estate, or they may be situated on a route used by people going to and from work. Open for long hours, they are handy for people calling in for newspapers, confectionery or snack foods, or an 'emergency' purchase such as milk or sugar, aspirin or cigarettes – items that do not justify a trip to the supermarket. And people who call in for just one item often make other impulsive purchases. It's a case of convenience outweighing cost.

Ultimately, when you launch your business, to maximise your profits you will need to think creatively and strategically about your pricing structure to make sure, if possible, that you can charge the maximum by offering a premium product or service that is niche to your area. If there are larger companies offering a similar service, this will be a must.

INNERGY AND THE PRICE POINT

Company: Innergy
Owner-managers: Gez Walsh and Maurice Gardiner

It took a bit of convincing to persuade **Gez Walsh** he was entrepreneur material. Scared of failure and too comfortable in his day job, he was working as a national sales manager at a competitor of the energy business he would eventually go on to start with partner **Maurice Gardiner**.

It wasn't until a couple of years after leaving the energy industry before they plucked up the courage to start Innergy LPG, which supplies liquefied petroleum gas (LPG) to businesses and commercial users throughout West Yorkshire.

Initial research consisted of phoning competitors' customers to ask about the level of service they were receiving, and what Innergy could offer to improve on it. 'Unsurprisingly, price came out as the main concern,' says Walsh. 'Secondly, many customers told us they couldn't trust their current suppliers. LPG is subject to the same price fluctuations as any other fuel. But customers felt that prices only moved upward and that their suppliers were abusing the movement in the price of product.'

As part of its focus on pricing, Innergy now provides a system on its website where clients can check prices against the competition. The company now has around 1,000 customers in the West Yorkshire area, and plans to expand into bulk LPG across the UK. Projected turnover for 2008 is £1.6m, but in order to expand some further borrowing is on the cards.

TELLING THE WORLD

WHAT'S IN THIS CHAPTER

- With everything falling into place, from the completion of your business plan and working on the practicalities of where you will be based to considering the kind of people you may need to employ, it's time to properly formulate and implement your pre-launch marketing strategy – basically tell the world about your company and why they should buy from you. This will ensure you are perfectly placed to get your business off to a flyer. So it's important that you have an understanding of what marketing is all about and the options open to you. Read on to find out about the best approach to take…

What is marketing?

Marketing is the means by which your business identifies, anticipates and then satisfies customer demand. If carried out effectively it will not only ensure that your business is seen and heard, but will also give it the flexibility to adapt to fluctuating customer demands and a changing business environment. Companies that really succeed are those where the owner has a vision for the firm and is dedicated to seeing it through. A marketing plan will help achieve focus and establish the vision. Marketing will help you understand who your potential customers are, place and price the product compared with the competition and also position the company in the marketplace. It will also help identify future opportunities for self-promotion.

Although there are established guidelines to follow, marketing can be a difficult skill to develop. But in terms of successful impact on the future commercial effectiveness of the business, it is worth cultivating. It can offer improved returns and profitability and a greater understanding of realistic business development opportunities. There are no hard and fast rules for timetables for your marketing. As general rule of thumb, it's recommended that you think about what your business would like to achieve three years from now compared with where it would be if you didn't employ a marketing strategy.

With respect to how to set your marketing budget, there are several possible approaches, none of which can claim to be the right way. They include using a percentage of sales, the same spend as last year (which is unlikely to be relevant to a startup), a similar spend to key competitors, and the dubious 'what we can afford'. Of course, in the end it will come down to what you can afford, but initially you need to plan your strategy to find out how much marketing you think is necessary, identify the essentials and go from there. Also, as you see later in this chapter, there are some good marketing methods that don't cost much at all.

Sonja Garsvo, former public relations chief at Apple Computers and now a personal business adviser at Business Link London City Partners, recommends factoring the marketing budget into your

> " Businesses that really succeed are those where the owner has a vision for the firm and is dedicated to seeing it through "

business plan from the bottom up. 'If you can't afford a marketing budget, you have to ask yourself how viable your product is,' she says. One of the major problems for startups when considering marketing is quantifying in advance the expected result for a given spend. But consider Microsoft. While your ambitions may be more modest than those of Bill Gates, his company's domination of the software industry is a testament to the power of successful marketing. Gates targeted potential competitors, undercutting rival Apple Computers, while launching a sustained marketing blitz to become one of the richest men in the world, with PCs dominating the home computer market. Industry observers attribute Microsoft's success as much to its marketing prowess as Apple's lack of it. Of course, in recent years, Apple has carved itself a lucrative niche in the technology sector thanks not only to wonderfully innovative and stylish designs, but also because of – yes, you guessed it – excellent marketing. What's more, Microsoft is now a major shareholder in the company.

> "
> **A marketing plan should be a statement of intent – where you are, where you want to go and how you are going to get there "**

Building a marketing plan

Any marketing plan should include the four Ps:

- Product
- Pricing

- Position
- Promotion.

Building a marketing plan also means drawing up a blueprint for effective marketing. It can also be a useful way of ironing out differences between colleagues about where the business is heading and creating a common goal.

Product and pricing

The key to product and pricing is research. The more thorough your marketing plan is, the better. If your business is going to operate within a specific locality, will the market support it? For example, if you plan to open a restaurant, how many already exist, what type of service do they offer and what are their prices like? How do they position themselves – greasy spoon, haute cuisine or takeaway? Will the locality support another restaurant, or is the area already saturated? Check out your rivals' prices, too, and position your product accordingly.

You need to check whether once you have started your business and want to introduce new products or expand into other markets, the prospects for growth are viable. Perhaps there is a niche for the product/service or the competitors have the market sewn up. Think about how you will sell the service – directly, mail order or via an agency, and the distribution method you will use, where your office will be located and whether you will need to supply after-sales service.

Position

Positioning means creating an identity for your business. You want to stand out from the crowd and be distinctive, so you need to develop a brand identity that is instantly recognisable. This will build a platform from which to launch your product. A business name is important and should reflect the value of the product or the service. See Chapter 6 for more on this subject. To create the brand identity, find a good local designer who can come up with letterheads, signage design, business cards and packaging.

Although design is one those trades that many people think they can do themselves, a professional designer should be able to create a unique identity and appearance for your business. A good local designer need not be expensive and is likely to be a small business itself, sympathetic to your needs and ambitions. To make sure that your logo and brand identity reflect the visions and values of your company, you will need to give the designer a clear brief about your company and what you want it to achieve, including the market you are targeting – as this should all influence the design they come up with. In fact, if a designer doesn't ask for details about the values of your company, your market and your competition – and perhaps examples of logos and branding you admire – then think twice about commissioning them. Ultimately, they should be producing a look and feel for your company that is significantly different from your rivals, appealing to your target audience and also right for your business.

All of these considerations have to be factored into a marketing plan and will form the foundation on which the fourth P – considered to be the classic marketing tool – promotion, is built.

> **You will need to give the designer a clear brief about your company and what you want it to achieve**

Promotion

Customer targeting is the first and most important step in planning any kind of promotional activity. **Jeff Holden** of the Chartered Institute of Marketing recommends asking the following questions to provide a clearly defined target audience:

- What kind of people buy or will buy your product?
- What do your best customers tend to have in common?
- Can you reach all of your customers through the same communication channels?
- Do customers fall into different groups?
- Are there different buying circumstances, for example, planned, impulse or special occasion?

On answering these questions, you will recognise who your customers are. The next step is finding effective channels to communicate your message. These fall into three categories: media advertising (above-the-line), non-media communications (below-the-line) and public relations. Media advertising consists of television, radio, the press, cinema, outdoor and transport. Non-media consists of sales literature, direct marketing, sponsorship, sales promotion and point of sale. Public relations involves a range of activities that attempt to generate a positive attitude towards your company or products.

Initially, you are unlikely to be able to sell to all the people or businesses you have identified as potential customers, simply due to resources. This means that it's important to look at your audience and hone your niche by identifying the best prospects – those you are most likely to get business from. They will not only be those prospects who are most likely to need your product or service, but also those you can reach most effectively and efficiently in terms of both time and expense.

Think carefully about how much time and effort you can afford to put into promoting your business and evaluate the most effective way of getting your message across to the most appropriate people. The internet means that you can reach more people than ever and you have greater potential to take your business to the global level. But the reality is that you need the resources to be able to service such a demand, so initially it's worth scaling down ambitions. In some cases, if you are offering a service that requires your physical interaction with customers, geography will play a key role in delineating your audience, as you will be restricted to how far you can physically travel. So it's best to start by focusing on marketing your business to a core group of prospects well, rather than overstretching yourself, as this is likely to affect the quality of the message you are delivering, with the consequence of reducing its effectiveness.

> **Start by focusing on marketing your business to a core group of prospects well, rather than over-stretching yourself**

CONTACT

Chartered Institute of Marketing
www.cim.co.uk
☎01628 427120

Getting your message heard

There are three key points to remember when advertising:

- Reach
- Frequency
- Impact.

> **A message must have impact to cut a swathe through the myriad of distractions that confront consumers every day**

Reach means getting through to the right audience, in the right circumstances and at the right time: 'Who wants to know about investment products when they are cleaning the kitchen floor and don't have the money to invest?' asks Holden. So successful reach is about selecting the right media and scheduling advertisements for appropriate times. Frequency is about giving the audience a reasonable chance for the message to sink in amid the hubbub of everyday life, while impact pretty much speaks for itself. Your message must have impact to cut a swathe through the myriad of distractions that confront consumers every day, and it must be presented at the most appropriate time.

Media advertising

The three major aims of above-the-line promotion are to inform, remind and persuade your customers about your products, services and the company itself.

The measure of advertising cost is the amount of business that you can generate per pound spent on advertising. Cinema advertising can be ideal for a local restaurant bringing in late evening diners. A recruitment agency can benefit by advertising on panels on local transport and can reach thousands of people in the right categories every day. Many small businesses are finding that local radio can also be a cost-effective medium. However, Garsvo warns against the scattergun approach. 'Shout as loud as everybody else and get attention but be focused about it, don't advertise for the sake of it;

think about who you want to reach and the best way of reaching them,' she says.

Non-media communications

Non-media communication takes a number of forms and its methods are within the reach of every startup business. Sales literature is a familiar tool, ranging from the glossy company brochure to the single-sheet product flier dropped through the letterbox, stuck behind the windscreen wipers of cars or direct mailed. It should be designed with a specific target audience in mind and should convey what the product's key features and benefits are. Direct marketing can be the most effective means of communication, and it embraces all forms of promotion where the buyer is required to respond directly to the advertiser rather than through a retailer or dealer. It includes selling off the page as well as direct mail and telephone sales. Don't forget *Yellow Pages*, and you may want to consider online information services such as Scoot.

As mentioned in previous chapters, it's also worth setting up a website for your company. Getting someone to design and programme a basic one shouldn't be that expensive, and, anyway, keeping it simple is the best strategy as overly complex websites can actually deter visitors. You could also create one yourself, as there are lots of software packages around that can guide you through the process. However, if you are going to set up a website, you will need to let customers know that you are on the internet.

One of the clear advantages of below-the-line marketing over media advertising is that responses can be measured. However, it is worth noting that a 2%–3% return rate is considered the average, 5% is very good and 0% means something is seriously amiss. Sales promotion and point of sales can be used to offer something extra and build in loyalty, such as buy three curries and get one free during the following week. This also has the added advantage of blocking out the competition. Offers such as these can be made at the point of

CONTACT

Yellow Pages
www.yell.com

Scoot
www.scoot.co.uk

DOSH SOFTWARE AND THE DIRECT APPROACH

Company: Dosh Software
Owner-manager: Jonathan van der Borgh

Dosh Software was set up by accountant **Jonathan van der Borgh** to develop new accounting packages for small firms (and subsequently successfully sold to MYOB). Van der Borgh was keen to get a retail presence, but the company was fighting for space on the shelves at stores such as PC World. He quickly realised that direct marketing would be a quicker and easier way to establish the brand. As a new company, explains general manager **Tony Trevillion**, Dosh had to cut the cloth finely and any expenses had to be justified. That is why direct marketing had so much appeal. Dosh could mail to discrete groups, targeting the recipients and honing in on their customer base of accountants and bookkeepers.

One of its first promotions was through an accountancy publication. Dosh placed an advertisement in the magazine (which is distributed to 70,000 readers). In addition, it refined that list and placed a further 10,000 trial copies of its software on the cover of the publication, but only to be received by smaller accountancy firms. The results of each campaign were tracked, and within just one or two weeks the company knew how successful each mailing would be. The mailings were then followed up by telephone calls, both to customers who responded as well as those who did not.

sale or via mail drops, and are often a useful means of giving a startup business a leg up.

Sponsorship can also be an effective tool. Is there a local nursery or community project that needs some equipment in your area? You can provide it and in return work out a deal in which your company gets some promotion. If the cause is worthy it can generate positive word of mouth approval, too. However, do not make too much noise about the sponsorship and your generous donation, as this is often viewed cynically and considered opportunism.

Public relations

PR takes a number of forms, with its purest form viewed as the means by which a company can communicate honestly and accurately with its audience. It includes media releases, product launches and premises openings. To do it effectively, there are simple guidelines to follow. Send a press release to the local paper, or hold a launch event and target the appropriate trade journals. To find out the relevant titles, consult the business section in your local library. Check out the media directories *Pimms* and *PR Newswire*, as both list trade journals, then call the title and find out which journalist covers your area.

Keep press releases simple. Journalists are bombarded with hundreds of press releases every week and have tight deadlines to meet. If your press release is too long, there is a very good chance it will end up in the bin before the third paragraph is reached. Do not make any grandiose claims, as these are usually seen through very quickly. Simply explain concisely and clearly who, what, where

> **PR is generally a cheap form of communication**

KIRSTY'S STORY
We decided to do the early PR ourselves

While the website and creative brand were being developed and then refined, **Kirsty McGregor** started concentrating on marketing her business Entertainthekids.com, designed to inspire parents. Deciding PR was key, she chose a specialist agency from a selection of four. 'We had quite a few ideas for them, but we really didn't get the supportive response we were hoping for from our chosen agency. In the end we decided we should just try to do this early PR work ourselves. After all we had the ideas and the enthusiasm, and we would do as much as we could with virtually no budget. So this is what we did and the results we achieved:

- 'Approaching celebrities (via their agents) with children for an endorsement. *Result:* Kym Marsh provided us with a quote.
- Approaching the monthly parenting magazines for a chance to show them our idea with a view to building a relationship with them in readiness for our launch. *Result:* We met two magazines whose editors were willing to review the site and have made personal contacts with several others.
- Asking my son's nursery, and begging our old primary school, to allow us to carry out some market research on their parents. *Result:* 320 questionnaires distributed, nearly 20% returned, all very positive and they proved we have priced the product accurately.
- Writing a blog and getting it published by a business magazine. *Result:* You are reading the results which first appeared on the startups website.
- Entering the inaugural *Manchester Evening News* Venture Award for young (!) up and coming entrepreneurs, making it into the final three and getting great coverage in the newspaper.'

and when. Invite the reporter along to an opening, but make sure it doesn't clash with press days because they will not turn up.

Try to build a relationship – you may have other information that a reporter could turn into a story and in return you may get a free plug. Remember that the editorial content in newspapers and magazines carries a lot more weight with readers than the advertising. So make the time and effort to send out regular press releases, try to identify individual journalists to cultivate relationships with, offer your services to publications as an expert commentator, propose that you will write a free series of useful (and short) articles or sponsor newsworthy local events. Letters to the editor can also be a surprisingly powerful marketing tool, although its effectiveness may take time to develop. If

! TOP TIPS
SUCCESSFUL MARKETING STRATEGY

For successful marketing, bear these simple rules in mind:

! Start by setting clear objectives for where you want your business to be, in say, three years

! Define your target market and identify your audience

! Decide on the brand and the values you want to transmit, which will be the platform for your business

! Plan your promotion strategy

! Set a budget

! Devise a schedule

! Decide how the strategy will be measured, such as through increased sales, direct responses, coverage received in local press, etc.

! Implement the programme according to the schedule

! Monitor and evaluate the results, so you can assess effectiveness and make more informed future marketing decisions you have a local market, you probably read the same local newspaper as your target audience does – and both of you are likely to read the letters page, as it is often the most popular part of a newspaper. Don't write in unless you have something constructive to say, but you can make sure that you have by reacting to news items, commenting on new government policies and legislation, and any local issues (traffic and the environment are good candidates for a business's viewpoint). Your letter can apply a spin that reflects your business's concerns, and always ensure your business's name is part of your signature.

Low-cost marketing strategy

A good business marketing strategy doesn't have to cost that much. At its simplest, a marketing strategy is all about improving your chances of making sales – usually by making more potential purchasers aware of your products or services, or by making them aware of its desirable qualities (perhaps including its price). In any case it makes sense to optimise your budget. Given the choice between big-bang and little-but-often, good business marketing is less about getting big bangs and more about producing smaller amounts very regularly.

You don't, however, need to spend big, as most of the ideas in your marketing strategy are likely to involve moderate costs. But it will require quite a lot of time and effort from you on a regular basis. The key is to choose the ones that best support your marketing plan, and mix them in with more expensive options to help keep your costs down. Most (but not all) take advantage of the fact that you have a computer and an internet connection.

> " Good business marketing is less about getting big bangs and more about producing smaller amounts very regularly "

Build a mailing list

Collecting the names is the hard part, so give your prospects a reason for them to provide you with their name and address – competitions, an emailed newsletter, the promise of advance information and

CONTACT

Information
Commissioner
www.information
commissioner.
gov.uk

discounts, maybe even a loyalty card. Work at keeping your list accurate and up to date. Try to get hold of email addresses as well as (or even in preference to) postal contact details. Email is cheaper and more versatile than postage, and it can be integrated more efficiently with other aspects of your marketing, notably your website. If your database of names has been gathered in the normal course of business, you might not have to register under the Data Protection Act. This is a complex area, however, and you should check the situation with the Information Commissioner.

Once you have your list, use it. Concentrate on customers more than prospects as they will be more valuable to you, both for repeat business and because they will act as a reference. Looking after your customers so that you retain their custom is actually cheaper than attracting new ones. So be personal. Remember birthdays and anniversaries. Say 'thank you' when they buy (if only by email). Offer them the chance to comment and criticise. Give them special offers not available to anyone else. Make sure they know that your Christmas 'thank you' gift is going to a select few, and that they're in this group.

Ask them to check out new products or services, because they will appreciate being treated as special, and the risk is lower because they're more likely to buy. Look at their past purchase history if possible, and tailor special promotions to them. Find out whether they prefer you to use their first names or a more formal mode of address, and make sure all your mailings and other communications use the appropriate salutation.

Use discount vouchers

A good way to bump up sales volume is to offer discount vouchers, but they can also send a message about your business. It could be customer care (distribute them to favoured clients only), but coupons work better as a value-for-money flag. Distribute them in print advertising ('cut here'), by direct mail, by hand (on the street corner, if appropriate, or at trade shows), and even by email or via the web ('quote this reference to get your discount'). You can also include 'next purchase' coupons with customer orders. The coupon can be a fairly cheap production in terms of design and print, as its main selling point is usually the low price it offers.

Distribute postcards

Postcards are also cheap and easy to produce, especially if you use colour on one side only. They can be mailed to prospects, stacked in help-yourself dispensers, and you can use them for a variety of marketing messages, such as 'see our new product', 'gasp at our new prices' or 'look at our short-term cut-price promotion', and 'enter the competition or the free prize draw (and get two entries if you give us a friend's name and address)'. A reply-paid licence makes it easy for someone to return the card, and these are simple and economical to set up with the Post Office.

CONTACT

The Post Office
www.postoffice.
co.uk

Run competitions and giveaways

People love competitions, even if someone else wins. They are an excellent way to garner mailing list names, while sending branding messages, as the kind of contest your run implies the kind of company you are. Contests can also make for good PR, especially if there's a fun element that will attract media coverage. Of course, you can also simply give them something free, as people like to get gifts, even if they have to pay a premium price for a more expensive item to qualify for the freebie. This could be a free makeup purse with purchases, wine and fruit in your room if you book the weekend break, a CD of business tips with every seminar booking, or a pizza with every DVD film rented.

The aim here is both to boost sales and to tell the world that you are a generous, value-conscious supplier. It also improves your

> **The aim is to boost sales and to tell the world that you are a generous, value-conscious supplier**

competitive sell, since it becomes more difficult to compare like with like.

Start a loyalty programme and a club

The customer gets a good deal from a loyalty scheme and you get a keen customer (and their contact details). A simple approach is to give customers a card that is marked after each purchase and results in a free or reduced-price offering after a specified number of regular-priced purchases. Easier to operate is a loyalty card scheme where regular customers get a discount on purchases on presentation of the card.

You can extend the programme into a full-blown club, sending out newsletters, launching exclusive special offers (great for shifting slow-moving stock), discounts on related products or services (it's generally easy to find other suppliers willing to give your club members a 10%–20% discount in return for capturing the buyer's details for their own database) and seminars and other get-togethers.

Work on your elevator pitch

Every entrepreneur should prepare a short presentation that sums up the great things about their venture. As mentioned earlier in this guide this 20–30-second piece is called an elevator pitch, as you could potentially deliver it while ascending a building in an elevator before the lift stops at your floor. Work on this so that you can recite it in your sleep – but not as though you are delivering a canned presentation.

When people say: 'So, what do you do?' the question they're really asking is: 'How do you make money', but actually saying that is regarded as impolite. So your elevator pitch should answer the unspoken question, but in such a way that identifies the problems you solve or the benefits you can offer, and implies that your business is very successful because it's so good at those problems and benefits.

Make a fun screensaver

Try Xara Screenmaker 3D and give the screensaver away to customers, prospects or anyone who visits your website. All those PCs suddenly become advertising billboards for your business. Screenmaker is recommended because it's cheap, very easy to use and good fun. It also produces pretty good screensavers from your text and/or images (logos, photographs and drawings).

CONTACT

Xara
Xara Screenmaker 3D
www.xara.com/products/screenmaker3d/

Make a mini CD

Instead of handing out a parcel of brochures and your business card, give your prospects and customers all they need on a single disk. And it doesn't have to be a conventional CD-Rom, as you can get neat half-size mini-disks, and 'business card' CDs, which are rectangular but still fit into a standard CD drive. Both have enough storage space to fit at least 30MB of content, which will most likely be enough for your whole website and/or lots of product information.

Work on your website

Search engine marketing has become a specialisation that commands fairly high prices but cannot guarantee success. Search engine 'optimisation' (SEO) involves tweaking your website so that it's more likely to appear early on in the list of results when someone enters a relevant keyword, but that's as far as it goes. In fact, most websites (especially business-to-business) get a minority of visitors from search engines and directories. Rather than spending time and money on a programme of promoting to them and buying keywords, you might be better to concentrate on your own mailing list and make sure that any other marketing materials reference your website – sign-written vans, business cards, promotional flyers, Christmas cards, promotional gifts and so on. In any case, there's quite a lot that you (or your webmaster)

SEO AND MAXIMISING YOUR WEB PRESENCE

Use META tags for keywords, title and description. All these should emphasise three or four key concepts using words that you also repeat in the text and the headings on the page.

Make sure you are listed in all the relevant free directories. The operative word is 'relevant', so don't submit your website to every free directory, or you will be bombarded with junk mail and solicitations to buy further services. Once you've identified the best ones, you might think it's worth taking the inevitable offer of paid-for fast-tracking to get your listing in there sooner.

Most visitors go to commercial websites for information, not for entertainment. Good web design starts with easy, obvious navigation and relevant, easy-to-use content, so avoid jarring colours and idiosyncratic typefaces, over-elaborate grammar and any humour unless it's been thoroughly tested. Include 'click for more information' rather than over-long pages scrolling down to infinity.

Refresh your website regularly. Give the punters a reason for returning, with frequently updated information and tips they will find useful that relates to your business, new products, downloadable freebies and competitions. Redesign it thoroughly once a year, and tell everyone on your mailing list about all major updates (and most minor ones too). You could even send out a regular e-alert about what's new on your site, but avoid doing this too frequently as it could prove annoying.

Choose the right names for your website. That's right, more than one name, with the separate domains all redirecting visitors to your main website. Many businesses will have a slogan or catchphrase, many will be known by contractions, abbreviations or initials, and most are prone to at least some misspelling. Get domain names for as many of the possibilities as you can, because registration is so cheap right now that you might as well cover all the bases (see Chapter 6 for more details about this).

For each name, set up a separate webpage that almost immediately takes your visitor to your main website. With judicious use of the right keywords in the webpage's test and its HTML META tags, this will greatly improve your chances of appearing on Google and other search engines when someone enters the relevant search term. Why? Because Google gives a lot of weight to 'site popularity', the number of webpages that link to yours. The more links to your website, the higher you will be in the results list.

can do without calling in the expensive pros (see box). See page 238 for more on getting the most from your website.

Work on your references

Marketing should focus on benefits rather than features, meaning what you can do for your customer rather than how you do it, so use case studies and testimonials to prove your point. Ideally you need real clients. You can use a photograph and direct quotes to prove they exist. However, a startup could get by with some hypothetical situations, but make it clear that these are not real. Customer stories are good business-to-business website material, and you can use clickable links for specifications and other non-chatty material to prevent the reader being inundated with statistics or technicalities. You can also produce them as single-sheet case studies and include them in brochures, but they should be both relevant and up to date.

Keep up with your email

People who use email expect a speedy response, and providing one is a simple marketing technique that supports lots of good messages: we're alert, responsive, aware of customer concerns, professional, up to date and so on. If you can't reply to incoming email within an hour or so, use an automated system to provide an instant response of some kind. This could be a simple: 'Thanks, we'll get back to you as soon as possible'. But if you've organised your email addresses correctly, a more targeted response should be possible, meaning that incoming mail addressed to products@yourcompany.co.uk could elicit an automated response that includes a PDF document containing product details or an appropriate website link. You can do quite a lot with Microsoft Outlook rules, or check out some of the autoresponder packages on offer.

Always use email signatures

A couple of lines at the bottom of a message identifying you and your company is a simple way for sending out your contact details. Make sure every email carries your 'signature' (including replies to incoming messages) and that everyone in your organisation uses the same signature format. It shouldn't be too long, but should give two or

> **An email doesn't carry the materials and overhead costs of a paper mailshot, and you (probably) don't need the expensive and risky element of visual design**

three alternative ways to contact you and your company, your website address and include a marketing message of some kind, such as 'Sale now on' or 'Winner of the Best Company Prize 2007'.

Email marketing

This is among the simplest and least expensive marketing options. An email doesn't carry the materials and overhead costs of a paper mailshot, and you (probably) don't need the expensive and risky element of visual design. You know almost immediately whether the address is 'live' – still active, or spelled correctly – and you can ask for a read receipt to indicate whether your target has received the message. What's more, you stand a good chance of getting an immediate response, since the easiest time to click on 'reply' or a link to a webpage is while you are actually reading the mail.

This doesn't mean that all email marketing is inherently good, however. For a start it is indelibly associated with spam – unwanted and unrequested junk mail. Make sure that the people on your list actually want (and preferably are expecting) the material you are sending them. There are laws about this now, though they are depressingly feeble. The 'From' and 'Subject' lines are crucial in email marketing. The recipient must recognise the sender – company name or brand are good options if your own name will mean nothing. And the Subject is what will persuade them to read on, so put real effort into finding the right words. People don't read emails, they skim them. You still need good copywriting in an e-newsletter or a sales letter, but if possible you should also include clickable links or buttons for instant access to key online areas.

You can send a test mailing to a subset of your mailing list using two different subject lines. When you track the response, you can see which subject worked best and use that for your main mailing. The same holds true for other marketing methods such as banner advertisements and paid search campaigns. You can start with a low investment, track your returns, and make changes before deciding whether to invest more or try a different tactic. Internet marketing is useful to marketers on a budget because it is flexible, trackable, and offers vast reach for little investment.

Finally, always include an 'Unsubscribe' option in your message, but you may as well make sure that people know what they're missing when they do unsubscribe. Clicking the Unsubscribe button should take them to a webpage which asks them to confirm their decision and to identify what they specifically want to remove. They might not want to unsubscribe from everything and may want your occasional product updates, but not the regular newsletter.

ACTION POINT
KEEPING HOLD OF YOUR CUSTOMERS

Looking after customers is far more important than attracting new ones, according to **Alastair Campbell**, managing director of The Ideal Marketing Company. 'It is far more cost effective to target your resources towards holding onto a customer you already have than to spend a fortune trawling the country to attract a new one,' he says. 'After all, it costs seven times more to attract a new customer than to maintain an existing one. A whopping 75% leave because of "perceived indifference". That means that they stop doing business with you because they feel that you aren't interested in them; that you don't make them feel special anymore. So while you may think you are treating your customers well, most of them probably think otherwise and could be quickly tempted away by a competitor.' Here are Campbell's five easy-to-implement ways on how to keep hold of your customers:

Capture their details and keep in touch with them: At least once a month write to them about a special offer, special product preview, clearance sale, new product line, open evening or whatever. This lets them know that you are thinking about them and looking for new ways to serve them.

Ask them how you are doing: Conduct a customer satisfaction survey on an annual or regular basis depending on your customer base. You can even offer an incentive if they complete the form.

Conduct regular customer forums: This allows you to tell your best customers more about what you are up to and to find out from your customers what they like about your service and products. It can also be a useful opportunity for customers to meet your staff (especially background staff) and of course other customers. If you are feeling brave, let them talk about you while you are out of the room for an hour and then listen to their feedback on what they like and don't like about your company.

Develop more than one contact point: If a buyer leaves or your contact leaves, the relationship between your two organisations disappears overnight, but if you have more than one point of contact, the relationship is far stronger and can withstand the odd member of staff moving on. When a company pairing system is carefully planned your two organisations become so closely intertwined that no other company will get a look in (as it does with Northern Foods and Marks & Spencer).

Be honest: Own up to mistakes, and don't pretend to be something that you are not. You can't build a long-term relationship based on mistrust. A customer would prefer you to hold your hands up to making a mistake rather than trying to shift the blame where it doesn't belong.

Remember: Most companies spend their hard-earned marketing and sales effort attempting to attract elusive new customers when they probably have most of the business they will ever need sitting on their database.

ATTIK AND THE ART OF TAKING RISKS

Company: Attik
Owner-managers: James Sommerville and Simon Needham

Attik is a brand business creating advertisements and design-led identities for many of the world's most successful companies. Formed in 1986 by two 19-year-olds, a £1,000 business grant from The Prince's Trust, some practical advice and a mentor, **James Sommerville** and **Simon Needham** opened their first office in Sommerville's grandmother's attic, hence the name. Needham also cites self-promotion and a 'no holds barred' approach to selling themselves 'in the early days' as a crucial factor.

'We tried PR companies to see if they suited our needs and shared our vision, but it didn't work so we took on an internal PR person who understood our way of thinking and working. When we first started we also had quite aggressive marketing campaigns, such as going around the streets and sticking flyers on walls and buildings, and we'd also do this to recruit people – something no one was doing at the time. We've even got a 6m by 4m poster on the wall next to our Sydney office. We didn't ask, we just put it there.'

This may not be an everyday method to establish brand recognition but it ties in neatly with Needham's fearlessly opportunist nature. 'Taking risks is all part of the game,' he says. 'You can be comfortable and run a business with 10 people and not aspire to grow any further, but you can also be prepared to take a gamble, although you should always have a plan in place in case it doesn't work.' To increase brand recognition as well as revenue, Needham created a separate concept entitled *Noise* seven years ago. Billed as a design bible, *Noise* is an annual publication containing the creative thoughts of all five Attik studios and sells thousands of copies each year.

'The industry needed something more ballsy instead of a standard brochure,' Needham explains. 'We gave it away to begin with, but when people actually came to us and asked if they could buy it, we stood back and let them'.

Opening up outdoor advertising for start ups

Jenny Nguyen, Marketing Manager, Signposter.com

Outdoor advertising is no longer solely the territory of big national advertisers. Through Signposter.com, a revolutionary new service designed to make outdoor advertising easy and accessible for all small businesses, every business can have a big – and well-designed – poster and take advantage of billboard advertising's brand-building, awareness-raising, sales-driving benefits.

Outdoor advertising working twice as hard

Small businesses often assume that local press is the only advertising avenue open to them to reach their target market. However it is more costly than outdoor ads, with the average cost of reaching 1,000 people standing at £22 against outdoor advertising's £2.75; and, in the current economic climate, press advertisers run the risk of surrounding their company's message with uncontrollable negative editorial, which can cast an unwelcome shadow. Outdoor advertising has no editorial accompaniment: all potential customers see is the message you want to get across.

Where could I advertise?

Through Signposter.com you can access 98% of the UK's billboards, so you have complete flexibility to use your local knowledge to decide which site is best for your business.

For example, you could choose a site on the busiest street in your target area or a particular bus shelter that you know is very busy throughout the day.

What makes a good outdoor ad?

Top tips, templates and an editing tool to allow you to adapt existing printed material for a billboard site are all available on the Signposter.com website, but some basic 'rules' to bear in mind are:

• Keep it simple! What is the one thing you want to say, and what is the the easiest way to say it?
• Use a big, striking image and the least possible number of words – it all needs to be legible from a distance
• People read from top left to bottom right so put your 'sign-off' – your logo, perhaps – on the bottom right
• Think about what will appeal to your customers and design your ad around them
• Have fun – if you enjoyed designing your poster, people will enjoy looking at it

---

Contact us:
Signposter.com | 08450 72 82 92 | customerservices@signposter.com

How to make the most of your website

Small businesses often make classic mistakes with their websites, assuming that having built one, even a custom design solution, that they will instantly appear highly in Google and win loads of work. While this can be the case in some situations, it is far more likely that you're going to have to put some legwork in to getting noticed by Google.

Google and the other search engines rely highly on other people linking to your website in order for them to establish how popular your website is. The more popular the website, the higher you return in the search results.

A great way to build these links is to look for forums and blogs that relate to your services. Look for business directories and social networking sites such as LinkedIn and Facebook, and build links to your website that contain the words you want to appear for. This way Google will quickly find your website and know what it's about.

Get out networking and build a list of contacts and regularly (maybe once or twice a month) email them offers or incentives to go to your website such as insights into your area of business – for example a HR company might send one out commenting on the latest change in employment legislation linking through to the full article on their website. This traffic will help Google to establish your websites popularity and will help you move up the search rankings.

Other great ways to promote your website is to advertise your website offline in flyers and promotional literature and drive people to it using call to actions such as 'check out our website for the latest offers'. This will allow people to check your website out and be reinforced by it and convert into paying customers.

You can manage all of this online using Google's Analytics software to track your websites traffic, what people are finding your website under and the pages they spend time on or leave your website from.

Whether you're looking to spend £25pcm or £25,000 on a website make sure you have a good web designer on board. For more hints and tips on how to make the web work for your business visit: **www.plugandplaydesign.co.uk/hints**

OPEN FOR BUSINESS

WHAT'S IN THIS CHAPTER

■ After months of preparation including researching the viability of your proposed business, finding the appropriate name, putting together your business plan and implementing your pre-launch marketing campaign, the time has finally arrived to open your new company for business. You will be feeling a mixture of trepidation and euphoria, and will have to prepare yourself for a few months of heavy work to get your business off the ground. Key to your early success will be setting up effective processes for invoicing, and the vitally important payment collection, not to mention setting yourself a realistic salary. Read on to find out how to approach these essential tasks… we start with the issue of paying yourself.

Paying yourself

Few people start their own business solely for the purpose of be-coming wealthy, and even fewer actually succeed in achieving this. So right from the start, it's essential to consider how much you should be paying yourself.

When starting up you are likely to want to plough everything you can into making sure you give your business every chance of succeeding, but aside from the issues of needing to keep enough back for running costs and marketing, etc., you need to live. The first 12 months, or however long it is until you think you will be in profit, will be a difficult period – in fact, there are more people who scrimp by than make a bucketload of cash straightaway.

Essentially, you need to be realistic. If you have given up the comfort and security of a regular salary, you can't suddenly survive without any income at all. You are also likely to have financial commitments that you will still need to meet, in addition to the new ones you will be taking on by starting a business, so it's important to make sure you take enough to support sensible living costs. If you don't, you may be tempted to borrow more or build up another debt on a credit card – something that will inadvertently place more pressure on your business. Starting a business is also one of the most stressful things you can ever do. Failing to ensure you have enough money to relax when you are away from it will only increase the strain, and again, will prove detrimental to your business.

So how much should you pay yourself? This will be dependent on the sector you are going into and is probably the best place to start looking for answers. Talk to others in the trade or to people with similar sized businesses and ask how much they were able to pay themselves at first, and what they can afford now. If they are not willing to tell you, try contacting trade associations, who should be able to help.

Once you have some idea of what others in the sector are earning, try to fit a similar figure into your financial estimates and see if it's

> **You need to consider, right from the very start, how much you need to live on and what you can afford to pay yourself**

viable. If it isn't, it could be that there's a problem with your business plan as a whole, and it is something you will need to address before you take the plunge. The key is to plan ahead.

Don't be afraid to treat yourself every now and then, but don't go overboard. You will need every penny of your startup funds and profits to put back into the business to help it grow. But don't undercalculate what you can live on either. Be honest about what you need to 'get by' and incorporate that into your costs and your business plan.

Making a sale

Some people seem like they were born to sell, while for many the thought brings them out in a cold sweat. But if you want to make your business a success, then you need to sell what you do – at least until you have the resources to build up a sales team. And even if you may not consider yourself a salesperson, if you can launch a new business you can probably also sell your product or service. In fact, when you speak to your bank, and potential recruits and suppliers, you are essentially selling your business to them to get them to work with you.

A lot of businesses – from clothes shops and online retailers to cafés, bars and restaurants – don't need salespeople in the classic sense, with sales driven more by marketing, such as advertisements in the local press, calls to action on websites, direct mail flyer drops, etc. But for many more businesses, salespeople are a key aspect of generating income and driving profit.

In many cases, simply having the best product or service is not enough. You still need a marketing strategy to raise awareness, and once you've launched, you will need a sales plan alongside it to build up a list of key prospects and sell directly to them. In fact, this is where any sales effort should start – drawing up a list of potential customers. This should consist of people you think should buy from you. Initially, buying in a database of contacts that fit your criteria from one of the many list brokers can be a good way to start.

With the list in place, create a sales story or pitch before you start making contact. You have launched a business on the basis that people would want to buy what you offer, so revisit those reasons. Write down brief points about what you offer, how it can benefit your potential customers and what sets you apart from your competition. Hone the points down to three or four and devise the best way to build them into an engaging story.

Having drawn up the first draft of your pitch, try it out on friends or colleagues who know a little about your sector and canvass their opinions. Tell them to be honest, and ask them to suggest improvements, which you can consider taking into account to make your sales story more effective.

Making contact

Cold calling can be effective, but it isn't for everyone. If you feel this way, you may find it useful to send an introductory email, which you can then follow up, giving you a reason to make contact and also providing a softer opening question: 'Did you receive my recent email about…'

One problem is getting through to the right person. If the list you've bought is what it claims to be, this should be easy, but as people frequently change job or roles within an organisation it's important to ensure the contacts are up to date. However, there is often someone – the 'gatekeeper' – standing between you and your contact. This could be a receptionist or PA who has been instructed not to put salespeople through. This means the less you sound like a classic salesperson the better, so clearly introduce yourself and where you are from, and be polite and friendly, perhaps saying you have only a few questions and won't take up much of your target's time. Don't open the conversation by asking them how they are and not telling them who you are – this will be highly unproductive, even though it is standard cold-calling fare. Ultimately, if you befriend the gatekeeper, you are more likely to get through after a few calls.

POWERCHEX AND THE COLD CALL

Company: Powerchex
Owner-managers: Alexandra Kelly

The service **Alexandra Kelly's** business offers could be used by many types of company, but strategically thinking about the best sector to sell to, and not being afraid to cold call, laid the platform for future success.

Kelly founded her employment-screening firm Powerchex after being made redundant and spotting a gap in the market. Powerchex screens the histories of new recruits to the finance sector, validating everything from credit and police records to employment references. Kelly's team offers a guaranteed five-day turnaround – a promise that impressed the 2007 Startups Awards judges enough to name Powerchex the Service Business of the Year.

When starting up, once she had the IT infrastructure in place, it was time to get some customers on the books. But Kelly wasn't willing to offer her services to just about anyone; she was determined to specialise in helping financial companies, an area that she thought would want her service more than most. And selling her services to the right contacts in the right market has worked wonders. 'It was hard to turn down people that approached us from outside the financial sector,' she explains. 'When you don't have any clients, turning down money isn't easy, but it paid off in the end. We're now asked to bid for contracts as a result of how specialised we are.'

Kelly already had a lot of contacts in the very industry she was pitching to from her previous job, but found that, for her business, cold calling was still more effective than networking for getting the first client on board. 'Even people that were willing to meet for lunch and chat didn't want to sign up,' she says. 'Yet, some of those same companies became clients through us cold calling junior members of their team.'

The point of the initial calls is not necessarily to make a sale, but to nurture a key contact that you can arrange to visit to guide them further towards a sale. Although it depends on your product or service, few businesspeople will agree a sale without at least one face-to-face meeting.

Presenting well

Once you have a meeting arranged, you need to work on a short, engaging presentation that adds key points to your initial phone conversations.

Pre-presentation preparations

Try to keep your presentation to no longer than 20 minutes – even shorter if possible – and then be prepared to field questions. PowerPoint presentations are effective, but a little old hat these days, so if you can use more engaging graphics projected, say, from your laptop, you may make more of an impact. And remember to say that you will need a few minutes to set up, and find out if they have a plain white wall or projector screen you could use.

First impressions do count, so it's important to come across well at that first meeting. Good preparation will help build your confidence and calm your nerves, and always begin by taking a deep breath and smiling, as this will help to relax both you and your audience.

> "Always begin by taking a deep breath and smiling, as this will help to relax both you and your audience"

During the presentation

Speak slowly and calmly, making regular eye contact, as this engenders a feeling of trust and helps you maintain their attention. You should also come over as enthusiastic and passionate, as this can be infectious, but don't overdo it. Also, pay attention to the mood of your audience all the time, and adjust your presentation accordingly. For example, if they start fidgeting or looking bored, move on swiftly if you have more key points to make and wrap up as quickly as you can.

After the presentation

Once you've finished and invited questions, try to answer confidently and knowledgeably, but also don't be scared to say you don't know the answer to a particular query, as this is better than bluffing your way through, and won't come back to haunt you later. You can always research the answer and get back to them.

Lastly, close the meeting effectively. Ask your audience for their opinions and if they are going to buy. Whether they say yes or are undecided, find out what the next steps are, what additional information they need and what factors they will be basing their final decision on. This will help you at the next meeting, if necessary.

Of course, rejection is just as, if not more, possible than clinching a sale, so be prepared for it and take it on the chin. Try to ask your audience the reasons for them not wanting to buy from you, as this can be key information in the development of your offer, and will mean you will get something productive from the meeting. Also ask your audience if they would mind if you contact them in six months or a year's time to review the situation.

Once you've got your first few sales under your belt you will start to build up a network of customers, and further sales should be a little easier – you could well have some good testimonials to back up your pitch.

It is easy to think that once you have closed a sale, you can relax. But the reality is far from it. Often, shaking hands is simply the first in a series of steps to ensure the deal goes through smoothly. Remember to enter the sales negotiation armed with information. If the value or risk of the business transaction is high, it's wise to get as much financial information about the client as possible, to minimise the level of risk to the business and protect against bad debt. Closing the sale is not simply a matter of asking for an order, and establishing terms of delivery and payment. You should also re-state your credit terms to the buyer and present them with your credit application form (free samples are available at the Better Payment Practice Group website: www.payontime.co.uk/collect/collect_cash.html), while establishing a named contact responsible for payment.

> **Shaking hands is simply the first in a series of steps to ensure the deal goes through smoothly**

The importance of getting paid

Half of all new businesses fail during the first two years. All too often the cause of failure is not the quality of the product or service, the effort and talents of the people, or the sales and marketing. It is quite simply down to financial failure – running out of money – which leads to closure, if not bankruptcy. In many cases, this failure could have been avoided by simple but effective planning from the outset. In too many new businesses, well-qualified people enthusiastically develop their goods or services, but pay insufficient attention to cashflow. Late payment erodes profits and stifles growth.

EXPERT OPINION

ACCEPTING ONLINE PAYMENTS

Shai Meijers, Marketing Manager of ChronoPay offers advice on accepting online payments for internet businesses.

With growing usage of the internet, for many businesses accepting online payments provides major benefits. Customers increasingly expect this facility and it can improve your online sales.

Accepting credit cards online will mean that you will be able to attract both regular and impulse buyers. Setting up a system in order to accept credit card payments online will also provide security for conducting your transactions.

Getting started

Setting up a merchant account

To accept online credit card and debit card payments on your website you must set up a merchant account with an acquiring bank (this means the bank will accept all credit card transactions, regardless of which bank has issued the card).

A merchant account is an agreement with a bank that allows you to accept payment by credit and debit card. This is a separate account from your business bank account and because not all banks are acquiring banks, you can have an internet merchant account (IMA) at a different bank from the one where your business bank account is located. The bank deposits the daily proceeds from your online sales into this account, deducting all service charges and fees as well.

The payment gateway system

The next step for accepting credit card payments from your customers is to use the online payment gateway system from your Payment Service provider. The payment gateway gathers all the information necessary to process the card, encrypts the information, and sends that information to Visa or Mastercard. The payment gateway allows the transmission of all the necessary information to the Payment Service provider who then handles the actual transaction on behalf of the website and the person buying the product and/or service.

Why you need a shopping cart

Probably familiar to you as a consumer, a shopping cart is a series of scripts that keep track of products a customer chooses to buy from your site until they move on to checkout.

A shopping cart acts as a front end which passes information via a secure connection to a payment gateway. Shopping cart scripts come in many shapes and sizes and at many prices too. A good shopping cart script will guarantee security and stability at any stage of a transaction, handling the complex data encryption processing while providing an easy-to-use shopping cart interface for your customers.

Fraud prevention

E-commerce fraud has increased significantly in the past few years. It is therefore important for you as a merchant to protect your online business against possible financial loss caused by fraud.

Chargeback fraud is an increasing concern especially for online retailers, where people buy something online with credit and then report the purchase as fraud. The Payment Service Provider

can help you avoid chargebacks with their fraud screening services, which is included in your monthly fee. Most payment gateways now offer real time fraud prevention.

Fees

The fees associated with various merchant accounts vary widely and can change depending on the e-commerce website's average ticket size and average number of transactions per month. Typical fees include transaction, discount, and set-up or application fees and could range in price according to the Payment Service Provider and your business (credit history, type of business, transaction volume).

Lastly, Online Payment Service providers will let you know what is required from a merchant to open an account in their bank; e.g. business account, business or a reseller licence, proof of a return policy, tax return document, etc. Once your account with a merchant provider is setup, you can start charging and processing credit cards in your online store.

For more information on the best online payment gateway contact Chronopay at www.chronopay.com

LUXTECH AND THE WISE MOVES

Company: LuxTech
Owner-manager: Russell Lux

The quickest route to sales isn't always picking up the phone and talking to someone directly. In **Russell Lux's** case, the environment in which he set up his IT support services company LuxTech was ripe for networking, and he exploited this to the full. Starting up in the spare room of Lux's London flat, LuxTech was founded in January 2001 and raised its first invoice in July 2002. Embellished with £2,000 of funding, which came from Lux's savings, the business was initially simply equipped with a computer with broadband connection.

Lux first gained clients through word of mouth. He targeted solicitors and accounts as they are client-based businesses and could recommend his services on to others. 'I built up a good reputation,' he recalls. 'London is a huge market to attack, but I had to do business through an introduction. It was very difficult to walk in off the street and introduce yourself.'

The increasing number of clients saw the business naturally outgrow the flat, prompting LuxTech to relocate to a small serviced office. It turned out to be a smart move, which saw a sharp increase in clients. This was because Lux used his networking skills to win the business of 22 other startup companies who also used the serviced offices within the first six months. It's a trick he repeated when moving to larger serviced offices in Camden, north London. LuxTech took on 42 extra clients – every business in the building.

'We moved into serviced offices because we didn't have any infrastructure costs – we didn't have to pay for desks, chairs or telephone systems,' Lux explains. 'We found the place through the internet and made lots of business contacts while there. It was great for them because we were on their doorstep – they had IT support literally down the corridor. It was like a large corporate – you had an IT department, a finance department and a marketing department there.'

A sale is not really made until it has been paid for, so the discipline of ensuring prompt payment, called credit control or credit management, has to be a priority if a business is to succeed, rather than payment being an afterthought. Establishing it as a priority means you can then consider granting customers credit where appropriate. But this should be calculated risk, never a gamble. You must know who you are dealing with, and this should be part of the preparation before a sale.

> **Late payment erodes profits and stifles growth**

Credit and creditors

Granting credit to a customer involves the risk of non-payment and so should only be done after checking and assessing that risk. A bad debt means that a company could have to make sales five – or even 10 – times the value of that bad debt just to recoup the loss. Research shows that the longer a trade debt remains unpaid, the greater the risk that it will never be paid. For many companies, their receivables – the money owed to them by their customers – are their largest assets. Figures from BACS – the banks' automated clearing system – show that growth businesses have a combined overdraft of £4bn. Reducing the amount owed by debtors cuts the overdraft and frees up capital to be used to finance the business, and reduces the stress of running the business.

You can get some basic training in credit control even before you have made your first sale. Local chambers of commerce usually have courses available, including such topics such as how to collect a debt over the phone. These are open to non-members. The government-sponsored Better Payment Practice Group (BPPG), which was formed to reduce late payment of commercial debt, publishes advice on the subject.

From the outset, establish procedures for credit applications by customers:

- Produce a credit application form: you can download an example at www.payontime.co.uk/collect/collect_cash.html
- Make credit terms very clear
- Ensure that all staff are aware of your credit policy
- Make payment terms a condition of sale
- Make sure that every buyer signs, agreeing to your credit terms.

Then, to help ensure you receive prompt payment:

- Design a clear invoice, which will always state agreed payment terms
- Send out invoices promptly and keep paperwork up to date

CONTACT

Better Payment Practice Group www.payontime. co.uk

- Establish a timetable for chasing debts, starting with the first request for payment: the invoice.

Establishing customer credentials

It is important to establish a potential customer's credentials. Obviously if your sales are low value/high volume, this will not be practical, but many companies have a small number of major customers, the effective management of whom is crucial to success. In these cases, a visit to a potential customer's premises will usually tell you a lot. The annual report of companies is also useful (although the information could be out of date). For particularly high-value or high-risk orders, obtain a credit report from a credit reference agency. Such reports cost between £3 and £25, depending on the level of information.

For very small orders, buying a credit report may be uneconomical and you may wish to take the risk yourself, but for significant orders, it's well worth the expense. Bank and trade references should always answer specific questions, such as: can I grant £500 credit, or what proportion of this firm's payments to you are overdue? However, they should not be solely relied on. If you have a new customer, confirm their address to avoid fraud, and find out how long they've been trading. If they are on a short lease, they could disappear with the goods. Also confirm that they have the cash to pay. There's no need to check their profit and loss account yourself, because a credit reference company will do it for you – and they will suggest a credit limit and a credit rating. For potentially high-value orders, take a credit report prior to negotiation, to avoid wasted effort. Credit costs and knowing the risks in advance helps in pricing.

Remember that credit control is a continuous process. Always monitor your debtors as their circumstances may change.

Deciding a credit limit

A credit reference agency may recommend a credit limit or you can do it yourself, deciding whether a firm is high risk – a late payer, for example with adverse information such as county court judgments against them or dubious individuals involved – or low risk, with a good

> **Credit control is a continuous process**

payment record and strong credit references. If you decide to grant credit, set up an account and write to the customer confirming this. Always have delivery of goods confirmed through a delivery note and follow up with a phone call, confirming that goods were delivered satisfactorily. Then invoice immediately, re-stating credit terms, and quoting an order number if appropriate.

Dealing with debtors

A new customer can equal more profits to your firm, but it could also spell disaster if they turn out not to be what they originally seemed. It may sound obvious, but it's vital to be sure of customer's identity to help avoid the heartache of receiving a 'gone-away' notice in response to your invoice. Start by getting complete and correct contact details for every customer via a proper account opening form. This must include the correct address and telephone details, which should be checked against alternative sources, such as the *Yellow Pages*. In the case of a limited company, request the full limited name and registration number, and for a proprietorship and partnerships, ensure that you take private address details and telephone numbers. The Better Payment Practice Group has a sample account opening form on its website (www.payontime.co.uk/collect/credit_app_pre. html). Using a credit reference agency to check the credit viability of new and existing customers will often reveal any address anomalies, which can then be confirmed directly with your customer.

Once you have established the new relationship, maintaining regular contact means you quickly become aware if a debtor relocates. Do not just issue invoices and wait for payment. Contact customers by phone to enquire politely whether your invoices have been received, and in doing so, you can verify that the address and telephone details you have remain accurate. Ask delivery staff to alert you to anything suspicious about the way goods or services are delivered, such as if the customer insists on collecting the goods, without adequate verification of their trading addresses.

TRACING A DEBTOR

If a letter is returned via Royal Mail marked 'Addressee not known' or 'No longer at this address', never assume this is actually the case. Many practised debtors simply return a letter as 'gone away' to give themselves more time. Start by taking the following steps:

1. Check your own information to see if you have made any errors on the original details. If you identify an error, re-issue your invoice immediately using the correct details.
2. Dial telephone numbers and re-check via a directory enquiry facility to ensure that you have the correct number.
3. Try a recorded delivery letter, as this may be accepted and thus confirm occupancy.
4. If the debtor appears to be no longer trading from the premises you have details for, then consider the following:
   - Contact the debtor's local Royal Mail sorting office as it may have forwarding addresses, or may confirm that the subject is still at the original address.
   - If you operate in the vicinity, use your delivery drivers or staff to seek information from the address or from its neighbours. However, you must have due regard to the Data Protection Act 1998. In particular, do not divulge any information about a debt to non-interested parties. You should say that you are seeking general information on a 'private matter', asking if there a forwarding address that they know of.
   - If you know any other suppliers that your customer uses, contact them to enquire if they have been notified of their change of address.
   - For businesses rather than individuals, use the *Yellow Pages* for the area of enquiry to identify and telephone businesses/newsagents in the locality who may well know the business or have useful information on the business's status. Again you must have due regard to the Data Protection Act when making such enquiries.
   - Look at the status or credit reference report you may have obtained when opening the account as this may give you alternative addresses. In the case of a limited company, you are entitled to contact the directors, particularly the company secretary, who has an obligation to inform any interested party of the status of the limited company.
   - You can contact these individuals at their home address or an address lodged with Companies House, but you cannot make them individually liable for any debt. A polite question should help you establish whether, for example, the company has entered liquidation, or a Creditors Voluntary Arrangement. If this is the case, you may need to seek professional advice about your rights as an unsecured creditor to a limited company. If these efforts fail then you could seek the help of a professional collection/tracing company who may quote costs, usually from £50 to £60.

Handling debt collection and your debtors professionally and effectively can help protect your company against a bad payment that could send the business under.

CONTACT

Credit Services
Association
www.csa-uk.com

> **Future growth always depends on cashflow**

> **Some customers will pay promptly while others are habitual late payers**

Late payment and how to avoid it

Whether you have a manual accounts system or a computerised one, it is important to prioritise debts, chasing the largest first. It is crucial to establish strong relationships with major customers to ensure prompt payment. Remember, the longer a debt is outstanding, the less likely it is to be paid.

So when payment is due, don't be afraid to ask. After all, it's your money, and if you have done the job right, you are entitled to be paid. Any disputes or complaints that delay payment must be addressed immediately. Some customers will pay promptly whereas others are habitual late payers. Establish a timetable for chasing debtors (see the box for an example) and to keep receivables under control. The suggested procedures should be supplemented with phone calls – one of the most effective methods of chasing debts – and faxes, emails and visits. Some businesses choose not to undertake their own credit control, but have someone else do all or part of it for them by outsourcing.

Techniques worth considering are debt collecting agencies, credit insurance, factoring, retention of title or payment in advance. 'There are a range of ways in which third-party outsourcers are being used,' says **Colin Thomas** of Graydon UK, a credit referencing agency. 'If you have limited resources, you can bring in an outsourcing company that can provide some immediate level of expertise. Future growth always depends on cashflow. Outsourcers can cover the entire order-to-cash cycle. You can choose whether your outsource partner operates in your name or in their own name. In the cash collections field, you may prefer them to operate in your name at the receivables stage and then in their own name for accounts that become overdue.'

Debt collecting agencies

'We're very much involved in advising small-to-medium-sized firms in ways to tighten procedures and collect debts,' says **Trevor Phillips** of consultancy Credit Professionals. 'Debt collection requires pleasant persistence. It's a selling job. Companies have to persuade customers

---

TIMETABLE FOR DEBT CHASING

Here's a sample schedule for chasing money you are owed:

- The sale: send out invoice
- 21 days: send statement reminding payment due after 30 days
- 30 days: if not paid, send reminder statement, re-stating terms and pointing out payment is overdue
- 45 days: send reminder, re-stating payment is overdue
- 50 days: stop supplies until paid
- 60 days: send final reminder
- 90 days: assign debt to collection agency

---

that they have to be paid. Once a debt is more than 60 days overdue, a company has probably exhausted all its own internal resources for collecting the debts, therefore, it is necessary to intervene with a third party.'

Many debt collection agencies have relationships with credit reference agencies giving them leverage to collect. Of course, there is a cost, typically between 1% and 5% of the sum, depending on circumstances. Under the Late Payment of Commercial Debts (Interest) Act 1998, a company can charge interest to its debtors on late payments. Many collectors have solicitors associated with them and can handle litigation if it is necessary to sue for a debt. It shouldn't be seen as a sign of weakness to pass on a debt to a collection agency. Simply view it as an extension of your business. A new business should be equally as professional as a large one in pursuing outstanding debts.

Credit insurance

Credit insurers, such as Euler Trade Indemnity, will insure against the risk of bad debt. Insurance companies can be contacted through the Association of British Insurers.

CONTACT

Association of
British Insurers
www.abi.org.uk

Factoring and invoice discounting

Factoring is a popular choice for new businesses because it helps avoid cashflow problems. In both factoring and invoice discounting, small businesses borrow against sales as a means of sustaining cashflow. Invoice discounting also involves a company loaning you a large percentage of the money for each invoice as soon as it is raised, which is then repaid plus a commission fee when payment is received from your customer within a specified time period. Under factoring the company will also chase the debt for you, for a larger commission payment. The key difference between the two is that in invoice discounting you continue to chase the payments yourself and the service is usually undisclosed to customers.

There are two types of factoring: recourse factoring, which excludes bad debt protection, and non-recourse factoring, which includes it. In the latter case, if a credit-approved customer fails to pay an undisputed debt, the factor will credit you with the amount of the debt.

Retention of title

Retention of title – keeping ownership of goods until they are paid for – has only limited application. It can't be used where you are supplying a service such as cleaning or architecture, or where the goods supplied are then made into something else, as in flour in a bakery.

Payment in advance

Credit is a privilege, not a right, and in some circumstances it may be appropriate to ask for full or part payment in advance – for example, when making a large order, which would extend the supplier's financial resources, or if a customer is not deemed creditworthy. In other instances, credit terms could be reduced to, say, one week, instead of the normal 30 days.

Credit is a privilege, not a right

EXPERT OPINION

CONTROLLING CASHFLOW

Matthew Holmes, Managing Director of Liquid Accounts offers advice on keeping the money coming in.

When you are starting out in business it's very easy to get carried away with the novelty and excitement of it all, and forget about the more mundane stuff such as admin and accounting. So it's important to get some systems in place right from the beginning (ideally using some software, even if it's just a spreadsheet). It's easier to do it now while you've still got the time, and can get into a habit, regularly setting some time aside to get your finances up to date, and review what they're telling you. (Are your sales going up and down? Are you making enough money to cover your costs?) Liquid Accounts regularly gets clients coming who only realise they've got a problem when they've got their first VAT or tax return to do, or their business adviser cannot help them until they've got some up-to-date figures. Here are Liquid Accounts' top five tips for getting it right:

Make sure you bill as soon as possible: It may sound obvious, but as soon as you've done the work, send the invoice! Don't be afraid to be prompt – you are only asking for money that's owed to you, and they're not going to pay you unless you ask for it. If your payment terms are 30 days (see below), and you wait another two weeks before you raise an invoice, you are only going to get your money after 44 days at the earliest.

Set payment terms and stick to them: If you decide to put on your invoices when you will like the bill to be paid (normally 'on receipt', 7, 14 or 30 days), known as payment terms, don't be afraid to make a quick call on the first day that the invoice is overdue to ask when you can expect payment. If someone is a habitually bad payer (or you need to improve your cashflow), don't be afraid to shorten your payment terms, or use your rights to charge interest (under the Late Payment of Commercial Debts (Interest) Act 1998). Big companies in particular can be particularly bad payers, and so don't be afraid to use these rights – that's why they exist.

Have a debt collection system in place: To make sure that all the above happens you need to have good accounting software that flags up for you when people haven't paid and someone keeping an eye on things and doing the chasing. Early on, this is probably going to be down to you, but as you grow you may consider having someone do this for you, such as a professional debt collection agency.

Consider using sales order processing and purchase order processing: On a basic level, this can mean anything from making sure that you get a signed letter of confirmation for everything you sell and everything you buy, through to issuing a full contract for each piece of work you do. Whichever route you take, it will make it easier for you to chase a debt or dispute a bill if a problem arises, and even without a full contract in place, it will be easier for you pursue a legal course of action. And you will be more likely to get a result (if they've signed for it, they can't say that they didn't want it!). Big companies will automatically have these processes in place, so don't put yourself, as the little guy, at a disadvantage. Any good accounting software should have sales order processing and purchase order processing as an option, and so it should only mean an extra five minutes' work – think of it as an insurance policy. Your accountant, lawyer or debt collection agency should be able to advise you on what you need.

Consider changing to cash accounting: Liquid Accounts' top tip is that if you are VAT registered, consider changing to cash accounting. This means that you only pay the VAT on your invoices once you've received the money, and it will really help if you don't know exactly when you are going to get paid. Obviously you would need to take advice from your accountant and check the rules of cash accounting before switching, but the good news is that you don't have to notify Her Majesty's Revenue and Customs (HMRC) of the change. Again, any good accounting package should have cash accounting built in as an option.

For more information contact Matt Holmes on 0845 450 7304; matt.holmes@liquidaccounts.net or visit www.liquidaccounts.net

Private limited companies and their subsidiaries are obliged to publish the time taken to pay suppliers in their annual report and the Federation of Small Businesses produces annual league tables of companies' payment records, while credit reference agencies focus on recent payment trends. Adverse information, such as county court judgments or previous insolvencies involving directors, clearly indicate high risk. This information is available from official sources such as the Registry Trust or the Insolvency Service for a fee, and is also included in credit reports. Basic information can be obtained from Companies House, but, again, a credit report includes this information. Good credit management should aid, not inhibit, the sales effort. The key is obtaining good information and setting up effective procedures. Making the effort at the beginning can save much wailing and gnashing of teeth later on.

CONTACT

Better Payment Practice Group
www.payontime.co.uk

Institute of Credit Management
www.icm.org.uk

Asset Based Finance Association
www.abfa.org.uk

Federation of Small Businesses
www.fsb.org.uk

Companies House
www.companieshouse.gov.uk

! TOP TIPS

ASSESSING CUSTOMER RISK

If your sales are high value and low volume make sure that potential customers can pay, by:

! Confirming their address

! Establishing how long they've been trading

! Visiting their premises

! Consulting their annual report

! Running a credit check through a credit reference agency

! Collecting payment

Travel and expenses

Few people actually know how much they spend each year on travel and expenses and most would have to take valuable time researching to get the answer, and they should. Travel and entertainment – or T&E as commerce likes to call it – amounts to the third largest controllable corporate cost, just behind salaries and data processing, and as a small business, it could be a leakage in your profits and something you need to keep under control. You are also likely to spend more on T&E than advertising. So it's even more concerning that so few companies can actually put an annual total on such a vital part of their operation. As a startup, this is your opportunity to redress the balance and keep a close track of T&E from the start.

MINIMISING TRAVEL COSTS

Whether you work by yourself or run a company employing several people, travel expenses will need to be minimised wherever possible. Here there are a number of easy steps that you can take to help control your costs.

Don't just take the most obvious route: A business can save almost a third by sending an executive via Paris to Los Angeles instead of flying direct from London. If you operate away from London and would be paying for a connecting flight, say from Aberdeen or Manchester, it may well benefit you to skip London and go direct to Paris.

Think about downgrading: When arranging business flights, ask yourself if business class is really necessary. Of course, for many startups 'slumming it in the back' may well be the only affordable way to go – but it can make better business sense anyway. Equally, using secondary airports or 'no-frills' airlines can cut costs significantly. For example, a return flight to Geneva, from London Gatwick, is six times cheaper with a low-cost carrier.

Loyalty schemes: If you will be travelling to see the same client several times a year, there may well be an opportunity to negotiate a better rate. It is also important to remember that a travel policy is more than just about the flights. Using the same hotel chain on a regular basis can also cut costs with a negotiated rate. And for individual travellers, who happen to be with the company too, loyalty schemes are worth using. Free points towards flights and hotel bills all help the bottom line.

Get in the professionals: You could use a company, such as American Express, which will help you to implement and follow a travel policy, organising travel for you and negotiating better rates on your behalf.

A formal travel policy and improved T&E management. With any travel policy, the balance is between the benefit of the travellers and the cost saving for the company. And this isn't simply a cost issue. Time out of the office has to be managed efficiently. No one can afford to miss too many important calls and it may be difficult to hand over to anyone else to 'hold the fort' while you are away. Then, of course, these days there is concern over a company's environmental impact, of which travel can play a major part, particularly with respect to air travel.

Bookkeeping

One of the most daunting things about giving up full-time employment to start your own business is the prospect of looking after the company accounts. For an ex-employee who is used to having his or her tax and National Insurance contributions (NICs) deducted at source via PAYE (pay as you earn), the prospect of dealing with the vast, looming shadow that is HM Revenue & Customs can be quite daunting.

It's tempting to say that there's no need to worry and that the entire bookkeeping process is child's play, but that wouldn't be strictly true. If it were, accountants wouldn't be paid so well. But HMRC is not – perhaps contrary to popular belief – a bullying, authoritarian organisation. On the contrary, its aim is to help businesses manage their accounts as effectively as possible. To this end it publishes regular newsletters and leaflets giving tips and guidance on bookkeeping, and has teams of advisers on hand to help out over the phone should you run into difficulties.

> " HMRC has teams of advisers on hand to help out should you run into difficulties "

Sole traders

If you are setting up as a sole trader rather than as a company with employees, then your bookkeeping work can be kept to a minimum. There's the added advantage that sole traders pay less tax than any

> **You can manage your accounts by hand, but it's easier to do it using a computer**

other class of working people, although you have to be careful that you don't fall foul of the IR35 regulation. This rule, which quite simply states that if you look like an employee, you are an employee, was introduced to prevent contractors working on site for single clients for long periods of time, effectively acting as employees, but invoicing as sole traders or single-employee limited companies.

As a sole trader, you have to keep track of monthly income and expenditure, which means holding on to all invoices and receipts. You will also have to talk to HMRC about National Insurance Contributions (NICs) – the easiest way to handle these is by setting up a direct debit, and the amounts involved are quite small. You could manage your accounts by hand, but it's easier to do it using a computer. A spreadsheet will suffice, containing columns for income, expenditure and VAT (if you are VAT registered). This means keeping track of all invoices (along with the dates they were issued and paid) and all receipts for work-related transactions, including any ground rent, telephone bills, heating and electricity costs and so on. If you work from home, some of your household expenditure may be tax deductible. This is all the information you will need to fill in the tax return form each year. You can then either attempt to calculate the amount of tax owed yourself or send the form to HMRC and let it do it for you. It's actually all quite easy and shouldn't take more than a couple of hours each month.

Partnerships and limited companies

Things get a little more complex once you start employing people, because you will have to look after their salaries as well as the general company accounts. You will have to manage the deduction of their tax at source, payment of employer and employee NICs, plus any pension schemes, bonus arrangements and non-salary expenses. The process is far quicker and simpler than it ever was thanks to bookkeeping software packages, which also let you plot graphs of profit and loss or income and expenditure, track overdue payments (both incoming and outgoing) and the more advanced tools can even automate the submission of the relevant forms to HMRC. Options available include QuickBooks Mind Your Own Business (MYOB), Sage Instant Accounting/Payroll and Liquid Accounts (online accounting software), which can all be used for companies of up to 20 employees – and don't be put off by the relatively low cost of these packages. Most of these packages are powerful accounting tools that can double as business assessment and stock control systems, giving you a real feel for which areas of your business are doing well and which are failing. For the sake of convenience, it's best to ask your accountant which software package he or she prefers to use and then buy that one for internal use.

When it comes to doing your company accounts, you will be better off finding a good accountant. Note that they won't do the donkey work of everyday data input for you, unless you are prepared to pay extra – a lot extra. What they will do is take the figures you have provided for the year and plug those into various forms to tell you the amount of money you have to pay for each class of tax. See page 272 for more on accountants and finding the right one.

VAT considerations

For companies, and sole traders for that matter, with annual turnovers exceeding a certain amount (currently £68,000), quarterly VAT returns must be completed and sent to HMRC along with any payment due.

The VAT form is very simple – just a single page – and usually works in the company's favour. This is because, although you must pay VAT on any income generated, you can claim back VAT paid on some goods and services, such as office supplies, vehicle servicing, fuel and so on. So the extra accounting is definitely worth it and even companies with turnovers less than the VAT limit can still register voluntarily. Remember that the standard rate of VAT was changed recently to help kick start the economy during the recession. Having been 17.5% for years, it was reduced to 15%. However, not all products and services attract the standard VAT rate, so ask your local

CONTACT

For the most -up-to-date VAT registration information: HMRC http://www.hmrc. gov.uk/vat/start/ register/index.htm

ACTION POINT
KEEPING ON TOP OF TAX AND ACCOUNTS

In your first year of operation it will seem as though there's an endless array of forms to be completed and taxes to be paid, whereas in fact there aren't really so many. Although your accountant will guide you through the process, it pays to understand the tax and accounting demands on your business, and if you bear in mind the following basics, you won't go far wrong.

During the tax year you must:
- Deduct the correct amount of PAYE from your employees' pay
- Work out the amount of NICs that you and your employees have to pay
- Keep a record of your employees' pay and PAYE and NICs due
- Make monthly or quarterly payments of the total PAYE and NICs due to the Accounts Office
- Manage VAT return completion and payment on a quarterly basis

At the end of the tax year you must:
- Send a Return (form P35) and an End of Year Summary (form P14) showing details of each employee's total pay and the PAYE and NICs due, to your HMRC office
- Send details to the Inland Revenue office about expenses you have paid to employees or benefits you have provided (forms P11D and P9D)
- Give each employee (who has paid PAYE or NICs and is still working for you at the end of the tax year) a certificate showing their pay, PAYE and NICs details (form P60)
- Give each employee a copy of the information you have given your HMRC office about their expenses payments and benefits provided (duplicate of form P11D)

At the end of your company's accounting year you must:
- Send a formal return for your company's accounts to your HMRC office
- You should receive copies of the *Employer's Bulletin* from HMRC along with the Employer's Annual Pack. Request the copies if you haven't received them within a month or so of starting your business, as these provide useful tips on the above duties, plus contacts and advice for business owners
- The percentage of companies audited each year by HMRC is quite small, but the organisation has effective ways of tracking suspicious returns. The auditing process is thorough and time-consuming, since all receipts and invoices must be checked against the returns and shown to the investigating accountant. Also, the Statute of Limitations is biased in the auditors' favour, so you may have to dig out paperwork going back many years. This means that you may want to take out auditing insurance with your accountant. The work involved during an audit is considerable – allow for three days at the very least – and could become very expensive if you pay your accountant by the hour.

HMRC office for its introductory video that explains the basics of VAT accounting. If that's not enough, you can also enrol on a brief course, again run by HMRC, which will go into greater detail.

Try to keep track of changes to tax regulations. This means listening to the entire budget speech! Your accountant should do this for you, but it doesn't hurt to know about VAT limits, along with changes in basic tax rates and company car regulations yourself. Above all, tempting as it may seem, don't ever attempt to 'cook the books'. Penalties for tax evasion are high. It's not worth the sleepless nights and feelings of guilt just to shave a few pounds off your tax bill, and there's always the chance that you will be found out, especially if you are audited.

Ultimately, you should remember that you are expected to account for every single business-related penny spent – this includes invoices for trade magazines and newspapers, for example. Although there may be some discretionary leeway, you are expected to show each month's transactions in sufficient detail that your profit and loss, income and expenditure – and therefore tax – can be clearly calculated.

> **Above all, tempting as it may seem, don't ever attempt to 'cook the books'**

Why you need an accountant

You might think that a startup or small business isn't big enough to warrant an accountant, but unless you are an expert in tax and finance – in short an accountant yourself – this simply isn't the case. An accountant can provide your business with a great deal of essential support. If you are just starting a business, your accountant will take the form of another business adviser. As mentioned in previous chapters, they can give advice on your business plan and the tax issues of registering your company. Some accountants offer bookkeeping services, but if they don't or if you wish to handle this yourself, you can get help with setting up manual or computerised bookkeeping systems. And most importantly, you need an accountant to assist on things such as whether it is necessary to register for VAT or PAYE and the procedures involved. You can also ask them for help with budgeting and forecasting cashflow, as well as credit control and general financial advice. They can also offer you up-to-date information on any general or legal enquiries.

An accountant can also advise you on the best way to arrange additional finance without putting your business at risk. Once you have the finance in place, there needs to be some control to ensure the growth of your business is handled in the right way. Many of your concerns will be financial – adequate working capital, good stock control, invoicing and so on – and an experienced accountant's advice can prove invaluable in such matters. Furthermore, can you honestly say that you are on top of all the essential taxation issues? Well, that's also an accountant's job – taxation is a large business expense and an accountant can effectively minimise these costs.

Finding an accountant

A simple internet search will throw up lots of accountants in your area. There are many ways to track down the right accountant for your new business, one of the best of which is through recommendation. Simply ask friends and contacts if they would recommend their various accountants. Also ask businesses around you if they use someone locally. Your solicitor and bank manager will be working with accountants all the time, and they will probably have a good idea of the firms most suited to your type of business, making them also a good source of recommendation. Equally, your local Business Link or Enterprise Agency will be able to help you in your search.

Make sure you ask people what they use their accountant for, as you might not need the same kinds of services. You should also quiz them on what they would recommend about them, their weak points, and if they are always on hand when needed. Most importantly, it is advisable to choose someone who is a member of one of the main professional accounting bodies. There is no legislation to stop anyone

"

Your accountant should be a good investment"

setting up as an accountant, so asking for member accountants in your area will ensure you are getting someone fully qualified.

Qualities to look for in an accountant

You need to make sure that the accountant you choose for your company is at least familiar with your business sector so that they are aware of any specific legislation. Also, look at the size of the firm. As you are a startup, look for a small- to medium-sized business accountant as they will probably specialise more in small business work, charge less than a larger firm and give more direct access to more experienced partners.

Make arrangements to visit several firms in person to meet the people you will be working with and to make comparisons. 'A lot comes down to personal chemistry,' maintains **Paul Watts**, corporate finance partner at HLB Kidsons. 'The accountant needs to be able to get into your business and show an interest in it, as well as just doing your accounts, if they are to advise you properly.'

You are likely to be working closely with your accountant, so if you don't get on at a basic level, your professional relationship may be more difficult than it needs to be. It's good to ask if you can speak to other clients, in the same way that you would ask for references, and this will be a real test of the calibre of the firm. If they are confident that their service has impressed, they shouldn't have a problem referring you to a few people. Equally, a good accountant should want to make an appointment to come and see your business. 'It's important to go out and see clients,' says Watts. 'You can't fully understand a business until you have been taken round it.' And allow each accountant to pitch to you, as it isn't just about what you want, but also what they are prepared to offer.

Business Link

www.businesslink.gov.uk

Enterprise Agency
Each region has their own agency; search online for the one nearest you.

Agreeing terms

When you are considering taking on an accountant, it's important to establish who your contact will be at the firm and who you can speak to in their the absence. This, along with the services they are offering you and the fees they will charge, should form part of the engagement letter. Like the contract, this should be signed by both of you, and will form the basis of your working relationship. As such, it is important to get as much information on it as possible. If the accountant is to handle your tax, your accounts and your payroll, it should say so.

This is also the point where you talk about money. Traditionally, accountants charge by the hour with more for a partner than for a junior member of staff. However, many firms are prepared to be flexible with regards to payment, and you might negotiate a fixed one-off fee for a full audit, for example, or pay monthly rather than all at once at the end of the year. The latter should be popular with both parties as it ensures regular payment when the money is available. However, going for the firm that charges the least can sometimes be a false economy, according to Watts. 'Don't always go for the cheapest firm, look for one that adds value,' he advises. 'For example, how much does the hourly fee vary for a partner and other staff and will photocopying and phone time be included in the cost or be extra?' Most importantly, don't be afraid to question anything on the engagement letter or to ask for something to be added. As with most contracts, it is in both your interests. In exchange for an hourly fee, you should get someone who saves you money, prevents you sitting up late with accounts that won't balance and who can provide general business sense. All the more reason to choose carefully.

Knowing whether you've made the right choice

So you have followed all the rules and carefully chosen your accountant, but this is the first time you have had one, so how do you know if they are doing a good job, and what do you do if you think they are not? To gauge their performance, look at what you are getting from them. At a basic level, are your accounts and tax returns prepared on time? Are you being billed as agreed and are your phone calls and letters answered? On top of this, take note of the advice they've given you. Have they come up with ideas you wouldn't otherwise have thought of? And if not, is that because you haven't liked the ideas, or because there haven't been any?

It is possible just to say to an accountant that you no longer want to work with them – you can effectively 'sack' the firm. But don't rush into doing this at the slightest hitch, as it's important to build a relationship with your accountant, which is difficult if you are changing every six months. Problems can often be ironed out, so keep careful track of the service and speak to your accountant if you need to. But, ultimately, remember that you are not paying for poor service.

Bizspace
Managed Workspace
that provides start-ups
with the flexibility they need

One of the biggest obstacles that any new business has to overcome is finding the right quality of workspace at the right location and, most importantly, good value for money whilst providing both the flexibility and agility for the business to grow and prosper in line with market conditions.

Against a background of tough trading conditions, and an economy in crisis, many existing businesses are finding it hard to make any long term plans, so why would an embryonic business want the hassle of being committed to a long-term conventional lease on workspace. Most new businesses find it hard to plan more than six months ahead, so the flexibility provided by managed workspace allows businesses to continually 'right size' their workspace in order to best meet the needs of their individual marketplace.

Bizspace is one of the UK's leading providers of managed workspace to businesses of all sizes and particularly the new start-ups sector.

We have a client base of more than 3,000 companies and over 7m sqft of space on 110 sites in England & Scotland, with each centre providing a range of flexible accommodation solutions for businesses requiring office or virtual office space; studios; workshops, industrial workspace; storage and self-storage facilities; mailboxes and meeting rooms.

Clients can usually move into their chosen workspace the same day they view it and with licensing and lease periods from as little as one month their start-up costs, as well as long term financial commitments, are drastically minimised. In addition to controlling the day to day costs, companies which relocate to flexible managed workspace sidestep all of the liabilities normally associated with traditional leases. There are no lengthy lease negotiation periods and your rent is fixed for the life of the contract for three months or longer, and there are no hidden building refurbishment clauses which are usually associated with long-term leases.

Contact BIZSPACE on: 0870 60 999 06
www.bizspace.co.uk

BIZSPACE

NEXT STEPS: REVIEW AND IMPROVE

Time management

It's not just owners of small businesses who claim that 24 hours are just not enough in a day – but do they seem to complain about it more than most? It almost seems obligatory that, when starting out, you will be at your desk late into the night, early in the mornings and throughout the weekend. Can you operate in this way for long at an effective level? The European Union (EU) obviously thinks not, as its many rules on working hours suggest that the evidence shows that people do not work effectively at such a pace, and it is unfair to expect your staff to do this. So why do owner-managers do it themselves?

How many working hours?

A recent Bank of Scotland survey found that entrepreneurs work on average a 50-hour week compared with the EU norm of just 35 hours work a week. For those businesses growing at over 10% a year the average working week is 52.3 hours. The survey reported that overall, Britain's 1.4 million small businesses are collectively putting in a staggering 31.2 million extra 'working weeks' each year. Seven in 10 (71%) small business owners claimed to feel stressed by running and managing their business, compared with only half (54%) in the previous year.

Without doubt, new businesses owners want to be efficient, and one way of keeping costs down is to take on as much of the workload as possible. And if, during the regular nine-to-five working day, you are handling customers or clients, then it is more than likely that the administration will follow in the evenings or at weekends. The increasingly global nature of business, particularly for anyone running a website as part of their business, for example, also means that working hours are extending – a work phone call at 9pm or even 4am is not unusual for website owners. But the key to making it all work is time management.

Imogen Daniels, an adviser at the Chartered Institute of Personnel and Development (CIPD), believes 'time management can make an enormous amount of difference to small businesses'. However, she also believes that you have to find the right solution to suit your business and your personality. Managing your time more effectively can be as simple as being more organised, such as keeping your desk tidier and having a more efficient filing system, or a good software package. However, if you are the kind of person who hates tidying, there's no point forcing yourself to keep everything on your desk neat, as you will simply resent it and soon stop making the effort. There will be another solution that suits you better, such as placing key documents in a certain place on your desk. As long as the important stuff is in one place, it doesn't matter if your desk is cluttered.

You are likely to have gone into business because you have a particular skill or want to do something you enjoy under your own supervision. Getting bogged down in all the administration and other chores that come with running your own company can be frustrating, prevent you from enjoying what you do and could result in you ultimately losing interest in the business. What's more, you won't be dedicating enough time to what you do best, which is running your company. And if you are stacking up the hours so you can fit it all in, you will be far from your best most of the time. So for the sake of your health, sanity and business, it is worth applying a few time management techniques to reduce time spent on administration and free up time to dedicate on the work you are better at and enjoy more. In the end, it's your business that will benefit.

CONTACT

Chartered Institute
of Personnel
Development
www.cipd.co.uk
☎020 8612 6200

Work rate

Any self-employed person, and certainly any new business, will agree that it is practically impossible to turn down work. Even if you are manically busy, it is very difficult saying 'No' because of the fear that all existing work will dry up and that you will be left with nothing. Unfortunately, although understandable, this approach has been responsible for bringing down many a good company. That's because, although business may be booming, individuals and companies that overstretch themselves are in serious danger of missing deadlines along with the faith of their clients – which means business won't be booming for long. However good the work, it is of little use when the deadline has passed. Clients are also quick to point out this failing to others and may recommend you, but with the words of warning: 'Good, but a hopeless timekeeper'.

The key is to be honest with yourself and your customers, and making sure that the people who are employed to carry out the key work that delivers your products and services – one of whom will be you – are doing just that, rather than taking on less productive roles that don't make the most of their skills. This will have the impact of maximising your work rate, allowing you to get through as much of it as possible, and so turn down less.

Ultimately, if you aren't confident that you can deliver good-quality work within the required timescale either don't take it on, for the reasons outlined earlier or be clear about your existing workload when talking to your customer. Being honest and saying you need a little more time doesn't necessarily mean the work will go else-where. A customer may decide to be more flexible and give you the time you need to do the work properly – and will appreciate your honesty and commitment to only delivering the best possible product or service.

Photographer **Jonathan Pollock** has built up a team of freelance assistants, whom he calls on at busy times. This frees him up to concentrate directly on his primary function, photography, and allows him to take on as much work as possible, without cutting corners. His assistants help with building sets and also staff the telephones when he is at work. 'You don't want to miss a call from your next potential client because you are too busy to answer the phone,' he advises. In terms of balancing work and personal life, which is essential to prevent you from becoming jaded and maintaining your work rate and hunger for the business, he advises that everyone books a holiday well in advance and sticks to the dates. This will give you plenty of

> "
> If you aren't confident that you can deliver good-quality work within the required timescale, don't take it on or ask if the customer can give you more time "

time to book in any necessary cover for when you are away or plan work around your break. He also suggests, 'Never tell anyone that you have no other work. Of course, as well as busy times, you also need to prepare for quieter periods, which using freelance help is ideal for as you simply won't employ them at this time.' Pollock's tip during leaner times is: 'Although you should never lie to customers, avoid revealing that that you have no other work. Simply say that you can fit them in.'

Be prepared

> **Never lie to customers – but you can avoid revealing that that you have no other work. Simply say that you can fit them in**

Another common problem among inexperienced owner-managers is underestimating the time a job will take and consequently undercharging. It is easy to think that a job will be cracked in a day or two, but it is much better to add on extra time to cover any changes that a client might request. Some people are afraid of charging for that seemingly unnecessary day in case they lose the work to someone else, but experience does prove that clients will be prepared to pay a little more for the confidence of knowing that a job will be done properly.

Often clients will ask: 'How much will you charge?' at a very early stage of negotiation. One tip is to throw the question back and ask what size budget they have and, if appropriate, how long they expect the job to take. Imply that you are flexible. You do not want to lose the work in a haggle over fees, but also stress that you want a decent rate for the decent job that they will get. Try to gain as much information as possible about what is required before naming your fee and timescale. Questions that may have seemed unnecessary at the outset can save a lot of embarrassment and heartache down the line.

The second of the MORI/British Gas Time surveys mentioned earlier showed that small owner-managers are setting aside more time to plan. Commenting on the findings, a British Gas spokesman says he believes businesses were dedicating more time to planning because owner-managers were 'working smarter'. Owner-managers were seeking more external advice and keeping a careful watch on spending as two ways of managing their time more efficiently. This is because they felt that forward planning was allowing them to allocate the right time to jobs, employ the relevant number of staff to achieve deadlines and give them time to chase up new contracts.

Keeping on track

Staying on top of your working schedule is hugely important, particularly with a newly launched company, as you won't have slotted into any kind of routine or work pattern, and taking your eye off the ball can harm your reputation before it's even built. It is all too easy to forget to send an invoice as one job is completed and the next deadline is on top of the list on your mind. Losing control of the cashflow in that way is bad enough, but worse still, a disorganised owner-manager could easily lose sight of a whole commission. Time management consultant **Gerard Hargreaves** is a great believer in lists. When working with British Gas on its biannual Time survey of small- and medium-sized companies, he suggested making lists as a top tip because it helps organise the tasks in your head and helps prioritise the tasks ahead. Keep the diary up to date, make sure that conversations with clients are logged and that agreed actions are noted somewhere prominent, so that those actions do actually go forward.

> Keeping lists and being aware of what is needed next does help to reduce the stress

Pollock has a page-a-day diary for just this purpose. 'It was one of the first things that I did when launching on my own,' he says. 'It sounds a little silly, but it is so crucial.' Each day is split into hours so Pollock can log meetings in the correct order and it has space for him to include priority tasks. He keep this diary up to date all the time, filling it in as he speaks to clients. 'I keep lists of props that are needed and tasks to be done, and I tick them off as they are completed so that, at a glance, I know what still has to be worked on,' he explains.

Daniels, from the Chartered Institute of Personnel and Development, is also a great believer in lists, claiming they organise events in your own mind, regardless of whether you actually keep the list beside you through the working day. She also finds that 'people gain a great deal of satisfaction from achieving listed goals and being able to tick things off'. Again, the answer lies in finding the solution that suits your character – some people prefer to use Post-it notes, sticking them around their computer and office, while others prefer accessing a complex diary on their computer. 'There is an enormous amount of fire-fighting that goes on in small businesses,' says Daniels. 'Keeping lists and being aware of what is needed next does help to reduce the stress.'

Delegation

" Learn to let go and trust others to take on some of the burden "

One of the biggest challenges facing entrepreneurs is delegating tasks effectively. When it is your own business, it is very hard to let go, but delegation is a sign of sound management. Even early on in the life of your business, it is pretty difficult to do everything and there comes a point when the cost of employing someone else to help is less than the cost of work lost because you can't cope. Chartered surveyor **Simon Smith** has first-hand experience of this. After setting out on his own, he quickly found plenty of demand, and a recent merger with another business has meant extreme pressure on his time. Instead of being out and about winning business and handling the tricky side of the operation, he found himself bogged down in administration and routine jobs that were taking up disproportionate amounts of his day. With a wife and three young children at home, he also found it hard to justify spending weekends at the office. 'I knew I needed someone to help out, but there has to be a balancing act between cost and help,' he says.

In his sector, Smith knew there was a history of recent graduates receiving low salaries and a consequent backlash of students unwilling to enter the profession. After months of seeking out the right person, he appointed a recent graduate who was going to the spend the next two years working towards full qualification. Smith knew he would have to give time to the new recruit to ensure he was in the best possible condition to pass his exams – and also give him the right sort of work to meet industry criteria. But he still got the benefit of having time to return to his core business and concentrate on doing what he did best.

Of course, you may not need to actually take someone on but simply to delegate the work to someone already within the business. And this shouldn't just be done for the more menial tasks. Passing on responsibility to staff can be a great motivator and often people rise to the challenge if given the chance. As long as you monitor the situation carefully and build in review processes, little damage to your business is likely to be done. 'Often owner-managers have a strong emotional

ATTIK AND THE FIVE PATHS TO SUCCESS

Company: Attik
Owner-managers: James Sommerville and Simon Needham

Attik is in the brand business, creating advertisements and design-led identities for many of the world's most successful companies. Today, the company is a complete 'brand communications group', designing and implementing creative design solutions for a host of large companies, such as BT and Infogrames. Attik has grown to such a level that it has five offices in three different countries, including the UK (London and Huddersfield), Australia (Sydney) and the USA (San Francisco and New York). But even though the company is one of the most recognised in its field, co-founder **Simon Needham** believes that the same principles apply today as to when it was a small business with only a few employees. Here are his five roads to success:

- When you take risks, prepare yourself for some losses by always having a back-up plan in place just in case
- In the initial stages of starting and running your business, never let your thoughts get past the first year of trading
- Get yourself known. If someone's already heard of you they'll come knocking on your door.
- There are times when things aren't going to go as well as you'd like but stick with what you've got and you'll get through it
- Grow reluctantly and only when you need to and use freelancers (no fixed overheads/costs) wherever possible

attachment to their business and it will have affected them in a lot of ways, from financial to family,' says Daniels, 'but they do have to learn to let go and trust others to take on some of the burden.'

Self-motivation

The key to the continued success of your new enterprise is maintaining the levels of motivation that drove you to launch the business in the first place. Motivation is more important than a business plan, or funding, or even business skills, according to entrepreneur **Leonard Tondel**, director of the Home Business Alliance. He believes that self-motivation is something you either have or haven't got. Successful owner-managers have it whereas frustrated employees don't.

However, as time goes on, entrepreneurs can suffer from a drop in self-motivation. This can be brought on by anything from too much success (if there is such a thing!), which can cut the drive to succeed, and delegation, which can result in a reduced sense of control, to failure and excessive stress, which can sap motivation. The key to avoiding this, and therefore maximising your potential, is to understand what motivates you. Ask any self-employed person what drives them, and the answer is likely to be simple: 'Money'. But owner-managers who think purely financial factors keep them motivated may be fooling themselves. 'Enthusiasm that's purely profit-based wears thin very quickly,' advises Tondel. 'So if you are going to start a business, make it something you will enjoy doing.'

Experts believe that the real source of motivation is likely to be rather more complex. Being your own boss comes top of the list for most small businesses, followed closely by flexibility and flexible hours, according to research by **Andrew Oswald**, Professor of Economics at Warwick University. Money comes a poor third for most self-employed people, including those who believe they are driven by the clatter of pound coins and the rustle of large cheques. A whopping 49% of the thousands of self-employed people he has studied call themselves very satisfied, compared with 29% of employees, and yet the popular view that self-employed people are happier to take risks is unfounded, Oswald argues. 'Their gambling behaviour is no different from the rest of the population,' he says.

Studies by **Cary Cooper**, Professor of Organisational Psychology at the University of Manchester Institute of Science and Technology (UMIST) and a director of business psychology at Robertson Cooper consultants confirms Oswald's findings. 'People who start their own businesses have typically worked in a larger organisation and enjoy the amount of control and autonomy that self-employment gives them, when they see the direct rewards for their labour,' he says. But although that autonomy may make most self-employed people happier than the average employee, Cooper's studies of top business people have shown that the desire to prove themselves is often what drives them rather than money. 'Many top entrepreneurs have had unhappy experiences in childhood, and are motivated by something negative. They want to go on and prove they can succeed, and are driven by control and power,' he says. Although those negative experiences may drive many to set up their own businesses in the first place, motivation grows with the enterprise, argues Cooper. 'As the business expands and they employ people, it's like an extended family with everyone depending on your success,' he explains. 'The drive that keeps you going then comes from your feelings of responsibility to everyone who depends on you.'

Although small business owners' lives have become more stressful, with increasing red tape and too little time to finish too many tasks, most would never contemplate working for anyone else, according to research by Abbey National Business Banking and the Federation of Small Businesses. Running a business now means longer working hours, less free time and a negative effect on family life, but the attraction of being your own boss still outweighs going back to working for someone else. Once the business is up and running, stress can undermine self-motivation unless you find some way to control it or channel it. Set yourself targets, recommends independent business adviser **David Street**, former director of the Institute of Business Advisers, and dig out that business plan, too.

> " Self-motivation is something successful owner-managers have whereas frustrated employees don't "

'Small businesses tend to use business plans only when they're trying to raise money,' he says, 'but they can also help you set realistic performance targets.' At the Royal Bank of Scotland, Head of Business Banking **Jason Oakley** agrees, saying: 'Your business plan should be the life and soul of your business and the key to targets you set.'

Formulating realistic goals for you and your team means you are more likely to achieve them, which will feed motivation all round. Gradual delegation of the jobs you don't enjoy or excel at will also boost your self-motivation, enable you to play to your strengths and boost the performance of your business.

! TOP TIPS
STAYING MOTIVATED

! Find a mentor to help you steer your self-motivation in the direction of success

! Set yourself realistic targets, and draw up a checklist

! Think positively by congratulating yourself on all the things you have achieved

! Visualise success by thinking in terms of what you will achieve rather than the obstacles in your way

! Make time for family and friends as strong relationships can help support your success

! Recognise that breaks are beneficial

! Look after your health – if it breaks down, so does your business success

! If you work from home, separate your working time from your leisure time

! Identify what really motivates you – money, independence or a fresh challenge – then pursue that goal

! Take a step back to gain a broader perspective

Enhancing performance

In the early days of a business you are likely to be highly motivated, which will drive you to work very hard. If you are not motivated you should seriously consider why you've launched your own business. Having said that, racking up the hours alone doesn't mean you are performing to your maximum.

If you are working long hours, make sure the effort you are putting in is as effective as possible, and that you are not wasting your time. So look at how you are spending your time during the day, and work out just how much of it is actually being spent productively. Then think of ways that you may be able to do certain tasks more effectively. For example, if you are spending a long time doing an essential, but rather repetitive or highly intense activity, there will be a maximum period when you will be at your most productive before you become jaded and distracted and your performance levels starts to fall off. Try to recognise when this occurs and recharge your batteries by taking a short break and then switching to another task, returning to the original work with more vim and vigour later on.

A great way to monitor the time you are spending on each task is by completing a time sheet for yourself. This is simply a sheet of paper (or you can do it on a spreadsheet on your computer) divided into the days of the week under which you write the times between which you have been working on a particular job, and the nature of that work, building up a list throughout the day. Many companies use time sheets not only to ensure their people are spending their time productively and to keep on top of which projects they have been working on, but also to assess the time – and therefore cost – spent in terms of person-hours on certain jobs, to inform decision making and assist customer costings.

'In the early days of a business you need to put the hours in to make it work, but you also need to analyse the quantity and quality of what you do in the day,' says **David Broad**, management consultant at M2R. Broad also recommends networking as a great way to gain

> **You need to analyse the quantity and quality of what you do in the day**

the necessary insight to improve your performance levels. 'Managers in larger companies have to motivate their staff, while in very small businesses often the owner just has to motivate themselves,' he points out. 'Going on a course or networking helps you to find a group of people who are all speaking your language, and can help enormously.' Networking can help to direct your motivation towards properly defined goals, and generate more business too.

'Keep in touch with other businesses and find out how they've managed to keep things fresh and meet their targets,' counsels Oakley. 'Exchanging views can inspire new ideas that apply to your business and may be proven winners.'

Personal development

Sometimes, it can be hard to get up in the morning when you are your own boss – late night drinking, a wakeful young child and extreme tiredness can all contribute. Motivation is one of the essentials for anyone working for themselves, but there is far more to it than simply gearing yourself up to start the day, and it isn't enough to keep your career on the straight and narrow. It is equally important to establish a career path that you work towards maintaining. It might be hard to envisage needing a career pattern when you are your own boss, but in reality, personal development is still important, and the same also goes for your staff – an employee who receives training will see that they are moving forward by gaining key skills, feeling valued and satisfied in their position, making them far less likely to leave than an untrained member of staff.

> " It might be hard to envisage needing a career pattern when you are your own boss "

Move on up

Its important to bear in mind that once you are your own boss it won't be enough to is simply keep working – as anyone who has survived a recession can tell you. As mentioned above, standing still in career terms should never an option, no matter how small your business. Take the example of a copy typist. There was plenty of work in the past on old style typewriters, but those who weren't able to become computer literate would have quickly found themselves, quite literally, redundant.

If you worked for a large company, you may have been offered training as required, with follow-up opportunities where necessary. Your employers might have even been prepared to give you time off for outside course work or even contributed towards the cost of independent training. Although your business may be no more than a one-man band, you can still adopt the same strategies for yourself. The only difference is that you will have to be more organised than if you were part of a large organisation. As a small business, attending a block release course will mean that no one is back at your desk, keeping the business going. The financial and practical implications need to be carefully thought out, too, but there is still no reason why you shouldn't better yourself and the same goes for your staff.

Personal development can help your business in several unexpected ways:

- Not only will you be better able to carry out the related task, but it may also help motivate you through a rough business period or provide fresh ideas if the business becomes stale.
- You never know when you might think of taking up a job again, for example because you have sold your business or you have been asked to join at board level – so keeping up to date with developments in the sector and by being seen as an industry leader, you have a better chance of winning a lucrative position.
- Your own business may be so successful that others will want you on their board as a non-executive director.
- If you sell your business on after the first flush of success, you may well want to start afresh and need to have developed your skills along the way.

> **"Many industries are experiencing calls for better quality and greater responsibility towards the consumer "**

Legal requirements

Besides personal development aimed at becoming better at the job and gaining confidence in your own ability to handle various situations, there is also an increasing need for gaining knowledge about the latest statutory requirements. The government has placed a lot of emphasis on the need for improved quality at all levels of business. Its new laws on corporate manslaughter (where individuals can now be prosecuted for the deaths of employees and members of the public in their charge) are just one example of where individuals are being forced to take responsibility. **Mark Redfern**, a director of training at Searchlight Solutions, has seen increased demand for senior management training to keep abreast with the new legislation. 'People are having to become very well versed on the legal side and keep up to date with current and forthcoming legislation, such as the Companies Act, the Data Protection Act and the Human Rights Act,' Redfern reports. He adds that Searchlight tries to address problems before they arise, so that trainees are in the best position to manage their businesses correctly.

Professional director **Martin Pedler** has strong views on the need for better quality directors and believes the recent legislation on corporate manslaughter mentioned above, in particular, will give a wake-up call to the nation's bosses. 'I think people have a fear factor about what they are taking on,' he says. 'It will not be long before the first corporate manslaughter case is taken against an individual rather than a company. It will set the cat among the pigeons.' Pedler adds that ignorance will be no defence for directors who haven't kept a close eye on what is happening within their businesses, and it could land them in jail. He believes that the first custodial sentence meted out will launch a surge in demand for greater training among directors. The same rules will apply to owner-managers and will put great pressure on all bosses to adhere strictly to health and safety regulations. If companies and directors can show they have tried to maintain proper standards, the courts will have no grounds for conviction, but cutting corners or non-compliance in any way will open the door.

Corporate manslaughter rules are not the only area that has been tightened up in terms of director responsibility. Many industries are experiencing calls for better quality and greater responsibility towards the consumer. The insurance industry, for example, has established its own self-governing watchdog, but in 2007 the government announced plans for the whole sector to come under the rule of the Financial Services Authority. One of the expected consequences is that industry pundits believe greater numbers will have to hold recognisable qualifications. Experience alone will not be enough to convince regulators that you are fit to run the business – you will need qualifications too. Insurance is not alone in this type of development, and it's something that could stop you operating your own business in the future.

Personal and staff training

Developing the skills of your workforce through training boosts morale and helps provide a better service to customers. They, in turn, are happier and more likely to return, swelling profits, which then benefits the business and encourages higher salaries. This is very much a win–win situation, and should encourage new owner-managers to view training less as a drain on resources or an annoyance that takes up employees' valuable time, and more as a useful investment.

In addition, it can help attract and retain the right people for your business. While unemployment levels are rising for the first time in years, making it easier to find applicants, recruiting is often expensive, disruptive and time consuming. So when you do hire the perfect candidate, it makes sense to try and hold onto them. Having a training programme or 'people development' strategy in place can help to both attract and keep key members of staff, giving your company a positive profile in the recruitment marketplace.

> **Having a training programme or 'people development' strategy in place can help to both attract and keep key members of staff**

CONTACT

For more details of
the IoD courses,
contact:
Institute of
Directors
www.iod.com

Bosses, too, can also benefit from career development and training as touched on earlier. Completing a course will provide a boost in self-confidence and renewed interest in developing the business. A better-trained boss will be more motivated, and this is reflected throughout the business, whatever its size. The director of development at the Institute of Directors (IoD), **John Weston**, calls it a virtuous circle. 'Better directors run better businesses and as a consequence you create wealth and employment,' he says. One of the IoD's prime missions is to improve professional standards across the UK, and Weston believes that by starting at the top, the professionalism will filter right through the business. The IoD offers a series of courses designed to cover most aspects of running a business, which are available to members. They are designed for like-minded people and many who have been through an IoD course say that the most valuable part was not the formal course work, but learning about other directors' experiences.

Choosing training courses

There are two ways to go when choosing courses: you can follow the structure of your chosen career or develop across a spectrum of skills. The options have led to the development of an IoD chartered director qualification, because, as Weston points out: 'Most directors have followed vertical career ladders, but our membership comes from a horizontal level of achievement and we needed a qualification that would appeal to that.' In other words, when you have become an accountant, lawyer, etc, you have a career structure that takes you up to the boardroom level, but once there you may well need the skills of a completely different career.

To follow your chosen career you need to make specific decisions about what to learn. Most fields have relevant industry qualifications and there will be a well-trodden route – one that you are likely to have done or have followed before you decided to go solo. Learning a new set of skills is likely to be more of a challenge. For example, it is easy enough to employ an accountant, but it might also pay dividends if you understand the basics of it as well. The UK has a raft of colleges offering full- and part-time courses and you can find out more by searching the internet. Bear in mind that different rules of entry (and payment) apply for mature students, and take into account your current workload before committing to a course – one or two evenings at college a week may not be feasible.

Local councils are another good source of courses. Many run a variety, specifically designed for part-timers. These are often evening classes that require a little, but not too much, homework between sessions. These could vary from a basic accountancy course to learning a new language – or a completely unrelated skill, such as upholstery, which could provide another source of income should the tough times arrive.

However, if you are looking for a more academically inclined qualification, then check out your local university, although part-time courses are usually limited. The other alternative that is quite popular is the Open University, as it allows you to work at a distance and at your own speed.

Should you consider an MBA?

If you want to learn more managerial skills, a Masters in Business Administration (MBA) might provide the solution. An MBA often takes several years to complete, but can be combined with a full-time job. Students complete course work in a series of block releases. An MBA is usually divided into 12 modules, comprising eight compulsory sections and four optional ones in which a student might choose to specialise in a work-related subject.

Nottingham University has a variety of MBA courses, and according to its Centre Director **Chris O'Brien** most students are in full-time work. Some choose to concentrate on the course – and there are attractive bursaries to help them afford the tuition. Most students are in their 30s, although there are both younger and older exceptions.

CONTACT

For nationwide information on MBAs, see: Association of MBAs www.mbaworld.com

O'Brien stresses that the aim of the course is to give a framework from which students can help run businesses. 'They have an understanding of business, which allows them to move businesses forward in a changing environment,' he says.

Online training

The time spent getting to and from a course and the inflexible times of lectures is often the reason why owner-managers don't take up training or education. This is where online training comes in, where you can work over the internet from any location, starting and stopping lectures when you choose. This mode of study is becoming more attractive, particularly when the cost of getting online can be as little as £12 a month.

DEVELOP YOUR STAFF FREE THROUGH TRAIN TO GAIN

The government has set up a national skills service called Train to Gain, which is designed to boost the performance of businesses by improving the skills of their employees. The aim is also to encourage companies to develop their staff by providing guidance and assistance on finding and organising training resources, making the whole process easier.

If your organisation is based in England, the government will assess your business and help you get access to the necessary skills and training. There's also help available to companies based outside England, but in the British Isles.

In this programme, each eligible company is assigned an independent business broker, who will offer free expert skills advice. Your business broker will arrange to visit your office at a time that suits you. They will:

- Identify the skills that will boost your business
- Create a tailored package of training
- Find reliable local training providers
- Find funding to complement your investment
- Evaluate the training to ensure real results.

For more information on Train to Gain call 0845 600 9 006 or visit www.traintogain.gov.uk. You can sign up online at http://traintogain.broadsystem.com

Companies such as E-Learnity work closely with an employer to provide the necessary training package for its staff. Others such as REDTRAY also offer courses on an individual basis. The downside is most of the courses are technology based, but this is beginning to change. Another criticism is the lack of one-to-one help, but a lot of online courses now offer telephone support, while tools such as Microsoft NetMeeting help course members share questions. The Open University is just one academic institution to make use of the internet as a way of reaching students.

CONTACT

E-Learnity
www.elearnity.com

REDTRAY
www.redtray.co.uk

ACTION POINT
KEY WAYS TO IMPROVE YOUR BUSINESS

You may think that once you have started up your business a lot of the hard work is over, but successful owner-managers are the ones who continually try to improve their enterprise. This is particularly important in a downturn, when you need to be able to respond to changing market conditions. Sitting on the sidelines while competitors make progress could prove to be disastrous for your venture. To help, here are 10 ways from startups.co.uk to help you get ahead.

Take on experienced staff: Since October 2006 it has been illegal to discriminate against workers on the grounds of age, so incorporate this change into your thinking when recruiting. Older staff offer maturity and experience, which could provide the keys to the success for your business. Don't believe that old dogs can't learn new tricks and remember that they might have a thing or two to show you.

Train up: The skill levels of your staff will have direct impact on the performance of your company, so it pays to continually develop your employees through training to make sure they are up to speed on the latest workplace innovations, such as IT, and on those in your particular sector. This is also vital during the current economic climate, as you need all possible resources at your disposal to attract business and fight off competition. The government has set up a scheme to help you do just this, called Train to Gain. For more information on this scheme, see the box on page 297.

Expansion through recruitment: Not every company is doing badly in the recession, and if yours is one of those that is performing well, perhaps you could update your business plan and take on a few extra staff. If demand is great enough and you can budget carefully, new workers could drive your business onwards and upwards. It will also mean you are ready to push on further when the recovery arrives.

Expand your offer: How about branching into other areas? If there is a niche market being ignored in your local area and your business is doing well, why not exploit it? Do some market research on demand and how any potential expansion would fare, but be careful not to over-stretch yourself. However, a targeted, well-thought-out expansion into a closely related field could prove to be very profitable – particularly if your existing market is slow due to the recession.

Don't just bank on banks: Although research has shown that the majority of small firms go to their high-street bank whenever they need new finance, many are now having to look at other options as the credit crunch has resulted in bank finance being difficult to come by. Equity investors, such as venture capitalists and business angels are a possible alternative, but they too have been hit by the downturn and have less to invest. This makes asset-based lending the best current option, where assets such as invoices, equipment, or even intellectual property can be used as security. See Chapter 4, pages 103–138 for more details about finding finance.

Go public: The government has announced that red tape on securing public sector contracts will be cut and that work will be awarded on a regional, not national, basis. Both measures are good news for small firms, who can now compete against a reduced field at a fraction of the cost for government contracts. From pavement maintenance to IT work, there is around £13bnn worth of contracts out there. What's more, the public sector is one of the few that has been actually growing during the recession.

Get your message across: If you have spent the last year relying on local newspaper advertisements or the *Yellow Pages*, it may be worth widening your options slightly to help boost your business. Cinema advertising often proves effective, as do panels on the sides of buses. Or you may want to put together a radio advertisement to reach out to local customers. If you come up with a targeted, attention-grabbing campaign at a reasonable cost, you should be able to boost takings significantly. See Chapter 8 for a thorough discussion on marketing.

Get supplied: Getting quality, affordable stock is essential in making your business profitable. If you feel that you aren't getting the best deal from your wholesaler, do something about it. Most are happy to negotiate over prices, particularly at the moment when business can be hard to come by, and good wholesalers reward loyalty by offering money off or extra products to repeat customers. If yours doesn't, try to find another one. Do some research on suppliers in your local area, and if all of them don't offer good value, then look further afield, as the savings you make could be critical. See page 206 for more details on handling suppliers.

Get paid on time: Now more than ever it's vital that you do all you can to maintain a healthy cashflow through your business. A big obstacle to this is that late payment has been seen by many businesses as acceptable practice for many years, putting small firms in debt that they can ill afford. So it's important that you act to get what's owed to you. The government has introduced legislation recently to tackle the problem, allowing firms to take clients to court for compensation. If all your chasing proves fruitless, consider using these laws. See Chapter 9 for more details on tackling late payments.

Keep the cash flowing: Debt is not necessarily a bad thing for small firms attempting to grow. However, it's essential that you keep up with repayments or your whole business could be at risk. Make sure you operate a well-organised cashflow system. Try to negotiate repayments so that you can pay in instalments when it suits you best, try to use a business debit or credit card to cut down on paperwork, make sure your records are well looked after, and ensure that you are aware of all outstanding debts. See Chapter 9 for more details on tackling debtors.

DOSH SOFTWARE AND THE GOLDEN CONTACT LIST

Dosh Software was set up by accountant **Jonathan van der Borgh** to develop new accounting packages for small firms. By constantly reviewing and updating the details it holds on former and existing customers it has developed a strong direct marketing database which is proving a great source of business, while helping the company deliver excellent service levels. 'If you buy a cold list, you will be lucky to get a return of half a per cent,' explains general manager **Tony Trevillion**. 'It is always easier to sell to someone that you have sold to before.' This has meant an investment in database technology to help Dosh keep up-to-date and accurate listings, but it has been money well spent. No opportunity is lost and Dosh uses every invoice mailing to existing customers to make full use of the postal charges. As well as an invoice, customers could receive additional information about the company or questionnaires regarding customer service, all within the weight limit allowed for second class mail.

'The nice thing about direct marketing, as an accountant, is that you can measure the success. You know all the costs–the creative outlay, the mail, the time involved and the envelopes,' says van der Borgh.

Over to you...

If you've read this far you must be serious about setting up your own business, but now it's up to you. You've taken the journey through this guide from idea to launch, and now it's time for you to put all the theory into practice – and perhaps flick back through these pages along the way to make sure you are on the right track.

You should now be under no illusions of the task ahead, and have a much better idea of what starting up involves. You will also have read plenty of examples of those who've gone before, and how they've overcome obstacles and faced challenges along the way, finally achieving what they set out to do – running their own company on their own terms.

Remember, no one has launched their own business without making mistakes along the way. This is all part of the process, and it's how you deal with these situations and learn from them so you avoid them in the future that matters. As for the challenges, you are bound to face plenty, but approach them in the right way and they'll make you even more determined to succeed.

This should be an enjoyable, liberating and ultimately exhilarating experience. And hopefully you will be making the webpages of startups.co.uk in the not-too-distant future as one of our entrepreneurial success stories.

Good luck!

INDEX

INDEX

INDEX